DATE DUE

The News of Detroit

The News of Detroit

How a Newspaper and a City Grew Together

William W. Lutz

with illustrations

LITTLE, BROWN AND COMPANY — BOSTON — TORONTO

FIRST EDITION

T07/73

Library of Congress Cataloging in Publication Data

Lutz, William W
    The News of Detroit.

    Bibliography: p.
    1. Detroit news. 2. Detroit--History. I. Title.
PN4899.D55N45   071'.74'34   73-1645
ISBN 0-316-53760-8

Published simultaneously in Canada
by Little, Brown & Company (Canada) Limited

PRINTED IN THE UNITED STATES OF AMERICA

Contents

	Foreword	ix
	Prologue	xi
1	For Two Cents Only	3
2	The Mayor Had Codfish in His Coattails	17
3	All about Honest Tom	32
4	The Tin Lizzie Was a Lady	49
5	Sit, Brothers, Sit	66
6	We Were the First to Sing on Raaadio	80
7	Bullets and Beer	93
8	Nancy (sob) Nancy	110
9	Trouble in Motor City	125
10	The Crime of It	143
11	Sports Heroes We've Had	157
12	We Helped Give the City a Face-Lift	176
	Epilogue	194
	Acknowledgments	199
	Chapter Notes	202
	Bibliography	211
	Index	217

Illustrations

(*between pages 76 and 77*)

Battle of the Overpass (*photo by James R. Kilpatrick*)
The Picket Line (*photo by Milton Brooks*)
Bootleggers Landing at Detroit (*photo by Monroe D. Stroeker*)
Gar Wood and Miss America I (*photo by William A. Kuenzel*)
Ty Cobb's Disputed Slide (*photo by William A. Kuenzel*)
WWJ's First Broadcast (*photo by William A. Kuenzel*)
Trouble at an Aldermen Meeting, 1900 (*photo by William A. Kuenzel*)
Teddy Roosevelt — Hats Off to Detroit (*photo by William A. Kuenzel*)
Woodward Avenue, 1915 (*photo by William A. Kuenzel*)
A Walk from Baseball Fame (*photo by Rolland R. Ransom*)
Arrival of the *News*'s Fish Train (*photo by Bernard Nagel*)
William A. Kuenzel — the First Aerial Photograph (*photo by Bernard Nagel*)

(*between pages 166 and 167*)

James E. Scripps
George G. Booth
William E. Scripps
Warren S. Booth
Peter B. Clark
The First *News* Office (*from a painting by James Scripps Booth*)
The Building at Shelby and Larned (*photo by William A. Kuenzel*)
Metropolitan Headquarters Building (Detroit News *Staff Photo*)
The North Plant (Detroit News *staff photo*)
When the City Went Wild, 1935 (*photo by Peter A. MacGregor*)
Joe Louis (*photo by Monroe D. Stroeker*)
Nancy Brown Draws a Crowd (*photo by Howard McGraw*)
Gerry Buckley's Funeral (*photo by Earl Barlow*)
A Riot Tragedy (*photo by Howard Shirkey*)
Bobby Layne (*photo by Drayton Holcomb*)
Mickey Lolich (*photo by James R. Kilpatrick*)

Dedicated to the more than
10,000 people who worked to make the *Detroit News*
America's foremost evening newspaper

Foreword

HERE IS HOW a newspaper and a city grew to mutual power and influence in world affairs. The facts will show that neither could have reached prominence without interaction in every field of human endeavor. The tragedy and the humor, the successes and failures of a hundred years — more than a third of the lifetime of the city — are woven into its fabric. This is Detroit and how it grew into modern times. And this is the city's largest newspaper and how it got that way.

Prologue

THE NATION'S PRESS thundered with indignation. The reason: an exposé of secret government deliberations over the past twenty years that reportedly showed the blunders and soggy thinking that led to the commitment of American troops in Indo-China. The people, many of the nation's newspapers editorialized, had been systematically kept ignorant of the thinking processes that sent more than twenty thousand American youths to die in the heat and jungles of an undeclared war. Now, as the result of a carefully plotted leak, high policy discussions that began in 1950 during the administration of President Harry S Truman were capsuled and made public.

The *New York Times*, for years the organ of the nation's intellectual elite, was the first to publish what would be billed as "shocking revelations."[1] These included the information that the United States had ignored eight direct appeals by North Vietnam's Communist leader Ho Chi Minh in the first five months after World War II. The Truman administration, the documents revealed, was the promulgator of the Domino Theory, which convinced succeeding administrations and most Americans that if one Indo-Chinese country fell to the Communists, all would tumble.

The war was escalated deliberately, the nation was told, although the Joint Chiefs of Staff had insisted early in the deliberations that South Vietnam "was a risk not worth the gamble."[2] In the long run the nation could not win a land war in Asia. The war progressed despite the warnings of top officials through the administrations of Eisenhower, Kennedy and Johnson. Although the Nixon administration followed a planned schedule of deescalation, it did not satisfy those Americans who wanted immediate evacuation of U.S. troops. To these Americans the secret papers, admittedly purloined by Dr. Daniel Ellsberg, a former Pentagon adviser, provided the sweet music of righteousness.

The *New York Times* printed the first of the condensed secret documents on Sunday, June 13, 1971. Editorials in many of the nation's newspapers hailed the *Times* for its bold stand. By June 16, the government had won a temporary injunction restraining further publication on the ground that certain revealed information might embarrass or jeopardize U.S. relations with foreign countries. But in the days to follow, other papers, also made privy to the documents, published new revelations.[3] Among the newspapers were the *Boston Globe,* the *St. Louis Post-Dispatch* and the *Washington Post.* Again court action halted publication.[4] The government, the defendants answered, was abridging the freedom of the press as guaranteed by the Constitution.[5]

On June 25, after nearly two weeks of national harangue and with the Supreme Court in session, Martin S. Hayden, editor-in-chief of the *Detroit News,* rode in an elevator from his third floor office in the newspaper's main editorial building to the office of the publisher, Peter B. Clark, on the mezzanine.[6] Clark, who held a doctorate in political science from the University of Chicago, taught there and at Yale before turning to the newspaper founded by his great-grandfather. Hayden, son of a former chief of the paper's Washington Bureau and former bureau chief himself, discussed the broad implications of what had been transpiring.

"There was no disagreement over how we stood," Hayden related. "The decision was simply a matter of whether we should make our editorial position known on the Editorial Page or move to Page One. In the paper's entire history it has editorialized on Page One rarely — only when it felt the issue was of great national, state or civic importance."

It was agreed that the paper's position ran so counter to the opinions broadcast throughout the nation that it merited Page One on Sunday. Hayden returned to his oak-paneled office and worked late into the night, putting down the paper's position in cold, methodical logic. When he finished he had written what amounted to the dissenting opinion in a case already affirmatively decided by the majority of the press. But like the remembered dissents of Supreme Court history, the *News*'s dissent was to gain wide attention.

The thrust of the *News*'s argument was that by irresponsibly publishing secret government conversations, many of which had not matured into policy, the press only invited government censorship in the name of protecting the democracy. There was a point when a responsible press must exercise restraint in the national interest and a point when its duty lay in exposing bad government. Clearly, nothing could be gained in revealing deliberations that might have resulted in decisions long since made. The greater danger lay in removing the government's diplomatic relationships with trusting allies.

Arriving early on Saturday morning, Paul Poorman, managing editor, set in motion orders to make three columns of space available in the Sunday edition. Boldly labeled An Editorial, the headline over the *News*'s dissent read, "Our Colleagues Err on War Secrets Issue." The editorial declared that the *News* believed "the *New York Times* and other involved newspapers did not act responsibly and in the public interest when" — without even trying to use established procedures for declassification of secret papers — they chose to publish an edited version of what it now appears was an incomplete account of our involvement in the Vietnam war.

What government is going to freely and frankly exchange views with us if it suspects the correspondence shortly will be published worldwide?

Even if the papers publishing them [the documents] did not so intend, the prospects are that the already obdurate Hanoi negotiators may feel that revelation of the alleged immorality of every U.S. President since Truman will so stir American protest as to force President Nixon to surrender now. Certainly, if a negotiated peace is in the American interest, none of the events of the last two weeks have helped our bargainers get one.

We do not defend the proposition that any government employee with access to classified material has a right to leak it for publication in the name of national interest.[7]

On the following Wednesday, the Supreme Court ruled in a 6 to 3 decision that publication could continue.

Overnight, Hayden became the spokesman of dissent on national television discussion programs and at public forums. The dissent was remarkable for its show of independence of thought in a nation where "follow the leader" is played not just by children but too often by many highly respected newspapers.

That the *News* was to think independently of the others was no surprise to its readers. For a hundred years, dating from August 23, 1873, the paper's spirit has been driven by precepts of independence that drove its publishers and editors in both editorial and business decisions. At a time when many of the nation's newspapers avowed party affiliations, and when editors of a number of party organs often were rewarded with plush political positions, the *News* struck out as a political independent.

Its founder called himself "an independent Republican." But he declared the paper independent of any party affiliation. Historically the paper's position has been to defend the people and the country. In doing so, it has crossed party lines as the occasion demanded. In booming one party's ticket, it has often played the maverick by supporting rival party candidates whom the paper felt could do a better job. Each has had to meet the test of bettering the city and the nation.

The News of Detroit

1

For Two Cents Only

No ONE but a stubborn man would have begun a newspaper in a town that already had four in the panic year of 1873. He was cautioned by friends, warned by bankers, discouraged almost to the point of giving up by everyone but Harriet — his Hattie — whom he had married eleven years earlier. Hattie said he had to have faith in himself; if he had faith he must do what he must do. Failure, said the woman who bore him four daughters and two sons (two of whom would die in childhood), would not destroy either of them.[1] He needed this support. At stake was the savings he had accumulated for fourteen years, first as commercial editor and then, in 1861, with the Civil War blazing, as part owner of the *Detroit Daily Advertiser*. In 1862, he had become business manager and managing editor of the combined *Advertiser and Tribune*, a position that pushed him closer and closer to the realization that eventually he must move on his own. Although he was wooed with the power that comes with editorial position and ownership of 40 percent of *Tribune* stock, his determination to form a newspaper of his own choosing continued to smolder.[2] Then, on Easter morning, 1873, the *Tribune* job plant that he had bought from two partners burned. It was now or never. Hattie kissed him tenderly. "Jim, we must work, not worry."

The next four months were frantic ones. But if the fire was a blow to his family's immediate well-being, it served also to spark his belief in the kind of newspaper that would be right for a city the size and composition of Detroit — a community of 80,000, lighted by gas lamps, with a transit system that was horse-drawn, an aldermanic government that took its orders from ward-heelers, log-rolling politicians and a rural legislature suspicious of the city.

James E. Scripps's idea of a newspaper that could succeed in the worst of times ran contrary to the concepts of the majority of contemporary newspaper publishers.[3] Daily newspapers in Detroit sold for a nickel, as did most of the papers in the nation. The cost per year — $13 on a weekly basis — amounted to almost two weeks' wages for the average laborer. A third of Detroit's hundred thousand people were not reading any newspaper. The market was there if he could create the demand at the right price. Now, how to do it?

Since leaving his family homestead in Rushville, Illinois, Scripps had gathered editorial and business experience, first by working for a cousin, John Locke Scripps, one of the three founders of the present *Chicago Tribune,* and then in Detroit. His idea of what a newspaper ought to be grew out of what he thought it should not be. He had grown to despise "those damn blanket sheets," an epithet he put down in his diary to describe the whole line of nickel papers in America. Readers found it impossible to open such papers on a trolley, or read as teams of horses clopped along. The articles were often arduous, the makeup unexciting. He had learned that any paper, if it was to succeed, must blend heroic idealism with business practicality. But, more than that, he believed that idealism in a newspaper was the greater part of its sales magic. The difficulty with the party organ papers was their limited appeal.[4] A paper that was critical of special interests when they worked against the total society would appeal to the mass of people, thus assuring its business success. His dislike of the "blanket" papers was more than esthetic. From a business standpoint, their size dictated large newsprint expenditures. Because of their cost, they were not reaching the lower income group of the nineteenth century. By reducing the size and the cost and creating a demand through a fresh approach, his paper would be in the vanguard of a new culture. His job was not easy; there would be times when everyone but Hattie seemingly would be against him.

Detroit had grown out of a fort into a hard-driving river town, populated by people who worked in the wagon shops, pharmaceutical companies, shoe factories, a railroad car factory; sailors, smithies, trainmen and common laborers. Its power establishment consisted of men who made fortunes in lumber and cement, "corporationists" who controlled the utilities, including lighting and public transit, and brewery owners who provided the elixir of life.

Here was a place to test a publisher's soul. Scripps saw Detroit as a workingman's town aching for an inexpensive paper that could play an important role in shaping the city's future. His compatriots at the *Advertiser and Tribune* failed to see his logic.[5] In many business fields the opinion prevailed that money could be made primarily by appealing to the moneyed class. He saw what other businessmen were to see toward the end of the century: that the average man was to provide a broad market in many fields of endeavor that would launch America and the world on a second industrial revolution and a new sociocultural era. The failure of Scripps's associates to see the opportunity made him the more determined.

When he founded the *Evening News,* which he later renamed the *Detroit News,* James E. Scripps's net worth was about $30,000, including $5,000 in cash; his equity in a house he had bought on Lafayette Boulevard, near First Street, just four blocks from Detroit's main thoroughfare, Woodward Avenue; and his holdings in the *Tribune* job plant, which had been insured for $30,000, a sum he split after the fire with his partners.[6] He was thirty-eight years old, nearly six feet tall, with large, piercing eyes, black hair and a full beard. To start a newspaper on his meager assets demanded a well-drawn plan and a tight business operation.

His first decision was to publish an evening paper, since three of Detroit's four papers were morning publications. The fourth, an evening paper, was the weakest of them all. The evening field had all but been abandoned as a lucrative market in America for a variety of reasons, including ease of distribution through the night and the belief that most readers wanted their paper in the morning. To conserve capital he did three things: He rented editorial office and composing room space in the morning *Free*

Press building on Woodbridge at Griswold, then let contracts to out-siders to handle both advertising and circulation. Then he gathered his staff: Michael J. Dee, who worked for the *Detroit Daily Union* (which Scripps was to buy in 1874); Robert B. Ross, a compatriot at the *Tribune;* Ashel H. Herron, a St. John's, Michigan, publisher and Fred H. Burgess, a Marshall, Michigan, newspaperman, both of whom were eager to move to a larger town; and John Swan, who had been a reporter on all of Detroit's papers at one time or an-other. The group was just right for the task ahead.[7] At times they gave the paper such an exciting flair, compared to the stodgy writing and makeup of its contemporaries, that even Scripps, who had hired them, became concerned. But he shrewdly refused to let his own innate conservatism stifle the group's editorial inventive-ness. The excitement did not happen overnight.

The first newspaper, published on Saturday, August 23, 1873, was tabloid size. The price was two cents — three cents cheaper than its competitors. Scripps's hope (later realized) was that cir-culation would grow to such an extent that he could reduce the price to a penny. About three columns of Page One of the first is-sue consisted of advertising, a newspaper makeup fetish that came to America from England but that died as competition for mass circulation forced a more attractive presentation. If Scripps had hoped for an immediate new product that would have dynamic appeal, he was bitterly disappointed. He went home at the end of the first day long after dark. He felt so embarrassed that he crossed the street several times rather than meet somebody he knew. He confessed to Harriet that the paper was a terrible flop. She tried to console him. He had carried the cash box home, and when he counted its contents he discovered that the first day's pub-lication of an optimistic ten thousand copies had grossed $126.69; costs were $175.73.[8]

The next day, Sunday, believing his venture a fiasco, he stayed away from the Reformed Episcopal Church, which he attended faithfully, to hide his disgrace. But on Monday he started a fresh week of publication by talking with Dee. "Have the boys write the paper," he told Dee, "as people talk in conversation." This was all the encouragement Dee needed; his own anxiety to break out of the old mold soon spread to his small staff. Scripps's confidence had been further bolstered by Hattie. She had told him that they would "cut corners"; he must give his idea more time to germinate.[9]

The losses continued at an average of $50 a day. By the fourth day, printing was reduced to nine thousand copies. But, although the paper did not meet the founder's early hopes, it was already making a mark on the city. Even at nine thousand copies, its printing was larger than any of its competitors. Within a few weeks, realizing his cash reserves were rapidly disappearing, Scripps wrote of his concern to his sisters and brothers in Rushville. The first to arrive was his half brother, Edward Wyllis Scripps, a spirited eighteen-year-old who was put to work as a sweeper. Eventually a number of cousins of varying degree arrived and were utilized in various niches of the business. But with the problem of capital still critical, Scripps's sister, Ellen B. — "Miss Ellen" — appealed to him by letter to write their brother, George H. Scripps, ailing from a Civil War injury, urging him to bolster the waning finances. George had bought 80 acres of the 160-acre family homestead and was the most affluent of the Rushville family.

After some hesitation George sold the acreage and arrived in Detroit bearing $2,000. Ellen followed after the death of the father of the brood, James Mogg Scripps, who had migrated with his family from England. She took her place on the copy desk and became the paper's first local columnist. So successful was her column that within a few years it became the basis of a syndicated feature service that developed into the nationwide Newspaper Enterprise Association. Of the group who were to join in the enterprise, Edward Wyllis Scripps was to make a mark in family and journalistic history as bizarre as his full stock of red hair and attire that turned staid Detroit's head. The nucleus of a journalistic adventure and the capital to give it a chance to develop, as Hattie had prayed, now had been put together. But the struggle was just beginning.

Noted as the family penny-pincher, George H. added this attribute to a business that needed a scrupulous accounting of funds.

A tobacco chewer, he soon acquired the reputation of a curmudgeon who punctuated his speech with emphatic splashes of tobacco juice which he aimed at a deskside spittoon. His most oft-used word was "No." Two months after its founding, the paper was printing forty-eight hundred copies, less than half the number it printed on its first day of publication. Unhappy with the paper's printing arrangement, Scripps decided to plunge further; he had no other choice. Using $5,500 he had acquired in notes on his personal property, he secured the two-story frame homestead of Judge John J. Speed at 65 Shelby Street, again close to the city's business center. Into the Speed garden, which had been remade into a pressroom, he moved a larger press than the paper had been printed on at the *Free Press*. He bought it in Chicago for $10,000. Some of this capital was secured through a loan from Governor John J. Bagley at an interest rate of 10 percent. By now the family had milked itself dry, putting "every last penny," as Edward Wyllis was to remark, into the operation.

The house on Lafayette became the family operation's center. Here editorial and business conferences often lasted late into the night, lighted by gas lamps. To keep a close eye on the enterprise, James nightly posted the books.[10] None feared to express himself, not even Edward Wyllis, the youngest of the group. He was paid $3 a week but he soon rebelled and quit, only to return when his wages were doubled. When the paper took over its own distribution, he was put in charge of city circulation at which he would soon prove most adept. Ever ambitious, Edward Wyllis also practiced writing, in the hope of disproving James's opinion that he was "terrible at it." He spent a year rewriting articles that already had been printed and presented them to James, who nodded his approval. Shortly, Edward Wyllis found himself city editor of the paper, an experience that was to pay off handsomely as he sought bigger and bigger challenges that were to bring him to national attention.

James arose daily at 5:00 and reached the *News* office at 7:00. After directing the editorial content and supervising the makeup of the pages, he hurried to the pressroom to assist in preparing the bundles. Then back to the editorial room to keep the interminable struggle alive one more day. At 6:30 in the evening, the tin cash box under his arm, he hurried home to count the receipts and register the results in a ledger. When Harriet worried about his health, his answer was, "I enjoy it." But the enjoyment eventually would exact its toll.

The first year's operation showed a net loss of nearly $5,000. But by the end of the second year the upstart newspaper that was daringly independent of party politics and private interests was showing a profit — $6,000 more than Scripps's original investment of about $21,000. It turned the corner editorially by following the original script — involving itself in public affairs and making the city its constant point of interest. And it succeeded on the business side with volume circulation. In his opening editorial, "Why I Started the *News*," the founder declared his interest in the broad market rather than in a particular reader elite.

Of party-oriented papers, he wrote:

> While it is necessary that we should have some such paper, there has been an error on the part of Detroit publishers in leaving the field of popular journalism entirely unoccupied. . . . In my opinion there should be papers in which only such things are published as are of interest to the great mass of their readers. . . . They will be useful to all classes who desire to keep up with the news of the day. . . . Popularity and usefulness are our only aim: the wants of the great public our only criterions in the choice of matter for our columns. . . . The "vox populi" will in the long run pretty certainly be found to be the "vox dei." Still there are times when the *Evening News* will speak out. . . .

The theory worked better than he expected, for special interest groups had to buy the paper to find out what others were saying about them. In various areas, the paper discovered plenty was being said. Two months after the *News* began operation, Jay Cooke, nationally recognized financier and adviser to Presidents, failed to meet his financial obligations to the Northern Pacific Railway. This, plus bank failings, precipitated a panic that continued to depress the economy until 1878. But instead of hurting the newly begun newspaper, the depression gave it an even

greater edge over its competitors because it was the least expensive paper in town. When advertising dropped off dangerously,
reflecting the depression, Scripps offered to publish want ad
notices free of charge. The move brought its calculated effect.
Swamped with ads, the paper announced that to accommodate all
its advertisers it was forced to return to the traditional practice
of charging. A rate of seven cents a line was established for Page
One, five cents a line inside. The period of free advertising had
proved to readers that the paper was a good medium to advertise
in. Meanwhile, Dee and his staff were working to create an editorial necessity for Detroiters to buy it.

The *News* campaigned for the purchase of Belle Isle, in the
Detroit River, as a recreation park, a crusade that won immediate
favor with Detroiters who could see the island, so close to the
city's population center, remaining in private hands as a playground
for the rich. At the same time the paper hammered away for the
right of its reporters to attend clandestine meetings of the board
of aldermen, where, it was suspected, private deals were made and
sanctified at the expense of the taxpayer.[11] These crusades boosted
circulation in a city saturated with special interest groups. From
1875 the rise of the *News* was meteoric. Within the decade the
receipts from the paper were sufficient so other opportunities for
investment were explored. In 1878, as the depression waned, James,
George H. and Edward Wyllis Scripps founded the *Cleveland
Penny Press*, built on the formula developed in Detroit. In 1880,
the Scripps papers expanded into Missouri with the *St. Louis
Chronicle*. In the next year the *Cincinnati Post* was founded. But
though James posted the books of the *Press*, the *Chronicle* and the
Post in Detroit along with the books of the *News*, the operation of
the chain papers presented philosophical differences he found
impossible to reconcile with his early success formula for a newspaper. The theory of a low-cost paper to meet a popular demand
had been proved not only by the Scrippses but elsewhere in the
nation as early as 1835 by James Gordon Bennett, founder of the
New York Herald, and later by such publishers as William Randolph Hearst and Joseph Pulitzer. To the theory of the penny press
Hearst, Pulitzer and others added the principle of syndication, the

idea that two or more newspapers could be published at greatly reduced costs by utilizing each other's endeavors. It was James Scripps's belief that such an operation would sap the strength of all the members of the chain and none would be stronger than its weakest link. On this point hung the future of the *Detroit News* as an independent paper, and it would not be resolved easily.

From James Scripps's humble start in Detroit sprang scores of newspapers as family members increased their holdings. He found some of his own capital immersed in outside papers as he answered family appeals for assistance. Yet this was not the success James Scripps was looking for. On the issue of the independent newspaper versus chain newspapers, he eventually was to split with Edward Wyllis and Edward's supporters in the family, including "Miss Ellen" and George H. Scripps. James's obstinance kept the *News* an independent newspaper. But it required fifteen years of litigation that ended after the death of George H. Scripps, when Edward Wyllis swapped his stock in the *News*, which he had inherited from George, for James's stock in the outside newspapers. Soon Edward Wyllis's theory of syndication resulted in a chain operation that bloomed with America's growing demand for a low-cost newspaper that would answer readers' desires to be informed, entertained, and, with the growth of cartoons and comics, titillated. The reward of Edward Wyllis's labors are the Scripps-Howard Newspapers, which bear the name of the founding family and that of Roy Howard, a reporter and editor, who eventually joined in the enterprise.[12] At its peak Scripps-Howard owned thirty-five papers, a group that today has been consolidated into eighteen papers in New York, Pennsylvania, Tennessee, Washington, Colorado, Alabama, Texas, Indiana and New Mexico. The *Cleveland Press* remains the hub of the far-flung network.

James Scripps's insistence on a locally owned and operated newspaper was total. To support the founder's conviction, the *News* for years published a line in its masthead: "Not Affiliated with Any Other Newspaper." The sentence was meant to establish in the reader's mind not only the *News*'s independence but its dedication to Detroit.[13] This philosophy carried over into editorial decision-making. When Scripps appraised the merit of a story suggestion he would ask the location of the setting, and if he didn't recognize it, he would inquire, "How close is that to Woodward?" Throughout the city's history Woodward has been Detroit's Main Street. The paper was never to forget the implied editorial tenet propounded by Scripps that readers were interested most in things that happened close to home. But he also was aware that national and world news often touched close to home. He was a testy fighter in the early efforts to break up the news-gathering monopoly of both the Associated Press and United Press, which at that time distributed its stories only to member papers. To secure an Associated Press connection Scripps bought the remaining stock in the *Detroit Tribune* in 1891.

By the mid-1880s the *News* was such a success that its founder could afford the luxury of travel to Europe and elsewhere. He also could heed his doctor's advice to "take the waters," advice often given those who could afford to bathe in spas for ailments that confounded the medical profession. His was a cranky gall bladder. In these instances, Edward Wyllis would be recalled from Cleveland, where he made his headquarters, and put in charge of the *News,* a decision that invariably led to frustration for James. Edward Wyllis's theories of syndication repeatedly got in the way of James's beliefs on how the *News* ought to be run.[14] Almost immediately upon his arrival in Detroit Edward Wyllis would raise the price of the paper and increase the amount of advertising. Letters would fly to James from family members and staff men. When James was sufficiently aroused, he would hurry home and resume command. Then he would live up to a saying repeated among family members that shows the Scripps family determination: "If a Scripps drowns, look upstream for his corpse." Almost as soon as James entered the door, Edward Wyllis was hastened back to Cleveland by worried top executives. Then James would issue a call for *News* personnel whom Edward Wyllis had dispatched to Cleveland. Next came a Page One announcement — they always were called "Announcement" — that reduced the price of the *News* and warned advertisers that they had to be more sparing in their demands for space. Such an announcement on September 8, 1879, suggested to advertisers that by reducing the size of their ads, they would cut their own costs and both they and the paper would benefit!

By 1877 the *News* had moved its editorial, business and printing facilities to a fourth-floor building at Shelby and Larned.[15] Within five years it would boast a daily circulation of 36,360 — the eleventh largest evening newspaper by circulation in the United States. Its Detroit sales were five times that of the *Detroit Post*, the *Tribune* and the *Free Press* combined. The Shelby Street building, despite numerous additions and renovations, was not representative of the paper's growing prestige in Detroit. It was drafty; soot from a neighboring power plant leaked through a skylight; and at night when the staff was small, rats ventured out of crevices in the woodwork to see what was going on. There was plenty to see.

In 1887 George Gough Booth, a salesman for a Windsor iron and wire works managed by his father, married James's daughter, Ellen W. Scripps, who had been named after "Miss Ellen." The two had met at Sunday church services. The next year, having been appraised sharp in business matters by both Edward Wyllis and James, Booth was asked to leave the iron works and take a position at the *News*. The day he arrived James Scripps escorted him into the paper's business offices and said, "This is where you will work." He then turned on his heels, leaving the *News*'s new business manager to figure out his duties. It did not take him long. The marriage of the Booth and Scripps families was to foster a publishing enterprise that would rival the most influential newspaper institutions in the nation. Booth, whose father, Henry Wood Booth, had operated papers in Toronto and in St. Catharines, Ontario, acted as a liaison between James and Edward Wyllis. Also, he saw the merit in the beliefs of both men. He approved James's conviction that a newspaper thrived when it was independent of outside influences. But he also saw the financial benefits that could be derived in a chain operation. Eventually Booth acquired eight newspapers in Michigan. He gave each a maximum of local autonomy, thus blending James's theory of independence with Edward's idea of a chain operation.

James Scripps's belief in a paper so inexpensive that the lowliest workingman could afford it was put to the test constantly as costs rose. In 1890, when the price of the *News* was two cents, James embarked on a plan to prove the paper could be marketed at a profit for a penny. To do so he began the city's second *Detroit Times*.[16] The first, a daily and Sunday paper, expired in 1884 when the *News* began publishing a Sunday edition. Scripps sold the *Times* for a penny and published it profitably for eighteen months. His point proven, he merged it with the *News* and reduced the price of the *News* to a cent. The next year he bought controlling stock in the *Tribune* and continued to operate it as a morning paper. (It was merged with the *News* [*News-Tribune*] in 1915 when the morning edition was discontinued.)

Booth arrived at the *News* at a time when James was devoting increasing attention to civic affairs. His moves in these years in seeking civic reform, in serving on public commissions and in state politics led his critics to declare he was "trying to run the town." Indeed, he was trying to do more than that: He sought to turn Detroit around from a city noted nationally for graft and corruption to a metropolis where "reform" was more than a gesture of posturing politicians. His backers hailed him for his civic spirit; his critics, often those whom the *News* attacked, charged him with stunting for circulation. History would be on his side.

Crusades begun at the turn of the century and earlier provided the newspaper with editorial policies that were to continue through the decades. Campaigns to make Detroit a better town were aimed at the "corporationists," an epithet that was cast in lead and transformed into the printed word thousands of times over. Lower utility rates, municipal ownership of the street transit system, a public lighting system, home rule — all were declared to be *News* editorial policies. So intent was the *News* on building a city that would serve all its citizens that Peter B. Clark, great-grandson of the founder, who became the paper's fifth publisher in 1963, remembers sitting on his maternal grandfather's knee and being warned "never to work for that socialistic newspaper." This grandfather, Albert E. Peters, was corporate secretary of the Detroit United Railway, with whom the *News* feuded for years. But times and events were to establish that what seemed socialistic before the turn of one century made sound governmental sense in the next. Lower utility rates, a public lighting system, municipal ownership of the transit system and home rule all were to come about as a newspaper and a city joined together in a common cause. Once gained, the philosophy that inspired such change was carried into state and national endeavors.[17] None came about without intense struggle both within the newspaper and without.

In 1890 Detroit was a city of horse-drawn streetcars with a population of 205,876, the fifteenth largest city in the United States. Its main thoroughfares were lighted by electric arc lamps mounted on tall stanchions. Pork was selling for eight cents a pound, butter for twenty-five cents a pound. In this year Samuel Gompers presided at the national convention of the American Federation of Labor, which met in Detroit. William McKinley was President. Some inventors were beginning to tinker with horseless carriages. But bicycles were the chief mode of private transportation, given a boost that year by the development of the drop frame for ladies and pneumatic tires. There were twelve thousand horses that drew private and public vehicles, including fire apparatus. The men of the town leaned heavily toward long sideburns and beards. They wore stiff collars and, often, bow ties. Attire was somber; suit coats sported narrow lapels, and vests were everyday dress for the white-collar worker. Dark, tailored suits were increasingly popular with women, possibly as a result of the women's liberation movement of the day. Women wore shirtwaists, sailor hats, high-laced shoes and fancy embroidered hose. *Hedda Gabler*, Ibsen's play about a most determined woman, and *Black Beauty*, a story about a horse, were popular on stage and in literature.

James Scripps now lived in a larger house on Trumbull Avenue and Grand River Avenue, on the westerly fringe of downtown Detroit. Here he gathered the paintings and pieces of sculpture he had collected in his travels to the spas of Europe. Hattie now sought more of his time, and on Sundays he would take her and the children riding in the Scripps's carriage. His coachman was John Fitzgibbon, whom Scripps soon was to transform into a reporter and correspondent in the Spanish-American War.

Hattie had joined the "then" generation. On Sunday outings she wore a dark tailored suit, with a blouse (often black) with large pearl buttons up the front. Her hair was cropped closely in the manner of the day and was a snarl of natural curls. At sixty-five, James Scripps's hair had turned gray, except for his beard, which was the last to show the telltale sign of age. But if the dress, the customs and the mores seemed to indicate this was the best of times economically and socially, history proved otherwise. Detroit was on the verge of change unparalleled by any city in the nation. The *News* would participate in that change to such an extent that a hundred years after its founding, it could be safely said that Detroit would not be the city it is had there been no *Detroit News*.

2

The Mayor Had Codfish
in His Coattails

IN A POCKET in the tails of his Prince Albert coat, Hazen S. Pingree carried dried codfish, which he chewed as a tonic. He was so convinced of its therapeutic value that once when his daughter was departing by train on a trip east he handed her a packet as she boarded. "Here, Hazel," he said, "take this, and if you get sick on the train chew on it and it'll do you good."[1] A shoe manufacturer, Pingree was destined to become Detroit's most respected, most despised, most volatile, most eccentric mayor in an era responsive to just such leadership. Drafted by the city's established elite to straighten out what Pingree soon was to call "Boodle City, U.S.A.," he took office in 1890, serving until 1897 when he was elected governor. When he found "the people cheated," he blasphemed, sometimes cussing out old friends in the heat of his rancor. Among the men he alternately praised and cussed was James Scripps.

For years the workingmen of Detroit had been seething over poor public transportation, poor roads, poor lighting, high gas and telephone rates, inadequate recreation facilities — all subjects that the *News* had been raging about almost since its founding. To attack these problems, Pingree struck frontal blows, accusing the "corporationists" of greed and politicians of being in their pay. He himself was a politician only in the sense that he held political office.[2] His lack of tact and irritating, high-pitched voice infuriated his targets. But the workingmen, reading of his exploits in the newspapers, loved him. They chose him mayor four times to take the city hesitatingly into the twentieth century. With major urban centers throughout the country suffering the malady of corrupt machine politics, his was not an easy task. As mayor he was alternately a roaring success or a dismal failure. He failed when he bucked odds that one man could not resolve, but he succeeded when he was able to gather the strength necessary to overcome his enemies. Measured in time, his greatest success came after his death as the result of his having brought evil to public attention, where others eventually could root it out. Although the city's newspaper gave vent to Pingree's venom, he attacked them unmercifully each time he failed to agree with them. He referred to the *Free Press* as "grandmotherly."[3] The paper, then avowedly Democratic, did not suit his politics or his disposition. He attacked the *Tribune* and the *News* because of Scripps's dual ownership and he assailed as untruthful the heavily religion-oriented *Journal,* which had been taken over in 1883 by William H. Brearley, the *News's* early advertising contractor.

Despite Pingree's tirades on behalf of honesty in government, James Scripps was skeptical of the Republican party's ability to clean its own house. The *News* opposed Pingree until Scripps, who was actively concerned in city government, was satisfied he would tackle graft and corruption regardless of party affiliation. It didn't take Pingree long. He soon won a national reputation for his headlong daring in assaulting the moneyed elite. Gradually the *News* warmed to the mayor's campaigns, which often jibed with its own. But the paper also defended private enterprise when it saw fit. Often as not the *News* and the mayor were at each other's throats. Only the passing of time showed the paper's role in furthering Pingree reforms, a conclusion observers of the era often missed. During the hectic years, Scripps and Pingree would be seen walking arm in arm one day and on opposite sides of the street the next.

Pingree wore a white vest beneath his copious coat, topped by a full beard and a white derby. Only his shrill voice betrayed his determination: the more he became angered, the more it grew high-pitched. Unlike Pingree, Scripps spoke in a low forceful voice that grew more testy as he became angered. On many issues both men thought almost as one, and each used similar tactics in slaying dragons. When Scripps started the second *Detroit Times* and sold it for a penny, the tactic was not lost on Pingree. In one of his many battles, Pingree started a rival telephone company, manned by his cronies, to force down the rates of the early Michigan Bell Company. Whether or not the use of these tactics was coincidental, it was no accident that each man turned to the broad mass of Detroiters to find the kind of support each needed to reach success in his own field. That Pingree even was nominated was an oddity of nineteenth-century politics.

Determined that the city would collapse under the weight of corruption, Detroit leaders in the Republican party met in 1889 to handpick the GOP's next candidate for mayor. After a lengthy harangue a voice from the floor called for attention. It was that of Elder Francis A. Blades, city controller and presiding pastor of the Methodist-Episcopal Conference. "Mr. President," shouted Blades, "I can name the next mayor of Detroit and not go out of this room. . . . His name is H. S. Pingree, and he sits right over there." Pingree disclaimed the honor immediately. "No, no," he retorted, "I was never in the City Hall except to pay my taxes. I'll double my subscription [to the Republican party] but let me out." Then, prodded to accept, he went on: "Mayor? Why that's political. What in hell do I know about politics? I'm too busy making shoes."[4] He soon showed Detroit and the nation that political savvy was an acquirable art.

Appearing in saloons, where much of the politics of the day was decided, he struck at Detroit's ethnic-political problems, drank "red-eye" whiskey (because that's what it gave you — red eye) to show where he stood on the rising question of Prohibition. He swept the election.

The *News,* which had been suspicious of Pingree during the robust campaign, found the election results nevertheless delightful. "The gang has been overwhelmed," the paper chortled.[5] "Tierney [whom the paper opposed] is beaten in the twelfth ward, Jack Shanahan [also opposed by the paper] was buried in the sixth. . . ." Then the *News* reported that Pingree's chief backers, James and Hugh McMillan, Dexter M. Ferry, General Russell A. Alger — all names that would leave a mark on the city and the nation — had scandalously made campaign contributions "in four figures." But "votes were bought on both sides," the paper editorialized, which seemed to equalize the corruption at the ballot box. Then the paper warned that Pingree "had better devote the time at his command between this date and the day he takes office to acquiring familiarity with local affairs of which he declares himself ignorant." In the manner of the press of the era, which freely attacked its competitors, the *News* reported that "the *Free Press* finds occasion to account for former Mayor John Pridgeon's defeat by holding the *News* responsible for it. The *News* gives the sagest and wisest device," the paper crowed, "on all matters that come within its scope [!] . . ." On Page One of the *News* that day the G. R. Mabley Company, the city's premier men's furnishing store, advertised hats at a dollar discount "to pay election bets."

In his inaugural address on January 14, 1890, Pingree decried Detroit's poor paving, a complaint voiced repeatedly in the *News*.[6] The campaign for better streets eventually brought Detroit to the forefront of cities with improved roadways. In 1909 it laid the first stretch of concrete highway in the nation — one mile long on Woodward Avenue. Pingree rumbled from one festering sore to the next. Taking on the powerful Detroit school board, he painted its corruption in glowing terms. "Why, actually members of this board have sold themselves out regularly to this and that and the other contractor. It is frightful. . . . After they had been bought they frequently sold themselves again, and left the parties they first sold to."[7] Because he was colorful and attacked evils often before he had garnered the facts, Pingree was both the butt and the darling of newsmen. All of this provided circulation ammunition for the *News,* which often delighted in passing on the mayor's charges.

Early in Pingree's term the *Journal* published an article that led him to excoriate the press and perhaps colored his judgment for years.[8] The paper piously declared that the mayor had poisoned two of his horses to avoid feeding them throughout the winter. "It is cheaper to purchase new horses in the spring," he was quoted as saying. In a time when the horse was not only the chief means of transportation but a beloved family servant, howls were heard nationwide. Pingree vehemently denied the story. Whatever the result, it did not hurt him with those who admired him for his sorties against corrupt government. He stood alone in a nation where machine politics created urban political bosses with virtually unlimited power. While the *News* was supporting reform in Detroit, papers such as the *New York Times* were generating steam for reform elsewhere, but not always with such singular success. Scripps's determination to place the *News* in the role of enlightened leadership in Detroit brought the dual rewards of greater readership and satisfaction of ethical purpose, the big canons of journalism. In 1890, grasping a popular chant of workingmen everywhere, the *News* strongly supported labor's campaign for an eight-hour work day.

Circulation soared. Across the nation readers were more than willing to accept the leadership of newspapers they trusted; for the newspaper became the court of last resort in a democratic society that was moving from control by the few to government by the true majority. The *News* was expected by its readers to lead in every area touching their lives. It seldom disappointed them. In the twenty years since its founding, the population of Detroit more than doubled and its circulation had increased tenfold to fifty thousand. That newspapers everywhere grew to wealth and power in exposing evil did not escape many eyes. It was a point to attack when being attacked. When the *News* conducted an unceasing campaign against the old Detroit United Railway (DUR) in the struggle to bring Detroit a less expensive and more accommodating transit system, Jere C. Hutchins, the DUR president, sarcastically declared that it did so because the issue was "a circulation gold mine."[9] Yet William P. Lovett, for years the executive secretary of the Detroit Citizens League, which worked in behalf of voter enlightenment, declared that "the *News* has been the recognized outstanding organ of municipal ownership" of the transit system. At one point in the struggle Pingree got the board of aldermen to charter a rival line, using a well-recognized tactic. The new line's fares were three cents, two cents less than a ride on the DUR. The transit fight was to boil for almost thirty years. The *News* was in the forefront with almost daily articles and cartoons.

The Panic of the winter of 1893 added hunger to the list of subjects on which Pingree and Scripps could merge their talents. The following spring when Pingree advocated "Relief by Work," and proposed a program in which the city's poor could use vacant lots to produce potatoes and other vegetables, cartoonists around the nation lampooned him, picturing him in the shape of a huge potato. The *News*, though skeptical at first, bounced to the mayor's side on June 13, 1894, by publishing a page headlined, "This Page Belongs to Pingree."[10] On it was a story reporting that the mayor planned to hold an auction on the steps of city hall to raise money to start garden plots and buy seed. He would put up one of his prized and well-publicized horses as a starter. Another article declared that potato patches "were catching on in other cities." And there was the usual critical article against the *News*'s chief rival, the *Free Press*, which had ridiculed the idea. The headline, quoting Pingree, read, "I Don't Give a Cuss" [about the *Free Press* criticism]. "Cuss" was the strongest four-letter word allowed in the *News*, which already had become "the family newspaper." But Pingree's page also carried a cartoon of the seal of Michigan. Where the Latin word, *Tuebor* ("I will defend") normally is found, the artist had lettered in "Tuber," a not-too-subtle jest. The patches proved most successful. Detroit's large colonies of immigrant poor took readily to the land and produced bumper crops.

As Pingree moved more and more toward the zealot, he ran into increasingly stiff opposition from the city's establishment. Even friends who had proposed him for mayor found his bombast intolerable. When the newspapers did not leap to his support, he cursed them from public platforms. At one point he declared of the *Free Press*, "I wouldn't believe its weather reports." He attacked the *News* just as unmercifully, and in 1895, summing up his first five years in office, he declared "the newspapers did not fight for the city." It was the talk of an impatient man who saw too many fights end futilely. The papers in Detroit and throughout much of the nation gave important space to the issues of reform. Besides the ethical principles involved, support of reform made plain business sense. Only the foolhardy newspaper defended the obvious evils of the day. It was the *News*'s opinion that no business could

long survive in a city whose citizens 'had lost faith in its government. It set out to reaffirm that faith in every way it saw fit.

The role of Scripps and the *News* is evident in the series of reforms initiated during Pingree's years as mayor. In 1893, while
keeping up a running fight with the private transit companies,
Pingree began looking into the price of gas in Detroit and in other
cities. He found that Detroit's rate was the highest of cities its
size. By doing so he made an enemy of William C. McMillan, president of the Detroit Gas Company, an amalgam of several firms.
McMillan, a member of one of Detroit's leading families, was able
to rally much of the composite wealth of the city to his side. The
issue erupted during hearings in Lansing in which Detroit sought
approval of a new charter. Articles in the *News* called the legislative maneuvering "a circus." Some two hundred anticharter lobby-
ists filled the capital and bribery was charged daily by Pingree
forces. Digging by the *News* uncovered an agreement dated in 1848
that gave Detroit's board of aldermen a voice on gas rates as long
as gas pipes occupied the public streets. The gas company was
furious and the battle lasted three years. In 1896 the Detroit Gas
Company voluntarily reduced its rates, making them commensurate
with rates in other cities.

Gas prices fell 30 percent.

The fight for cheaper electrical rates was equally vicious, lasting
from 1892 to 1895.[11] The *News*'s support was clear. It assailed private
contractors who were providing public electric lighting. "The
lights are all paid for as being 2,000 candlepower," it revealed on
October 19, 1892. "But they are often so dim that one candle
would be a fair rival to the sputtering, fizzling ball of light that
hovers between the carbons more uncertain than if the streets
were without any light except the stars and the moon." Before
three years had passed — on April 1, 1895 — the fight was won.
Public ownership of the lighting of streets and public places became a fact with the operation of a plant under Detroit's Public
Lighting Commission (PLC). In its first year of operation the
commission announced the plant had saved the city $80,000, and
greater savings were to come. Pingree had brought a top-flight
engineer to run the plant. Alex Dow, who years later became the

president of the newly organized Detroit Edison Company, not only managed the plant efficiently, but passed on the savings to the consumer. The PLC, which continues to provide limited lighting to the city, has served over the years as a benchmark of cost in appraising electric rates. From this beginning, utility commissions followed to regulate costs and profits in the public interest.

Pingree was in his fourth term as mayor when he tangled with the telephone company.[12] In conducting the battle he used an old stratagem: He got the board of aldermen to grant a franchise to a company manned by cronies. "Pingree's company" soon attracted twice as many customers as its well-established competitor. The rate war lasted until 1900 when "Pingree's company," with smaller capitalization, could not meet the rising need and was absorbed by Michigan Bell. But the competition had served its purpose. It brought enlightened management and the desired lower rates. Again the *News* had found an issue it could support. Extras appeared with each new revelation. The cry of the newsboys almost always began "Ping-greee" when the mayor was advocating something that would catch the eye and ears of the average man.

In 1897 Pingree and Scripps found another common ground — Free Silver. Although Scripps was opposed by members of his own board of directors, including Edward Wyllis, he joined Pingree in backing Democrat William Jennings Bryan for President in both the *News*, his evening paper, and in the *Tribune*, his morning paper. At the same time the *News* supported Pingree as the Republican nominee for governor, although Republicans nationally were against Free Silver. The Democratic *Free Press* bolted its party over the issue and supported Republican William McKinley. The *News* boasted that the *Tribune* and the *News* were the only papers in Detroit to publish all of Bryan's speeches, including his famous "Cross of Gold" address, a classic that was repeated year after year in declamation contests in the city's schools. It was an exciting year. In June, the *News* organized its own band, made up of newsboys. It appeared in parades and at concerts in a musical move to keep readers happy and interested. The paper's support of Pingree was accompanied by loud oompahs.

In November the reform mayor led the GOP ticket in Michigan while William McKinley, who won the presidency on his support of the gold standard, trailed in the vote count. Because he backed Pingree and Free Silver, Scripps felt the wrath of bankers, something Pingree, who earlier had been shut off from credit in Detroit, could understand. Local banks called in Scripps's loans, which had been made to expand the ever-growing newspaper, and advertising dipped sharply. He came within an eyelash of bankruptcy. But by mortgaging personal property and with newspaper economies, he weathered the storm.

Pingree's infighting with the "corporationists" was politically classic.[13] When a merchant canceled a contract with Pingree and Smith, the mayor's shoe factory, over a dispute with Pingree's politics, Pingree delivered a coup de grâce. Knowing that the merchant spent Saturday afternoons in a house of ill repute, he ringed it with guards, then ordered the house quarantined for smallpox. Marching down the street with a coterie of newsmen and cronies, Pingree saw the troublemaker in a window. The mayor, feigning surprise, declared, "I'll be damned." There was a quick huddling of heads at the door of the house. Suddenly it was discovered that there was no smallpox in the house and the quarantine was lifted. The merchant fled out the back door and the shoe contract was quietly reinstated.

While the key to Pingree's victories was his dedication to social reform, the rise of the *News* as Detroit's leading newspaper resulted not from figuratively riding Pingree's coattails, but often in pointing the way. The paper led in a series of crusades that changed the very makeup of the city. The paper's role was indisputable as a leading proponent of home rule, which would take city functions out of the control of the rural-dominated legislature. At the same time it argued for an art institute to broaden the city's cultural base and the reclamation of the waterfront, an eyesore occupied by railroads, flophouses, and industrial buildings. The reclamation campaign grew into a crusade for a civic center and downtown improvements aimed at keeping the city intact as a business, cultural and social entity.

Despite many mutual interests, Pingree and Scripps were not

blindly attached to each other's thinking. Far from it. When the paper felt Pingree had exaggerated some evil, it said so; when Pingree believed the *News* and other Detroit papers were not fairly representing his views or were hiding some dereliction, he posted his opinions on bulletin boards in prominent public places. When he ran for governor he sought to hang on to his position as mayor. He was prevented from doing so by court action.

As governor, Pingree's program was directed primarily at initiating legislation that would foster urban reform, give Michigan a system of primary elections and end the handpicking of candidates by political parties. And he never forgot the corporate giants. Always trying to lower transit fares, he sought legislation to limit the railroads to charging a maximum of two cents a mile. Then he tackled the trusts — a trust-buster years ahead of Theodore Roosevelt, whose antitrust declarations and heroics in the Spanish-American War were to ride him into the White House as McKinley's vice president. Pingree was successful in none of his proposals, many of them too far ahead of their time. Also, he was the epitome of the city slicker when the phrase neatly separated urban Americans from the "rubes" who lived in the country.

As if the trend of news was too doleful, in 1900 the *News* introduced a color comic supplement, Foxy Grandpa and Toyland, a circulation-begetting idea of Hereward S. Scott, a fellow Canadian brought onto the *News* by Booth. More syndicated comics soon followed. That year the paper started the first photographic department in the city. In 1901 William A. Kuenzel was hired on a full-time basis to capture the rapidly changing history on photographic plates. Kuenzel acquired a national reputation for historic pictures as the city moved into the rip-roaring decades just ahead. The crusades and the comics, which brought greater circulation, also created a demand for more space by advertisers. When Scripps reluctantly agreed to publish more advertising "as a public service," the *News* introduced other features to give the paper balance. A sports and a women's page were added along with other features that whetted the readers' interest beyond politics. But politics still commanded prime attention.

As Pingree's term grew to a close the *News* proposed him for the presidency of the United States.[14] In many ways the reform mayor had all the qualifications of Teddy Roosevelt, who would become President upon McKinley's assassination. But depressed at his lack of success in the state capital in Lansing, Pingree traveled to Europe to mull over his future. Before he left, he met with Scripps. The two shook hands in Scripps's office. Would the governor write for the *News* while he was overseas? Pingree agreed in an obvious display of friendship toward the newspaper. His articles began to appear on February 14, 1901, describing his experiences in the Madeira Islands, in South Africa where he shot an elephant, on the Red Sea and in Egypt. The articles ended abruptly on June 14. A dispatch from London declared that Pingree had taken ill, apparently from a disease contracted in Africa. Although he was attended by the king's physician, an obvious recognition of his world stature, he grew weaker and weaker. On June 19, 1901, the entire front page of the *News,* save the weather report and a short filler, was devoted to the death of Hazen Senter Pingree. A prominently displayed editorial, signed by Scripps, hailed the former mayor and governor for his role in the development of the city and called for "a suitable monument."

The monument, a seated bronze figure, was erected in Grand Circus Park, where shoppers and office workers pass it by the thousands every day. Yet only those who know the history of the city can grasp the significance of the wispy smile, the heavy jowls and thick eyebrows, the determined grip of the hands. In the making of a city he played a leading role in the search for truth and honesty in government, in stirring up skeletons that would continue to rattle for decades after his death. The *News* would help rattle them.

With Pingree dead, Scripps was determined to personally carry on the fight for civic reform in the state's capital. Although he had been defeated in an earlier try for office, he ran for state senator, and was elected in November 1902. Immediately he set about to initiate a series of reforms. If Pingree had upset the state legislature by his direct and high-pitched approach, Scripps would try a lowered voice and sound logic. He introduced bills, one after the other, that would have given Michigan a primary election law, opened the way for home rule and municipal ownership of the public transit system, and allowed urban communities to select their own commissions governing police, the parks, and the arts — all of which had been taken away from Detroit in 1901 by "Ripper Legislation," a term made popular by politicians to describe laws that uprooted the status quo. In all, Scripps proposed twenty-four bills. None of them passed. On May 5, 1903, he rose before the senate as the session grew to a close and lamented its failure to act on any of his proposals. "Just as cities are supplied with water economically without the intervention of private corporations," he declared, "so it is possible that many of the public utilities, gas works, electric light plants, street railways and telephones may likewise be owned and managed by municipalities advantageously."[15] The next day the *News* editorialized that Scripps's opinions on public ownership were bitterly distasteful to the party machine and its bosses. "His belief that the rights of the general public should dictate the action of legislative bodies is contrary to their practices and in championing that belief he has necessarily walked on some tender toes. . . ."

In polished words he was saying in the senate what Pingree had said two scant years before in a shrill voice, tattooed with his never-published "cuss words." As Pingree had insisted, Scripps declared that "these were no socialistic schemes." Both men offered their proposals as Republicans. At the close of the session, Scripps, then sixty-eight, announced he would not run again. As did Pingree, he vacated the capital disillusioned at the slowness of democracy. On his return to Detroit, he urged younger men to run for office and carry on the fight for reform. He left the public forum to go home to Hattie, who tried to comfort him.[16] But the struggle had taken its toll. A disease that affected his spinal column gradually sapped his strength, and three years later he was dead.

The irony of history is that many of the ideas subscribed to by Pingree and Scripps were realized in one form or another in the years following their death. In Scripps's case, he left the city's largest and most powerful newspaper to carry on battles on behalf of the commonweal. He had carefully laid plans to see that the paper would remain independent and in secure hands for the task ahead.

While he lay hopelessly ill, realizing he had only a short time to live, he dictated how he wanted the newspaper to be carried on. For thirty years, he ruled, the paper would be held in trust by those who subscribed to his basic thinking. Three men were charged with carrying on the newspaper's role of leadership in Detroit: his son, William E. Scripps, treasurer of the *News,* and his sons-in-law, George Gough Booth, Ellen's husband, who had served as general manager and vice president, and Edgar Bancroft Whitcomb, husband of Anna V. Scripps, who served as business manager of the *Tribune* when Scripps assumed full control of it. In the text of the testamentary trust, Scripps stipulated that he should be succeeded as publisher and president by Booth; and upon Booth's retirement, he hoped that the board of directors would see fit to elevate his son to the top position.[17]

Because of the age of the inheritors the trust virtually placed Booth in command of the *News* for the next three decades, important years as the city and the paper expanded far beyond the founder's early prescription of success. Scripps willed that after the duration of the trust, shares in the property that he controlled should be distributed to his descendants according to a formula recognizing the closest of kin. By the year of the dissolution of the trust, 1936, there were forty-eight descendants. Scripps then owned 41¾ of 50 outstanding shares with a par value of $1,000. He specified that 60 percent of his holdings in the Evening News Association and other properties managed by the James E. Scripps Corporation, a real estate holding company, and 24 shares in the Bay City Times Company, which he purchased in 1903, be distributed as follows: 60 percent to his four surviving children, 25 percent to thirteen grandchildren and 15 percent to thirty-one great-grandchildren. The Bay City Times stock subsequently was conveyed to the Booth Publishing Company, owned by George Gough Booth and his brother, Ralph. The trust assured that the paper would be closely held by members of the family through years when its independence would be tested sorely by nationally syndicated newspapers that built publishing empires by fulfilling the nation's need for an inexpensive popular press.

The trust was signed on May 4, 1906. In less than a month, James E. Scripps was dead. The four-page tabloid he founded in 1873 published twelve pages on the day of his death, May 29, 1906.

Among the mourners were Hattie; his daughters, Ellen S. (Mrs. George G. Booth), Anna V. (Mrs. Edgar Bancroft Whitcomb), Grace M. (Mrs. Rex B. Clark); his son, William E. and ten grandchildren. All were to live through the era ahead when many of the founder's early desires came to fruition. On January 11, 1915, stock in the *News* was raised from 50 to 500 shares with a par value of $100. On November 27, 1922, capital stock was raised to $10,000,-000. Early desires would not be realized quickly or without persistent struggle.

Hattie recalled the early struggle, how she had been called "the Mother of the *News*," when actually she seldom entered the *News* building, never wrote or proofread any of its articles. She explained her role most succinctly. Speaking of the first night of publication and despair, she said, "I think that if I hadn't stood back of my husband that night, there might never have been any *News*." It was a modest appraisal. She lived to see the development of a newspaper and a city her husband had nurtured in its infancy.

His son, William E. Scripps, the "Will" in his diary who was so bent on mechanical things that it appeared he might be lost as a newspaperman, remembered his father for yet another reason. Will recalled how his father tolerated Thomas E. Clark, a young Detroit inventor who tinkered with wireless telegraphy, when others wrote him off as a crackpot. In 1902 Clark sat in the elder Scripps's office and predicted, "The time will come when you will sit in your home and be entertained by music played thousands of miles away."

James Scripps looked at him suspiciously. But Clark went on. "Men will talk across countless miles of waste and water. Nations will be drawn closer together." Because Will, then twenty, was interested in such things, the publisher agreed to attend a demonstration in a loft Clark had rented. James and Will climbed the steps to witness the transmission of a message to the Chamber of Commerce Building a few blocks away. Amid a flurry of crackles and sparks, Clark signaled an operator at the Chamber of Commerce Building and got a signal of recognition.[18]

James Scripps wrote a check for $1,000, convinced there was something in the idea. He had become an investor in radio without knowing it. Will never forgot it, and eighteen years later he would capitalize on his father's investment.

3

All about Honest Tom

ON THE MORNING of July 26, 1912, a Friday, John C. Lodge, a strait-laced young politician left his apartment on Garfield, an east-west street intersecting Woodward, and walked to the nearest streetcar safety island. There he boarded a Detroit United Railway (DUR) "breeze scooper" for a nickel ride downtown where he transferred to another car whose final destination was River Rouge, a suburban community populated largely by descendants of early French settlers. The open trolley, the DUR's summer version of air-conditioned rapid transit, was the butt of many a cartoonist's joke.

As was his habit, Lodge had purchased a copy of the morning *Free Press*. In his twenties he had worked as a reporter for the *Free Press* and later was its city editor. He found nothing startling in the paper, certainly no hint of the civic storm that was at that moment about to engulf city hall.[1]

Lodge was one of thirty-six aldermen who represented eighteen wards, an electoral division soon to be expanded to forty-two aldermen in twenty-one wards. The wards, devised in 1825 as fire zones — just as they were in much of early America — had grown into political subdivisions by the simple process of evolution. While the ward system had its advantages in some communities, because it placed emphasis on neighborhood representation in city government, it had run amok in many of the large urban centers. Although a number of ward systems have persisted into modern times, they were fraught with corruption shortly after the turn of the century.

The clustering of ethnic groups created gardens of Eden for ward bosses.

Served by wardheelers, who did their bidding, ward bosses intervened for troubled people with various government agencies. The price of this service often was cash, more often the vote. The urban scandals of the early 1900s eventually spawned some of the nation's most domineering political machines. Out of them grew Tom Pendergast in Kansas City, Boss William Marcy Tweed in New York, Big Bill Thompson in Chicago. Yet a party machine of Big Bill Thompson's stature did not materialize in Detroit despite the presence of ethnic groups. Arriving to seek work in the city's growing industrial plants, nationality groups quickly were the prey of corrupt politicians. In 1900, 12 percent of the citizenry could not speak English. That Detroit moved to end the evils of ward politics was no accident. In July 1912, a chain of events began that eventually changed the very form of government in the city, making Detroit the first metropolis in the nation to institute a nonpartisan form of government. The *News*'s leading role in this resulted from a strange set of circumstances.

Detroit's ward bosses were its saloonkeepers and their masters were the brewers, competing private utilities and corporations lacking social responsibility. Lodge's own election to the council had been made possible by Billy Boushaw, whose saloon on Beaubien, at the Detroit River in downtown Detroit, was a gathering place of sailors and dock hands. When the grain and ore boats on the Great Lakes tied up for the winter, the deck and dock hands turned to Boushaw and his two-story unpainted frame waterfront bar and hotel for food, board and wintering-over money. In appreciation, the men voted as a bloc in the powerful First Precinct of the First Ward — Billy Boushaw's precinct. When Lodge ran for office in November 1910, Boushaw passed the word. Lodge was an easy winner. With many of the city's civic leaders, Lodge respected Boushaw as an especially honest saloonkeeper and philanthropist to the down-and-out. That Boushaw used his largess to garner votes was an acceptable element of urban politics. When in 1916 Lodge sought the election of his close friend

James S. Holden, who had begun to amass a real estate fortune, as number 2 on the ticket, he went to Boushaw. "Just leave it to me," Boushaw told Lodge. The vote in the First Precinct was 181 for Lodge and 179 for Holden, the two votes being the difference in Boushaw's respect for Lodge over the second nominee.[2]

Now in his second term on the board of aldermen, Lodge was aware of the usual petty thievery and conniving. Detroit's five newspapers had been pecking away at the skulduggery since the 1880s. Reform Mayor Hazen S. Pingree's nickname for Detroit, "Boodle City," had put the city on the nation's front pages, but to no avail. Stories of graft abounded; some were plainly humorous. Jay G. Hayden, who joined the *News* in 1907 and was assigned to the city hall beat, reported that he approached Thomas E. Glinnan, alderman from the Eighteenth Ward, after reading a story in the *Detroit Journal* accusing Glinnan of accepting graft. "Mr. Glinnan," Hayden said, "the *Journal* says that you've accepted a $50 bribe." Glinnan looked sharply at Hayden and began to laugh. "Jay, anytime it's that small an amount, you can just publish my denial. Now this guy Rosenthal [an alderman] — you can buy him for twenty-five bucks."[3]

But despite such denials, Lodge and others continued to hear enough stories to wonder about the extent of the corruption. What Lodge did not know as he got off the trolley in River Rouge, where he worked as secretary of his brother Edwin's lumberyard, was that the lid was about to be blown off. He entered the office and began working on the books. The business of the lumberyard had undergone a traumatic boom in recent years, reflecting Detroit's new position in the industrial world. The company's customers no longer were furniture makers but the city's budding new auto companies. Wood in body frames, die molds and pallets had become big business.

The storm that had been gathering was to hit with a sour splash when a newsboy deposited a late edition of the *News* on his desk. Nine aldermen had been caught in a trap baited by Edward R. Schreiter, secretary of the board of aldermen, who had confessed that as secretary he had played a key role in arranging the bribery of aldermen. He told the story to William J. Burns, whose detective agency had been quietly hired three months before by a group of civic leaders led by Andrew H. Green, Jr., manager of a downriver coke processing plant. While the plot was thickening in his midst, Lodge had been unaware of it. Of the city's newspapers, only the *News* knew what was transpiring. Its awareness of the impending entrapment came about in an unusual way.

With Hayden and Edward Fitzgerald reporting from city hall, the paper had been chipping away at the board of aldermen incessantly. Daily across the top of its lead editorial column it ran this item: "No more public service franchises on any terms, and the termination of all existing grants at the earliest possible date. Government by the people, and not by private corporations." The constant barrage worried Burns as he got closer and closer to his quarry. Two weeks before the detective planned to spring his trap, he complained to Green that the *News*'s "meddling" might uncover his plot. Green promptly went to the aged red-brick *News* building at Shelby and Larned and walked to the second floor office of Edwin G. Pipp, managing editor. The power of the paper was not reflected in the editor's office. It had stark, plastered walls, linoleum on the floor. Pipp, tall, with small, piercing eyes, considered "a horse of a worker" by his contemporaries, was making a career of ferreting out corruption in the city. He had the Pingree disdain for roadbuilders. As a reporter he could be seen with an iron rod probing the ground alongside new street paving to see if it met the specified thickness. Occasionally he would carry a sledgehammer to the site of suspected thin paving and break it up. His inordinate interest in the public weal moved him into the editor's chair of the newspaper.

Pipp sat at his desk and looked inquisitively at Green through wire-rimmed glasses. "Mr. Pipp," said Green. "I want to ask a favor." Pipp studied Green and intuitively knew this was not an ordinary visit. "What is it, Andy?" he asked evenly. Green hesitated for a moment, then began: "Well, we've laid a trap to catch the boodlers in city hall," he blurted, "and your paper is getting so damn close that we're afraid you'll scare them off. I want you to lay off city hall until we can make our move." Pipp stretched his long legs across the corner of his desk. "I'm afraid," he said, with a knowing pause, "that you had better tell me the whole story." The editorials that had jerked Burns to attention had warned that rumors of bribery were rampant at city hall in connection with a forthcoming vote on a petition to close Seventh Street, on the near west side near the river, to permit the building of a shipping terminal by the Wabash Railroad. The *News* was in favor of the terminal and the street closing. But if the rumors of bribery persisted, it warned editorially, the paper would throw whatever weight it possessed against it.[4]

Green now explained that his old friend, Glinnan, hailed throughout the city as "Honest Tom Glinnan," was suspected of taking bribes for various votes in the council, as were several other aldermen. Green said he did not believe Glinnan was involved. But to stop the rumors he had agreed to head a syndicate that put up $10,000 to hire the Burns Detective Agency. Burns was in Detroit, posing as a representative of the railroad. As "Walter Brennan," he had already passed the word that he was interested in getting favorable council action on the street closing. To confuse the situation and muddy the rumors, Burns had a detective working for him also named Brennan.

Green now provided a tempting piece of news for the editor. Schreiter, the board clerk, had given Burns a list of individuals he thought would accept a bribe. The list included the sum of money Schreiter thought each man could be bought for! The top price — $1,000; the lowest — $100; the average — $300. With this information Burns rented two offices on the fourth floor of the eighteen-story Ford Building on Griswold Street, then Detroit's Wall Street. When the trap was to be sprung, Burns, as "Walter Brennan," would sit in Room 409 and make the payoffs. His agents, including the real detective Brennan, were to wait in the adjoining office, peeking through a hole and recording whatever transpired on a dictagraph, called by Burns a "dectectaphone." This recorded conversation then would be played on a dictaphone in any court case.

Pipp received this information with some misgiving. There had been talk at the paper of backing Glinnan for mayor in the forthcoming election. Nothing on the record indicated Glinnan had a devious political background. Like Green, Pipp was not convinced Burns was on the right scent. But he was not about to let his feelings get in the way of plain common sense. Pipp now outlined to Green an arrangement by which the *News* would remain silent. The paper would halt its snooping and its probing as long as it received a day-by-day accounting of Burns's activities and, finally, an exclusive story when the trap was sprung. In addition, the *News* would cooperate with Burns, providing whatever information it possessed. Green agreed, shook hands with Pipp and left. Pipp immediately reached for his telephone and called Malcolm Bingay, city editor, who in later years became editor of the *Free Press* and a daily columnist.

As agreed, each morning Green turned over the complete record of Burns's activities of the day before. The reports continued for almost two weeks and unfolded a conspiracy in which an attempt would even be made to link strait-laced Pipp in some sort of chicanery in the hope of silencing the newspaper. The reports included the list of men whom Schreiter said would accept money. At one point it was rumored Pipp's name would emerge because of the paper's reported stance on Honest Tom Glinnan for mayor. Meanwhile, Hayden and Fitzgerald rented an office opposite Burns's in the Ford Building. On the day of the payoff, the reporters watched the comings and goings of aldermen as they slipped into Burns's office. The dictagraph was the first on record to be used as a listening device in a suspected illegal activity. There was discussion of whether it would clearly record the voices because of the distance involved. But nothing was said about whether its use might be construed as an abridgment of constitutional rights. Burns told his group that he would speak loudly to each alderman entering the office. He'd say, "Hello, are you Alderman So-and-So?" After receiving an answer, he'd add, "I've got you down here for $100" (or whatever amount Schreiter had indicated). By speaking loudly he'd make sure that the names and the sums would be recorded on the dictagraph in the words of the aldermen.

One by one the aldermen who had been listed entered the office and followed the script laid out by the detective. "That's right, that's what I told Eddie," or "That's the figure I counted on." That is, until Alderman David Rosenthal of the Fifth Ward arrived. "Hello, you're Alderman Rosenthal, aren't you?" Burns bellowed. No answer. Rosenthal, Burns later recounted, smiled wisely and nodded his head up and down. "And you are supposed to get $100, Alderman Rosenthal?" Burns persisted. Rosenthal said nothing. Instead, Burns later related, the alderman waved his hands and shook his head from side to side. When Burns appeared puzzled, Rosenthal held up two fingers. Although not a word had been spoken Burns reported he handed Rosenthal $200, and Rosenthal silently left the office without so much as a pantomimed "thank you." The only words on the dictagraph were Burns's.

As each alderman left the office he was arrested by waiting police. Each was relieved of the marked money in his possession. When the last man on the list had arrived and was arrested, Hayden and Fitzgerald scurried to the *News* office to write their stories. During the preceding day Bingay had had engravings made of the nine men listed by Schreiter. He also swore two printers to secrecy and much of the background information gleaned from the daily reports was set in type. When this copy was set, Pipp locked all the trays of type and the engravings in the office safe.

When Hayden and Fitzgerald reported the trap was sprung, Pipp took the trays from the safe and carried them into the composing room. In his hands was the story of the biggest government scandal in the city's history to date. The only other item on Page One would be the weather report.

When Lodge read the *News,* sitting at his lumberyard desk, he was dumbfounded at the magnitude of the charges. Schreiter had been the fixer. In his confession to the police, recorded on the dictagraph, he talked freely about "boodling operations in the council." Said the *News:* "Schreiter . . . told just how the money was distributed after each deal. Each grafting alderman knew just where to go on council nights for his share of the boodle. Some of the money was pinned behind the curtains in the council chamber. Some was hidden in the desks, some under rugs. All each alderman had to do when a 'divvie' was ready was to go to his boodle-trysting place and grab off the money. They knew just as well where to go as they knew the places at their dinner table. . . ."[5]

That same day Lodge told the *News* he would enter a resolution at the next board meeting calling for the elimination of the position of secretary, thus ending Schreiter's role of fixer. But this was just a minor step in the governmental changes to come.

Green, who dealt the story to the *News,* also was shocked at the outcome. For he believed even beyond the end that his friend Glinnan was above approach by bribers. The *News* told of his sorrow in an article reporting his actions as police led Glinnan away. "Tom," Green cried, "you know this town is rotten and it is up to you to tell everything. Tell everything, Tom, and when this is over I will take care of you down at the works, and you can start all over again in life." The statement was to haunt Green later.

The irony for Green was that his old friend's name was at the top of the list: "Glinnan — $1,000," the biggest of the accused bribetakers. The *News*'s role in the revelation was announced the next day on Page One in a letter from Green, addressed to the editor: "Dear Sir: I want to express my appreciation of the hearty cooperation of yourself and the *News* in working with me to uncover the graft in connection with the Wabash deal in the council. The work would have failed absolutely but for your readiness to work with me. The pointers you gave me and turned over to the detectives invariably proved to be right leads that resulted in success to the work. I want to say also that I would never have thought of going into the work of ferreting out the graft but for the suggestion given me by Mr. George G. Booth, of the *News,* some time ago." It was the first indication that the publisher of the newspaper had played a hand in the investigation.

The exposé spelled the doom of the old order. The hints of bribery that the city's newspapers had been publishing since the 1880s had now been brought to a dramatic head. Day after day articles struck hard at grafting in high places. Glinnan, the first to be indicted, was the plum to be plucked. But the plucking was not easy. The legal maneuvering was classic. For two and a half years the *News* pursued its quarry. Between 1912 and 1914, when Glin-nan's trial ended, the paper published more than five hundred articles — an exposé of corruption that could not be ignored even by the most callous citizen or politician.[6]

During the two years, more aldermen were indicted on charges of grafting. But the collapse of the house of cards depended on Glinnan's conviction. It did not come. As the case went to the jury, the *News* reported that the defense attorney, James McNamara, had made an impassioned plea, charging a gigantic frameup of Glinnan and all the rest. All, he said, had been lured into the Ford Building where money was planted on their person. He charged that Burns, the detective, was a slayer of character, who hoped to build a national reputation by his pseudo-exposures of graft in Detroit.

In his summation, McNamara brought the jury to tears. Looking at Honest Tom Glinnan, then into each juror's eyes, he began with a quotation from the Lord's Prayer, "Lead us not into temptation but deliver us from evil." Green's offer to take care of Glinnan was just a further example of the devious trap. An exhausted jury was poised to say, "Amen." Besides, most Detroiters already had made up their minds that the trouble lay deeper than Tom Glinnan or any of the others.

The trap proved to be largely ironical. The setting of it and the arrests resulted in national recognition of the William J. Burns Detective Agency, which had been founded in 1909. The Glinnan case made the Burns agency a strong rival of the long-famous Pinkertons. On April 27, 1915, the *News* ran its final "running" story of the trial. With Glinnan acquitted, the prosecuting attorney washed out the cases against the lesser aldermen. If the big fish could not be caught, none of the rest were catchable.

The irony was heightened when it was discovered that there had been no real reason for the bribery. In a straw vote taken before Burns had even arrived in Detroit, thirty-five of the thirty-six aldermen had indicated that they were in favor of the street closing. The only opposition came from the alderman representing the people on the affected street. Passing up a bribe for something you were going to vote for anyway certainly was more than a politician could be expected to endure.

The dismay in the *News*'s offices over the outcome of the litigation was tempered by the knowledge that forces had been set in motion to right the wrong that made it all possible — the peculiar makeup of the aldermanic system. During the long exposé, *News* editorials argued the need for a new city charter. Henry M. Leland, head of the Citizens League and an automobile pioneer, was urged to take a leading role. Enabling legislation had paved the way in 1912, six years after Scripps's death and ten years after the death of Pingree, who had also found deaf ears in Lansing. The Glinnan case highlighted the need for civic change, but more work remained to be done.

Daily articles pointed to the twin evils of a ward system controlled by "corporationists" and private ownership of the public transit system.[7] Leland's first charter commission proposal was rejected by the voters in 1916, not because they did not want a change, but because it was "too weak." A new commission was appointed in 1917 as the nation entered World War I. Despite the frustrations of the war, voters went to the polls on June 25, 1918, and adopted a new charter by a margin of eight to one.[8] With its adoption Detroit became the first major city in the United States to institute a nonpartisan form of government. In November, with the war drawing to a close, voters again went to the polls and chose a mayor, a city clerk, a city treasurer and nine councilmen, all elected at large. Leading the list of councilmen was John Lodge. Trailing and out of the running was Glinnan, who had won election in his ward three times following his indictment but failed in his first citywide test, last in a slate of eighteen. No longer could ward bosses such as Billy Boushaw, whose reputation was better than most, guarantee a candidate election to the council. While the new charter could not insure voters that future politicians would be simon-pure, men such as Lodge, who won respect during the years of greatest scandal, could run more easily on their record. They would not be forced to seek help from some of the city's least desirable citizens. Lodge's campaign was remarkable in that he did not make a single campaign speech, a promise he later admitted he had made to his mother before he ran for office. Mrs. Lodge felt that political speeches "were uncouth."[9] During the next forty years Lodge kept this record clear. He broke it only to deliver a State of the City address when he served as mayor, twice in an acting capacity and again when he was elected to the office in 1928.

During the long struggle to bring Detroit a nonpartisan city government, the paper hammered away at a pet hatred of its founder, the private transit systems. In 1904, the *News* hired Burt Thomas, who became a nationally known cartoonist for his illustrations that supported the paper's editorial attack on the discomforts and the expense of the old trolley lines. Thomas's first "Mr. Straphanger" cartoon appeared on January 5, 1912. "Mr. Straphanger" was a woebegone figure, unable to overcome the forces that ruled his life, the prototype of the Sad Sack of World War II. "Mr. Straphanger" became a symbol of the average citizen in his struggle against "Mr. Moneybags," who kept transit fares high and service at a minimum. The paper editorialized that the city could operate its own system more cheaply and pour the profits into better service.

Not everyone agreed with the *News,* including one of its leading advertisers, Joseph L. Hudson, a respected participant in civic affairs. The newspaper's editorial position on municipal ownership sent Hudson scurrying to the Shelby Street offices of the paper on numerous occasions. The first of note occurred in March 1906, when the clothier was president of the Detroit Municipal League, which he began. The organization fell out of favor by 1912 when the Detroit Citizens League was founded. Balding, the ends of his broad mustache twisted and upturned, he walked the five blocks from his store at Gratiot and Farmer and stormed into the office of Hereward S. Scott, *News* general manager. Scott peered from behind his veneer desk, over the tops of rimless glasses and through the pall of cigar smoke that always seemed to veil his face. Seeing the flush on Hudson's face, he stroked his red Vandyke beard (which had brought him the office nickname of "Pink Whiskers") and waited for Hudson to speak.

Ignoring the usual pleasantries, Hudson launched into the crux of his visit — the *News*'s opposition to the DUR. He ended with the threat that he would "pull my advertising out of the *News* unless you change your policy on this thing." The merchant, fearful the city's takeover of the transit system might result in the tearing up of DUR tracks on Woodward, hurting business, did not see the long-range benefits of the *News*'s demands for an improved city-owned system.

Scott, not known for his patience, was quick to react. The hair on the nape of his neck already had stiffened and his Vandyke spoke with a quiver almost before the words rolled over his lips. "Mr. Hudson," he said coldly, "you cannot take your advertising out of the *News* because it already is out." At this moment Hudson got up from the stiff-backed chair where he had deposited himself, turned his back and disappeared down a narrow passage in the direction from whence he had come. Scott tipped back in his chair and repressed the urge to call out, "Mr. Hudson, why don't you come back and talk this thing out."

Days later Hudson did come back. He told Scott he had been thinking about what had transpired, and he decided that both the *News* and his store were suffering by his precipitous action. Could he again advertise in the *News?* Scott sucked on his perpetual cigar and then emitted a phrase that was to become famous in the paper's history. "All right, Mr. Hudson, but never again on Page Three!"[10] It was a blow to the advertiser, who respected an early tradition that placed high regard on advertising on Page Three, where Hudson ads often appeared. After nearly a week's absence from the paper, Hudson ads reappeared — on Page Seven. The interchange between the two men never was allowed to be forgotten. It was something new reporters learned at one time or other in their apprenticeship. It let them know at once who was running *News* editorial policy.

This was not the end of Hudson's confrontations with the newspaper. Spirited, quick to anger when he felt he had been wronged, his first step to "punish" the *News* for an editorial grievance was to pull Hudson advertising out of the paper.[11] The disagreement over municipal ownership continued through the years. In January

1912, the *News* raged in its editorial columns against renewing the franchise of the DUR, to be decided by voters in an election on January 23. Although Hudson's views were given in the paper's news columns, the merchant decided to answer the paper's editorials with editorials of his own. Instead of the usual Hudson advertising of merchandise, copy for the January 12 issue consisted of an editorial condemning the *News*'s position on the transit system. Scott fumed. Ordering Hudson's copy withheld, he filled the store's usual advertising space with "An Explanation." In it *News* policy regarding editorials was explained:

> Mr. Hudson does not like the *News*' views on the street car question. The value of Mr. Hudson's business cannot be a consideration, therefore the space which would have been used today by his store in the *News* is devoted to this announcement that there may be no misunderstanding on the part of the public as to the disagreement between the *News* and one of our largest advertisers.[12]

Hudson ads reappeared twelve days later. When they did, on Page Nine, they discussed such things as the merits of the new style in men's clothing. Before leaving for England later that year, where he died, the highly respected merchant and philanthropist told his successor, Richard H. Webber, "Whatever you do, don't try to tell the *News* how to run its business."

The aldermanic fight and the campaign for municipal transit ownership spilled into the politics of the editorial columns. Here the paper scored a notable victory by successfully advocating the election to mayor of Republican Oscar B. Marx, who had strongly endorsed municipal ownership. Marx won despite the solid opposition of Detroit's other papers and a fierce campaign by businessmen dedicated to defeating municipal ownership. While advocating Republican Marx for mayor, the paper endorsed Democrat Frank E. Doremus for congressman.

If all this was not enough for *News* readers, Theodore Roosevelt chose this time to pass through Toledo on his way to the Republican national convention in Chicago. Reporter Jay Hayden boarded the train at Toledo. En route, Hayden found Roosevelt in a drawing room and asked him a question that was on the nation's mind:

Would Roosevelt bolt the Republican party if he were snubbed in Chicago in favor of front-runner William Howard Taft? Roosevelt explained he had promised New York newspapermen he would not give his decision until he reached Chicago. He then invited Hayden to breakfast with him.

When the train arrived in Chicago, it was greeted by a bevy of newsmen. A story that Roosevelt was drunk on the train had been circulated by Republican delegates who preferred Taft as a candidate. Hayden, who had been with Roosevelt for several hours, knew otherwise, and set the newspapermen straight. The attempt to smear Roosevelt before the convention had failed, but the former President was snubbed by the convention nonetheless. Turned down by his own party, Roosevelt ran on the Progressive party's Bull Moose ticket. The *News* promptly endorsed him.[13]

It was quite a mixed political bag.

Hayden, who had been engrossed in the Tom Glinnan affair earlier, now found himself deeply involved in the paper's campaign for municipal ownership. His city hall stories of the conflict read like reports from a war front. Marx's first act as mayor was to seek a charter amendment authorizing the city to acquire and operate a street railway system in competition with the DUR. Marx asked Henry Ford to serve on a three-member street railway board, but Ford, who had gained respect in Detroit as an increasingly influential industrialist, declined in favor of James Couzens, his vice president and general manager. Unwittingly, Ford had started Couzens on a long political career that would take him to the U.S. Senate.

On June 24, 1913, Marx made his first move. He presented the draft of an ordinance to the city council that would fix the rate of streetcar fares at three cents. When it appeared the ordinance would pass, Jere Hutchins, the DUR president, roared this advice to conductors: "If any passenger offers a three-cent fare refuse it at once." Police Commissioner John Gillespie countered by ordering his officers to "arrest all conductors who refuse three-cent fares and attempt to forcibly oust a passenger. If necessity demands it, the police will take charge of the cars and operate them."

As the battle warmed, Couzens threatened to furnish one thousand automobiles (Fords) to pick up passengers on the DUR's Fort Street line, a main east-west thoroughfare, unless the DUR agreed to reduce its fares from a nickel (or six for a quarter) to seven tickets for a quarter. The threat worked. But it only marked a one-round victory. Several more rounds would be fought before the city would deliver the knockout punch — ownership of the railway.

The first attempt by the city to purchase the DUR's holdings came to a head in the fall of 1915. Wrote Hayden about the hectic campaign: "From Henry Ford down to Eddie Barnett, proprietor of the city's most noisome café, and Billy Boushaw, boss of the 'foist of the foist,' the citizens screeched and fought. . . ."[14] In the midst of the campaign the *News* saw fit to attack Police Commissioner John Gillespie, an ardent backer of municipal ownership, for "failure to clean up conditions of vice" in the city. As it had displayed during the Pingree era, the paper had no intention of supporting a friend if that friend had gone sour.

As the struggle mounted, Belle Isle Bridge caught fire from coals dropped by a city tar wagon. The *Journal*, which opposed the purchase plan, charged that the city administration deliberately burned the old bridge in a devious maneuver to gain control of yet another bond issue — for a new bridge.

A few days before the election, the railway commission — consisting of Couzens, John F. Dodge, a Ford stockholder, and James Wilkie, general manager of Parke, Davis & Company — met with Mayor Marx and Police Commissioner Gillespie. Gillespie had a quick solution to ease worries over the vote. "Give me $5,000 to place with the saloon keepers," he said, "and I will win this election." Couzens and Ford looked at each other. Then, Dodge, who with Couzens easily could have afforded the expenditure, declared, "Not a damned cent. This is a good proposition. The people can take it or leave it." Like earlier proposals, however, the vote fell to defeat. Under the city's charter the proposition could not be submitted to the voters for another two years. By that time Couzens, having left the Ford company in 1915 in a squabble with its founder, was mayor.

The Detroit of 1918, when Couzens took office, was flushed with the victory of World War I. The pockets of workers, whose wages had nearly doubled during the war to sixty-five cents an hour, were jingling. The charges of gouging by the DUR aroused little interest. Nevertheless, in his inaugural address, Couzens did not back off. He vowed to institute new proceedings to enable the city to own its own street transit system. His first move was to make yet another attempt to purchase the system. His offer was $29,653,936. The DUR insisted on another $2 million. Couzens indicated publicly that he didn't believe it was worth the extra money, but he agreed to allow the voters to decide.

On April 3, 1919, three days before the vote, Charles E. Sorensen, Ford's general manager, announced that Ford was building a gasoline streetcar that would make the city's electric trolleys obsolete.[15] The announcement effectively scuttled the purchase of the electric streetcar system. It was quite a turnabout for Ford, who supported municipal ownership when it was first proposed and when Couzens was in his employ. Couzens was properly smitten by Ford's ploy. Voters turned down the plan on April 7. John Lodge, the council president, shook his head and asked, "What's the answer?"

Couzens soon came up with one. At his own expense he engaged engineers to lay out a competing but nonparalleling system of a hundred miles of railway. In April 1920, voters were asked to approve a bond issue of $15 million to build the railway. Supported by the *News*, condemned by the *Journal, Times* and *Free Press,* the issue received more than the necessary two-thirds votes. As the victorious proponents cheered, opponents of the system regrouped forces. The DUR launched nine lawsuits in quick succession in attempts to halt construction. One suit contended the form of the proposal was illegally stated; another charged that the ballots were printed on too thin a paper. All the suits were dismissed, the last on February 28, 1921, by the United States Supreme Court. Now the battle moved to the streets. Each time the city's line reached an intersection with the DUR's, work was halted because of threatened injunctive proceedings. But on January 15, a frontal assault won the battle. It occurred at the intersection of Mack and St.

Jean, on the city's east side. Learning that the city planned to cross the DUR line on Sunday, when the courts were closed, E. J. Burdick, the DUR's general manager, obtained a court order on Saturday evening. At midnight, under the light of acetylene lamps, work was begun. When Burdick tried to serve the court order Police Commissioner James W. Inches, who succeeded Gillespie, promptly had Burdick seized and taken by patrol wagon to a station on Belle Isle. DUR trucks that had been placed to block the crossing were towed away. By daylight Sunday the work was done.

On Monday, Burdick, released from police lockup, raced to court to seek justice. Inches and other city officials were cited to appear on a charge of contempt. To a man they denied ever seeing a court order. Burdick, they said, was arrested for disturbing the peace, according to the police report. On February 1, 1921, sixteen streetcars bearing the inscription "Detroit Street Railways" began operation. The purchase of the private system remained to be accomplished. This occurred after Couzens bought one share of DUR stock, allowing him to attend a stockholders' meeting at which the issue would be voted upon. Taking the floor, he made a final offer of $19,850,000 and set a deadline of March 10, threatening that unless it was met the DUR tracks on Woodward would be torn up. The company capitulated.

On April 17, 1922, after a thirty-year fight, a public referendum was passed enabling the city to purchase the private lines. The long struggle begun by Pingree and supported by James Scripps and his followers was won. Detroit's street railway proved itself in its early years of operation. Ford never produced his promised gasoline streetcar. But the growth of the automobile as a means of transportation was to hurt the operation within a few years. By the mid-1920s Ford's Model T was to give fits to transit systems across the nation. Whether privately or municipally owned, transit lines had to compete with the automobile, and nearly everybody was driving his own. In the 1920s it most likely was a Tin Lizzie.

4

The Tin Lizzie Was a Lady

As THE POPULAR PRESS provided a reading vehicle for the average American, Henry Ford's Tin Lizzie gave millions of Americans wheels to move into the new life ahead. Ford's refusal to follow others in building "toys for the rich," and the insistence of such men as Scripps, Pulitzer, Hearst and others to provide newspapers that, as Scripps said, "even the poorest man could afford," added up to a social development that was to shatter the sharp division between the rich and the poor, the ignorant and the informed.

Ford's Model T, selling in 1925 for as little as $240, was far below the cost of "cars for the swells" and began a rural revolution by bringing the farmer and the "city slicker" so close together that eventually they were to become almost indistinguishable culturally and socially. On January 5, 1914, Ford's announcement that his company would pay a minimum wage of five dollars a day, at a time when factory wages averaged half or less than that, gave impetus to the evolutionary development that would forever alter the economy of the nation and the world. It would change the very mores of society.

Others who contributed heavily to making the automobile an instrument of a new industrial revolution included such pioneers as Frank Duryea, the first man to produce more than a single hand-fashioned car; Ransom E. Olds, whose Runabout was an early, small, popular car; Henry M. Leland, who developed the Cadillac and the Lincoln; William C. Durant, who put together the General Motors Corporation (GM); Alfred P. Sloan, Jr., who gave GM its successful decentralized management concept; William S. Knudsen, a production wizard for Ford who later became president of GM; Walter P. Chrysler, a GM vice president who founded his own company; and John and Horace Dodge, early Ford stockholders who eventually formed their own manufacturing plant.[1]

For most of these automotive leaders, Detroit was their center of operation. The demands of these men and their companies comprised the driving force that pushed the nation's economy to unpredicted heights. The maws of their factories yawned for increasing quantities of steel, aluminum, upholstery, glass, rubber — all the elements that helped put the nation on wheels.

On June 4, 1896, Henry Ford, a lean, inventive engineer who was working for the Edison Illuminating Company, took an ax and broke out part of a brick wall of an old storage shed at 58 Bagley in what is now downtown Detroit. He had been working for three years to perfect a gasoline-powered vehicle that he had built too wide for the door. Steering the vehicle into the alley, he started the motor, threw in the clutch and bumped over the cobblestones for several blocks when motor trouble developed. He got out, made a few adjustments, and returned to the shed. The car utilized bicycle wheels, a two-cylinder, four-horsepower motor and a simple bicycle seat. It had no brake or reverse and was steered by a tiller. A gong had been installed should people or horses get in the way.[2]

Ford was not the first to drive a gasoline-powered vehicle. On March 6 of the same year, Charles Brady King became the first man permitted to drive an automobile in Detroit. Two years before he had tested the vehicle on Belle Isle, unable to win permission to use Detroit streets. Others were venturing forth elsewhere — Charles and J. Frank Duryea and Colonel Albert A. Pope, in the East; Elwood Haynes, in Kokomo, Indiana; and Alexander Winton in Cleveland — among thirty or forty inventors who were working on the "horseless carriage" in America and in Europe. Later in his life Ford was to say that the development of the automobile was simply an evolutionary process: The bicycle had been refined to such a point that there was no place inventors could go except to a new mode of transportation. The test rides of the inventors, "crackpots" to skeptics, took several years to acquire the recognition they deserved. Steam- and electric-powered carriages blazed the trail. When Ford and King took their first rides in Detroit (which by 1912 was designated by the U.S. Census Bureau the motor capital of the world), the city's largest newspaper, the *News*, failed to record the feats. On the days of their historic rides, the *News* made no reference to the events, nor did anyone else. The incident was not unlike the flight of the Wright brothers at Kitty Hawk on December 17, 1903, which was ignored by the nation's press for five years. The automobile had yet to prove itself something more than a gimmick. After all, something much bigger was happening in the field of transportation — a bicycle show and rally on Belle Isle. There was also concern over bribery in the juridical system and growing atrocities in Cuba by the Spanish. Even the want ads reflected life's current interests. The most advertised item — horses.

The dawn of the automobile did not come up like thunder 'crost the bay. In July 1899, more than three years after the test rides of King and Ford, the *News's* city editor, Patrick C. Baker, whom James Scripps had taken out of the paper's composing room because he was a huge man "and could handle men," assigned a reporter to do a "roundup" on the increasing number of Detroiters involved in attempting to perfect a self-propelled vehicle. On July 16 the story appeared on Page 22. The headline was simple: "To Startle Detroiters." The article is significant in the annals of the passenger car, for it posed some of the same alternatives that inventors were posing seventy years later: Should the automobile be gas or electrically powered? However, where the argument then dealt with the practicality of the engine, subsequent questions dealt with emissions and pollution created by the early mass acceptance of gasoline as a power source. The difficulties facing reporters in attempting to depict the automobile's development are evident in the article. Henry Ford was identified as John Ford as the result of a possible mixup in names with the brother of one of the other inventors listed or the name of Ford's brother, John. By 1899 Ford had moved from 58 Bagley to 72 Alexandrine, again in what is now downtown Detroit. Here is how the *News* appraised the growing phenomena:

"Detroit is on the edge of a genuine surprise in the use of automobiles.

"A long search last week about town showed that there were four or five local inventors at work on the great problem.

"John Ford, of 72 Alexandrine avenue east; Henry W. Koehler, [who lived with his brother, John] on St. Aubin avenue near Jefferson; Barton Peck, of Beaudien street, and several others are diligently working on carriages that will be run without the use of horses.

"By a singular coincidence none of these gentlemen were ready to give the details of their work to the public at this time. Nearly all admitted, however, that within a few weeks, or a month, they would have working models on the streets of Detroit.

"The answer returned in each case was about as follows: 'We have several patents to perfect, and we will not give our ideas to the public at this time.'

"In a general way, these Detroiters are experimenting with electricity and gasoline as motive forces. . . ."

The article went on to explain that electric taxicabs had gained the ascendancy in New York City and emergency wagons were rushed to cabs whose batteries had run down. Then came this insight of the unfolding drama in the streets of Detroit at the turn of the century:

The other night, there was an interesting scene on the boulevard in which a Detroit inventor of a gasoline machine and several park policemen participated.

The motor flew along with amazing rapidity, gradually gaining on the policemen, who were riding their bicycles at the rate of about 12 miles an hour.

Without warning, the huge horseless carriage, at the rate of 15 miles an hour, appeared in the midst of the startled officers, who at once set their strength against their pedals in a friendly bout with the motor.

The race was furious. It was manpower against the violent but noiseless explosion of gasoline. The motor made such a small, trifling noise that the warning gong had to be used to prevent a swarm of bicycles and pedestrians from being run down.

By and by, almost out of breath, one of the coterie of the pursuing park policemen exclaimed:

"You're running now over 17 miles an hour."

"That's easy," replied the man at the throttle of the horseless machine.

"But you can't outrun us," cried another officer, eager for a genuine race.

"We'll see about that," rejoined the man at the throttle, giving the steel rod a jerk and opening full head of power. As if by magic he swiftly left his pursuers far behind. He outran them as fast as though they had been standing still. His gauge registered twenty-two miles an hour. Looking back and finding himself alone in the race, he pulled up. In about five minutes the perspiring policeman came flying along.

"It's not a race," said one, as all dismounted and threw themselves on the grass. . . .[3]

There were more important problems in the world to occupy Page One. Although the Spanish-American War had ended in four months, in the summer of 1898, McKinley's decision to annex the Philippines resulted in three years of guerilla warfare. John Fitzgibbon, the bright young man who had been taken from his job as Scripps's coachman, made a reporter and later a war correspondent, was covering the U.S. occupation.[4]

One headline to greet readers was "OBDURATE!" The article described an incident in the running warfare between the *News* and the private companies operating the city's transit lines. Detroit had moved to electric streetcars from horse-drawn trolleys just three years before, long after they had been in use in such cities as Chicago, New York and Cleveland. Customers were finding the cars and the service discouragingly unsatisfactory. In winter, trolleys were cold; in summer, hot and dusty. A small stove that heated the cars in winter was but a token of comfort. Taking the windows out in summer afforded natural air-conditioning. But it could not compete with the clutch of bodies emitting perspiration. The *News*, not unlike other leading newspapers in the nation, was not omniscient about the impact of the horseless carriage. There were more obvious national and local issues of immediate concern. Nor did being in the eye of the hurricane increase foresight of what was to come. Events, however, were moving swiftly.

One week later, on July 21, 1899, William Kuenzel, then working as a free-lance photographer for the *News*, stood on East Grand Boulevard, his camera on a tripod, and snapped a picture of one of the new horseless carriages. Published the next day, the lines beneath it read: "Ford Automobile on the Boulevard . . . First correct picture ever shown of the Detroit invention which can propel the carriage 30 miles an hour and will carry its passengers from Detroit to Ann Arbor for four cents worth of gasoline."[5] In the car, but not identified, were Henry Ford and Frank R. Alderman, treasurer of Ford's first business venture, the Detroit Automobile Company, which later became the Cadillac Motor Car Company.[6] On April 7, 1901, the W. E. Metzger Company, producer of an electric-powered auto, the Waverly, ran the first automobile advertisement to appear in the *News*. "A most elegant and practical vehicle," ran the ad. "Can be run by Ladies." The price was $850.

By 1903, when the Ford Motor Company was founded, the hubbub over cars was loud and clear. Articles concerning automobiles, new factories, steel die and tool production, were scattered from Page One into other areas of the paper, including the financial pages. A new phenomena, car racing, was recognized on the sports pages. The *News* joined the excitement by purchasing its first gasoline-powered delivery vehicle, an Oldsmobile.

During the ensuing years more than two thousand auto companies were organized throughout the world.[7] The attrition of weaker companies and the attraction of others to Detroit was not a mere accident. At one time twelve different auto companies were at work in Detroit, among them a firm managed by Olds, who found suppliers for his small Runabout in the city. A plant founded by James W. Packard in Warren, Ohio, moved to Detroit in 1903, closer to the center of supply. Purchased by millionaire Henry B. Joy, the company moved into the world's first reinforced concrete factory building, designed by Albert Kahn, who became internationally famous as an industrial architect. That same year Leland's Cadillac Automotive Company took shape in Detroit and John F. Dodge won a seat on the board of directors of the Ford company. He and his brother, Horace, provided motors for Ford until 1913, when they parted company and the Dodge Brothers opened their own assembly plant. Among the pioneer cars that lingered for years were the Pierce-Arrow, the Brush, the Rambler, the Reo, the Leland, the Hudson, the Willys-Overland, the Nash, the Paige, the Maxwell, the Peerless, the Durant and the Studebaker. All eventually became dropouts or were absorbed by stronger companies as the stresses and strains of the industry demanded larger financial backing for greater and better manufacturing techniques.

Whether they were produced in Detroit or elsewhere, the early cars added a number of significant phrases to the American vernacular, the earliest being, "Why don'tcha buy a horse?" Other catch sayings, such as "Get out and get under" and "In my merry Oldsmobile," were turned into song, joining the ping, ping, ping under the hood to provide music for investors and buyers alike.

The Buick, the Cadillac, the Olds, the Chevrolet (arriving in 1911) and the Pontiac (formerly the Oakland) were gathered under the aegis of the General Motors Corporation, which was organized in 1908 by William C. Durant. In 1925, Maxwell-Chalmers was reorganized as the Chrysler Corporation, which eventually absorbed the Dodge company. The formation of what has been hailed as the "Big Three" — Ford, GM and Chrysler — had become a reality.

James Scripps Booth, who forsook the newspaper business of his father, George Gough Booth, occupied his engineer-oriented mind by developing the Scripps-Booth car in 1908.[8] In 1914 he brought William B. Stout, later famous for his aircraft inventions, to Detroit to redesign the Booth car, a two-wheeler, later altered into a four-wheel runabout. It was sold to GM in 1919.

What separated Ford from the rest, and gave the firm an impetus that by 1914 made it the world's largest producer of automobiles, was its founder's stubborn belief in volume production of a low-cost car that the greatest number of people could buy. Olds's

Runabout was the first car produced in any significant number (6,500 in 1905). But Olds could not convince his financial backers of the future of the average man's ability to purchase automobiles in any quantity.[9] At forty-one, having made a million dollars, he resigned in 1903. Roy D. Chapin managed Olds until 1906, when he quit, also unable to convince the firm's financial backers in the future of small cars. The Hudson Motor Car Company, which Chapin founded, was the result. His son later became the head of American Motors Corporation, an amalgam of Hudson and Nash-Kelvinator.

After running the alphabet of models from A to S, Ford struck upon a car in 1908 that soon put his company into the ascendancy — the Model T, affectionately called the Tin Lizzie. Ford called the T "the universal car." It was high enough off the ground to traverse muddy, rural roads. It was simple enough for a man handy with tools to repair. It was big enough for a farmer to haul small supplies from town. The first year's production reached 10,660, an industry record. By the end of 1913, the Ford company was producing half of all the automobiles in the United States. This fantastic demand became the mother of yet another invention.

In the summer of 1913, looking over the plant he had built three years before in Highland Park, a suburb within the city of Detroit, Ford reasoned that if each workman could remain in one assigned place, with one job to do, the T could take shape more quickly, with subsequent savings in man-hours. The theory, resulting from earlier assembly-line attempts at smaller parts, was tested by dragging a chassis by rope and windlass along the floor of the plant. It soon became apparent that with refinement the idea was sound. Eventually Ts were rolling off the line every ten seconds of every working day.

On January 5, 1914, Ford, flushed with the success of the Model T, made an announcement that supported his faith in the consumer. Declared the *News:* "Workers Get $10,000,000 of Ford's Profits This Year; 26,500 Will Share . . . No Man Over 22 Will Get Less than $5 a Day for Eight Hours. . . ." Ford not only had exploited a market others were slow in finding, but with the five-dollar day he was expanding his own market, making it possible to fulfill engineer William S. Knudsen's observation that "every-body wants to go from A to B sitting down." Ford considered the payment of five dollars for an eight-hour day the finest cost-cutting move he ever made. "I can find methods of manufacturing that will make high wages. If you cut wages, you just cut the number of customers."[10] Rather than being revolutionary, his think-ing was the result of an evolution long in the making.

His announcement of the five-dollar day brought laborers into Detroit by the thousands, packing the streets outside the Ford plant where they fought and rioted. The company was at a peak of its power and influence. Just two years before it had singly fought and won a suit that broke the Seldon patent, for the manufacture of a motorcar, after eight years of litigation. The patent was owned by the Electric Vehicle Company of New York. It claimed a royalty of 1¼ percent for every car built. Ford successfully argued that the patent was illegal and an infringement on free enterprise. His victory opened the door for the entire industry. From the first Model T in 1908 until 1927, the Ford company made 15,007,033 cars, by far the leader in the industry. Ford was hailed nationally as a genius and, being a genius, he was sought out for advice on every subject from fatherhood to fatherland. He sponsored a "Peace Ship" mission to Europe in 1915, and in 1918 bought his own newspaper, the *Dearborn Independent,* a country weekly.

He counted several newspapermen among his close friends, among them Pipp, the editor of the *News* from 1910 to 1918, whom he later hired to edit his paper. Pipp quit in a dispute over Ford's anti-Semitic views, which were expressed until 1922. In that year Ford gave a car to Detroit Rabbi Leo M. Franklin, an old friend, who sent it back, expressing his dismay at the Dearborn paper's anti-Semitic articles. As abruptly as they had begun, the articles stopped, and Ford apologized to Dr. Franklin. The *Independent* ended its role as a Ford mouthpiece in 1930.

James Sweinhart, a *News* reporter who kept Ford's friendship, appraised him as a man of indefinite moods and action. One morning Sweinhart looked out the front window of his home and saw a new Ford roadster at his front curb. In his mailbox was a set of keys. "I immediately called Mr. Ford and said I could not accept the gift as it would be unethical," Sweinhart recounted. "He could not understand why. He had lots of cars and he felt if he wanted to give one away he could." Years later when archivists pored over Ford memorabilia, they found a note in which Ford indicated he had given a car to the *News* reporter. But, alas, a check had arrived to cover its cost. Mrs. Sweinhart, it seemed, had fallen in love with the car at first sight.

During other moments of largess Ford gave cars to such prominent people as Crown Prince Gustav of Sweden, King Alphonse of Spain, Baron Von Krupp, Thomas Edison, John D. Rockefeller, Randolph A. Hearst, Fritz Kreisler and John Burroughs. From 1921 to 1942 he gave away more than two hundred vehicles, always careful to make a note and file it. Ford threw very little away. Among the things he saved were newsboy receipts — boxes of them. The result of years of collecting throughout the world is the Henry Ford Museum and Greenfield Village, just two miles from the Ford homestead.[11]

Henry Ford's emotional tie to the T grew so strong as the car reached undreamed-of sales that it almost destroyed the company. For nineteen years Ford would allow no fundamental change in the vehicle. Although he often has been quoted as saying, "You can have it any color so long as it's black," it was actually marketed first in red, then green and finally, from 1913 to 1926, only in black. His belief that the T was America's universal car was emphasized in the T's emblem, which read "Ford — universal car."[12] The philosophy of the Volkswagen — the people's car — which was introduced to the United States in 1949, is really no different. The problem for Ford was that America had changed in affluence, in social mores and, for most of the people, in economic status. The man who had helped this evolutionary development by producing a vehicle the mass of people could buy, and by giving impetus to an industry that accounted for 16 percent of the nation's gross national product, failed to see what he had wrought. That the VW would take a large share of a later market only proved once again that times, as they will, had changed, at least for the nonce.

On August 31, 1916, Ford told a reporter for the *News* (probably Sweinhart) that the company was discontinuing the payments of special dividends, which had brought quick wealth to early investors, in favor of reinvesting the money for expansion.[13] The Rouge complex in 1925, costing more than $350 million, was the result. But while Ford was building bigger and better facilities in Detroit and elsewhere, he evinced no plans to alter his "universal car." Ford production in 1925 was 20 percent greater than the entire industry's.

But while Ford was blind to the changing market, others were not. Already GM, with Chevrolet its leader, and Chrysler Corporation were making notable strides. In 1921 Ford sold 67 percent of all cars built in the United States, but five years later its share dropped to 46 percent. While Ford was developing a centralized one-man rule, aided by Harry Bennett, an ex-boxer who headed the infamous Ford service department, GM was having troubles with its founding genius, Durant. Durant's dictatorial rule was driving men from GM to other companies. In 1921 Knudsen, who directed the building of twenty-two Ford plants in thirty-three states, was fired in a power move among Ford cronies. He went to GM, where Durant had resigned to be succeeded by Alfred P. Sloan, Jr., and modern management practices that made GM the largest industrial organization in the world.

In 1919, Sloan foresaw the new richer consumer market, at last. In that year, GM instituted its own installment buying plan, the General Motors Acceptance Corporation. Buying on time, as history was to prove, was to underpin the American economy henceforth. But as late as December 26, 1926, Ford told an interviewer that credit buying was the bane of American business. He had not put aside his populist, rural upbringing in Dearborn Township. An article in the *New York Times* was headlined, "Ford to Fight It Out with His Old Car." Across the nation, skepticism grew that the man who had been hailed a genius could reverse the very changes he helped set in motion.

On May 26, 1927, the Model T assembly lines at Highland Park and the Rouge were shut down. Said the Ford company in the *News* in an unsigned statement penned by former *News* writer William J. Cameron, for years Ford's voice and public relations representative:

> The Model T was one of the largest factors in creating the conditions which now make the new model Ford possible. The worldwide influence of the Ford car in the building of good roads and in teaching the people the use and value of mechanical power is conceded. Nowadays everybody runs some kind of motor power but 20 years ago only the adventurous few could be induced to try an automobile. It had a harder time winning public confidence than the airplane has now. Model T was a great educator in this respect. It had stamina and power. It was the car that ran before there were good roads to run on. It broke down the barriers of distance in rural sections, brought people of these sections closer together and placed education within the reach of everyone. We are still proud of the Model T Ford car. If we were not we could not have continued to manufacture it so long.[14]

Cameron was calling on fifteen years' experience as a *News* editorial writer. His claim to journalistic fame had been an article, "Don't Die on Third," reflecting on a game played on April 18, 1909, between Detroit and Cleveland that the Tigers won 3 to 2. The hero of the editorial was George Moriarity, whose steal home won the game.

For Ford the handwriting was on the wall. The percentage of Ford sales had slipped badly. Although the Model T still was outselling the Chevrolet, Chevy — with a synchromesh transmission, four-wheel brakes and other improvements — was catching the public eye. Many Americans were angry that Ford even thought of changing the T. But change it he did. Nine months passed before the Model A, Ford's answer to the growing competition, came off the lines.

Although Ford had "retired from the company," much of his time had been spent in willful opposition to his son Edsel whom he had made president in 1919, and others in high command. During the layoff, the sales organization was demoralized, with many dealers deserting to GM and other companies. By 1941 Bennett was strongly entrenched in the power structure. He was Ford's "universal man," who, like the "universal car," was expected to do all things. In June 1941, Bennett was the company's chief negotiator with the United Auto Workers, which was seeking its first contract with Ford, having signed GM and Chrysler. The company had been hit by a series of walkouts as the union flexed its muscles. On June 19, Ford read the draft of the union's proposals and walked out of the plant offices in disgust. Upon leaving he told Charles Sorensen, who worked without a title but wielded great power, to "lock the gates and close the place down." Returning to Fairlane, Ford told his wife, Clara, what he had done. She was furious. She pleaded his actions would put "all those people out of work and create all kinds of hardship." He was obdurate. Then she threatened to leave Fairlane forever if he persisted. Ford thought it over for a moment, went to the telephone and called Bennett. "Settle with them tomorrow," he said. Later on he explained that he suddenly felt Clara had a vision of the total problem that people close to it did not have. And he respected the judgment of the neighboring farm girl he had married almost sixty years before better than his own.[15]

In May 1943 Edsel, who had been ailing for several years, died. Bennett's rule, with a company police force of hoodlums and shady former policemen, had become a national scandal. It ended only after Ford's grandson, Henry II, then twenty-six, was discharged from the Navy in August 1943 and was able to solidify his position. It did not happen immediately, nor as quickly as the government, worried about the company's vitality, might have hoped. The founder was then nearing eighty but was still very much in command. And Harry Bennett was his brigadier general. There was an additional challenge. In 1927, during the changeover to the Model A, Chevy passed Ford in sales. A seesaw battle after that left Chevrolet entrenched in the lead in 1936.

Young Henry's job seemed impossible. Many of the men who had helped Ford become No. 1 were gone. The firm's accounting system was a shambles; with only thirty-two employees there had not been an audit for thirty years. For years invoices for merchandise that cost under ten dollars were not totaled. On Ford's orders, these invoices were stacked and weighed. Then, by dividing the average weight of each invoice into the total poundage, the number of invoices was determined. By multiplying this figure by an estimated average billing cost (less than three dollars) a total figure was ascertained. It was later estimated that this system was off about 1 percent a year — quite a figure for a firm doing $3.9 billion in war production alone, including the building of 8,685 B-24 bombers at a specially built plant at Willow Run. Young Henry also discovered one department still making propellers for the old Ford Tri-Motor airplane whose production had stopped years before. To counter Bennett, he had the support of both Clara, his grandmother, who influenced her husband throughout their married life, and his mother, Eleanor, plus cash reserves of more than $645 million.

Early in 1944, having moved into the factory without official support, Henry II learned that his grandfather had drawn a codicil to his will; it directed that upon his death control of the company would pass for ten years to a ten-member board of directors — not including Henry II. In effect, Harry Bennett would head the company. John Bugas, who would play an important role in the rejuvenation of the company, had been hired by Bennett as an aide. Bugas left as chief of the Detroit office of the Federal Bureau of Investigation to take the job. Now Bugas, who supported young Henry, was invited into the inner family thinking. He would confront Bennett about the codicil. If Bennett tried to make the codicil stick, Henry threatened to call a meeting of Ford dealers around the world and members of the press during which he would outline the company's financial and managerial condition.[16]

Bugas walked into Bennett's office and quickly made his mission known: Did Bennett have a copy of the codicil? Looking straight at Bugas, Bennett opened a desk drawer and pulled out the legal document. Bugas related young Henry's threat. Bennett, who obviously had questioned the value of the codicil because of Henry Ford's advanced age, struck a match and burned it. "Here," he said, referring to the ashes. "Take it." Now Clara and Eleanor played their aces. On September 20, 1945, Clara begged and cajoled the elder Ford to relinquish the reins of the company to his grandson.

He was reluctant, still, to do so. Then Eleanor played her trump card. She would sell her stock to outsiders unless the founder agreed. Enfeebled by the passing years, he gave in and issued a call to his grandson to meet him at Fairlane.

Henry II, then twenty-nine, listened to the old man, and having been cautioned by Bugas to secure full control of the company if he got any at all, retorted to the offer: "I'll take it only if I have a completely free hand to make any changes I want to make." Old Henry argued for a while but he lacked the strength to make another fight of it. The next day the board of directors confirmed the selection and the vast company was in the hands of a young man who suddenly felt very sure of himself. "I never for a minute doubted we would make it," he said later. As the board meeting ended Bennett got up, turned toward the door, glared at the new president and growled, "You're taking over a billion-dollar organization that you haven't contributed a thing to."[17]

Within ten minutes Bennett was out of a job for the first time since 1915, when old Henry "had taken a liking to him." "I simply said to him," Henry II later recalled, " 'Harry, we've got to part company.' "[18] Although he left the company the next day, Bennett was kept on the payroll for a year and a half until he became eligible for retirement pay. The revitalization of the company did not end there; within a few months more than a thousand executives who were Bennett cohorts were invited to move on. While filling these positions with bright, young men of known engineering and managerial abilities, Henry II looked at properties his grandfather had dabbled in over the years. A Brazilian rubber plantation that cost $20 million, soybean farms, mineral and timber tracts were sold. By July 1946, the grandson had begun to put together a new organization that led the Ford company from a firm that was losing $9.5 million a month in 1945 to its current position as the nation's third largest industrial corporation with total assets of more than $10 billion, nearly a half million employees in 300 facilities worldwide and annual gross sales anticipated in 1973 — its seventieth year — of $17 billion. Quite a turnaround for a company whose profits had dipped from $80 million in 1929 to $6 million in 1941.

Bennett's vicious control over the affairs of workers ended with his departure. No longer would his spies probe the personal lives of employees to see if they met with Ford's rigid socioreligious beliefs. The company that had been run since 1903 with a strange mixture of paternalism and ruthless dictatorship joined the new society with a president and a new managerial team that understood the changes that had occurred and built a strong corporation to answer them. But instead of leading the pack in the small car market, young Henry found Ford chasing Chevrolet. GM had put its house in order some time before.

Shortly before midnight on Monday, April 7, 1947, death came to Henry Ford at the age of eighty-three of a cerebral hemorrhage. The setting was the Ford estate Fairlane in Dearborn, in the county of his birth, on the banks of the River Rouge, a river he had deepened and widened and on which he had built the largest of his manufacturing and processing complexes.

For several days it had been raining. The flooded waters of the Rouge gradually overflowed the banks, entering the mansion's power plant and shorting out the electrical system. At the time that death came the mansion was lighted only by kerosene lamps and candles. Clara and a woman servant were nearby. The house was without telephone and without heat, save that afforded by fireplaces. Clara and Henry had returned to Dearborn only a few days earlier from their Georgia winter home. The day before he had visited the Rouge plant, where workers cheered him on sight; in their eyes, despite all that had happened in the intervening years, he had contributed much to mankind and to their welfare. Significantly, lying in the Rouge below the turn basin he had built was the giant ore boat, *Henry Ford II*. The ship was symbolic of a new age he had helped to bring about but that he had such difficulty understanding.[19]

He retired at 9 P.M. — for the last time.

The *News*'s editorial eulogy read in part:

No other man ever so changed the face of the world in his lifetime as did Henry Ford. Of this we have the evidence of our own eyes, on every side, wherever in the world men live. . . .

He conceived that his own prosperity lay in that of others. To place in the reach of the greatest number of people a useful product which would lift the whole level of living was, therefore, a purpose to which he committed a boundless originality, an inexhaustible energy. . . .

His memorial is the face of America as he left it. In no other one lifetime has that face been so completely transformed. No other individual, while he lived, so radically affected the lives of so many as did the man who today lies dead. . . .[20]

There was no hint, as there might have been, that the *News*'s own founder and Ford had much in common — a mutual interest in the average man and a faith in his ability to buy as well as produce. But it was there for those who wished to see it.

5

Sit, Brothers, Sit

DETROIT'S EMERGENCE as the center of world automobile production did not occur without torturous growing pains. Before the aches were to subside into an acceptable system of labor-management bargaining, a new phrase — "sit-down strike" — became an important part of the workingman's lexicon. While sit-down strikes had been attempted in the United States as early as 1906, the tactic was not refined until the early 1930s during a series of strikes in France. The tool that effectively shut down a factory and even an industry soon leaped the Atlantic.[1]

On December 10, 1936, a woman employee of Detroit's Kelsey-Hayes Wheel Company who was a member of the United Automobile Workers union pretended to faint from exhaustion while she worked on an assembly line. In the confusion Victor Reuther, a union organizer, leaped onto a box and started to sell the importance of unionism. As he talked, his brother Walter Reuther, who was waiting outside, climbed through a window and took charge. The sit-down was short-lived and its significance was not immediately apparent. But it was a dress rehearsal for things to come.

Eight days later, on December 18, Walter, Victor and their brother Roy were in Flint, fifty miles north of Detroit, to direct a brazen labor caper at the Flint Trolley Coach Company, whose workers were represented by an AFL affiliate. Martin S. Hayden, Jay's son and a *News* reporter, was sent to find out what was happening. He found Walter, Roy and Victor in a room in a "flea-bag" hotel (Flint's Durant Hotel, named after GM's first president, was too expensive for the fledgling union). The trolley coach strike was a minor ploy, Hayden was told. Larger things were coming. "Wait till we hit the big one — GM," Walter said, matter-of-factly. Hayden lifted his eyebrows. It was easier said than done. He wondered momentarily if he should telephone the unionist's boast to the *News* office, then thought better of it. It was too preposterous an idea. No one would believe it.[2]

Within a week the UAW began a series of hit-and-miss sit-down strikes in GM plants in Kansas City and Atlanta while demanding collective bargaining conferences with management. They were short-lived and soon workers returned to their jobs. Then, on December 30, the union struck GM's key Fisher body plant No. 2 in Flint, supplier of automobile bodies for Chevrolet, the corporation's biggest seller. The sit-down had reached the big time, but its full impact was still to be felt. When the union listed its demands on December 29, the *News* published them on Page 10 of its first section. The next day when the UAW made good its threat, the story was moved to Page One and stayed there. Homer Martin, UAW president, was quoted as saying: "We mean business." There was a feeling even among staunch union members that he was whistling in the dark.[3]

As 1937 dawned the union struck GM's Detroit Cadillac plant. Inside, working as a plater, was a young man who had become known to *Detroit News* readers as "Boyd, the high school chronicler," through the "Listening in on Detroit" column of H. C. L. Jackson. Boyd Simmons, who had hoped to become a newspaperman, had to settle short of his ambition. Jobless in the midst of the Depression, he was happy to catch on at Cadillac and write part-time. When someone shouted, "Quit working, it's a strike," Simmons's curiosity was piqued. While workers who did not sympathize with the strike were allowed to walk out of the plant, Simmons decided to join those who remained. Then he remembered that he would be unable to furnish what had become a regular Saturday *News* magazine page article. He called Jackson on a factory phone. Reporter Paul Conrad was sent to the plant. "Jackson wants you to write about your experience as a sit-down striker," Conrad shouted through a window.

Simmons agreed. Taking a pencil and a pad, he sat on a box and wrote the first personal narrative of a sit-down striker ever to be printed. It appeared on January 14 on Page One. In it, Simmons described how the men slept on floors and passed the time away playing cards and talking. Food was sent to them from a union kitchen and "it wasn't bad." He said, "There's a determination to fight to a finish about a sit-down that sorta gets you." He revealed that the strikers had elected committeemen who would see that the men inside did not damage company property. He passed the story out of the window to Conrad, with the instruction to show it to Walter Reuther, president of West Side Local 174. Reuther read the story and told Conrad, "It's all right with me."

The next day Conrad appeared at the window and told Simmons that Fred Gaertner, Jr., the *News* managing editor, wanted to see him. Deciding he had seen enough of the sit-down, Simmons slipped out of a window, avoiding union men who had been posted at the exits, and walked home through a heavy rain. The next day the *News* hired him. His first assignment: general reporting, with an emphasis on labor.[4]

The UAW's sit-down tactic paralyzed the giant nationwide GM complex. Eighty-six days after the first GM plant was struck, on February 11, 1937, a settlement was reached. When it was over Hayden checked to see what had happened to a strike of the Standard Cotton Products Company, a small supplier of upholstery padding, which had been the first Flint plant to undergo a sit-down. To his amazement, the strike still was in progress. It simply had been overshadowed by the fracases at GM, so much so that at the peak of the demonstrations, UAW members who were assigned to support the upholstery company strikers forgot to deliver their regular 5 P.M. meal one day. It was midnight before someone remembered and the food was rushed to the hungry workers.[5]

After GM came Chrysler, the smallest of the Big Three. The

strike of sixty-five thousand workers lasted twenty-nine days. The big nut to crack was the Ford Motor Company, whose founder had publicly indicated he felt quite capable of operating his plants without union help. He was to find the task quite a struggle.

On May 25, 1937, Walter Reuther told Archie W. Robinson, who headed the *News*'s labor beat, that he planned to have union men distribute organizational leaflets at the Rouge plant gates. Robinson was aghast. "You'll be beaten to a pulp," he predicted.

"They won't dare," Reuther answered. "Not with all the photographers and reporters who'll be at the scene." Reuther had not properly assessed the determination of hoodlums and toughs who had been organized into the Ford service department by Bennett.[6]

The next day union men passed out leaflets on streetcars, handed them to workers in automobiles entering Ford parking lots, put them in car windows when workers stopped at intersections. At the plant were reporters from the *News*, the *Times*, the *Free Press* and representatives of leading papers throughout the country. The well-laid plans were to reach a violent climax because of a simple suggestion from *News* photographer James E. (Scotty) Kilpatrick.

Seeing the huge "Ford Motor Co." sign across the face of the plant, Kilpatrick asked Reuther, Frankensteen and other union leaders to gather in such a way that the sign would appear in the picture. They agreed. Then, looking up, Kilpatrick saw the overpass that carried Ford workers from a parking lot to Gate 4. "How about getting up on the overpass," he suggested. "It'll make a better picture." It did more than that. It led to what became known in history as "The Battle of the Overpass."

As Kilpatrick took the picture the unionists smiled. Looking to one side they had seen Ford servicemen approach and somehow found it amusing. Their smiles soon were wiped away. In the melee that followed, Frankensteen's coat was pulled over his head and several men punched and kicked him. Reuther was also beaten as an attempt was made to throw him over the rail to the street below. Clinging to the rail, he succeeded in working his way toward the steps. Two other photographers had followed Kilpatrick up the steps. All three were manhandled. One of the photographers, Al Anderman of the *Times*, finally retreated to the bottom of the steps to take an overall view of the fighting. When he looked through his viewfinder, he saw Reuther and Jack Kennedy, also a UAW leader, hurtling down the stairway toward him. Instinctively he threw out his arms to deflect their fall, and the three men ended in a pile at the bottom.

Kilpatrick, taking advantage of the confusion, simply walked down the steps and carried his photographic plates to a waiting *News* car. He slipped the plates recording the fight next to the cushion in the rear seat. When a Ford serviceman converged on the driver, demanding all the plates, he got only those Kilpatrick had left in full view on the front seat. "Get the hell out of here," Kilpatrick told the driver. And he did.[7]

The determination of Ford servicemen to destroy evidence of the battle did not end here. R. K. Arnold, another photographer for the *Times,* had run to his car in an attempt to get away with his pictures. He was chased into the police station of suburban Melvindale before his pursuers abandoned their efforts. Knowing they had failed to halt the flow of photographs to the papers, the servicemen notified Bennett, who passed the word to Ford.

Before Kilpatrick's plates had arrived at the *News* office, Gaertner had received a personal call from Henry Ford. The pictures would show, Ford said, that the strikers had been beaten by loyal Ford workers, not by Bennett's servicemen. Gaertner told Ford he would look at the photographs when they arrived. He was standing at the paper's city desk when a copyboy delivered the developed pictures from the photographic department. Gaertner called reporters who had been covering the strike and asked them to identify the principals in the pictures. The attackers clearly were Ford servicemen, downriver hoodlums in Bennett's employ and Dearborn policemen who had been summoned to protect the plant. One detective's handcuffs were visible as he lunged at Frankensteen.

"Print it," Gaertner ordered. Then to City Editor Arthur Hathaway he said: "Tell the boys to write it as they saw it." This decision to expose the brutality marked the beginning of Bennett's downfall. Kilpatrick's photograph showing Frankensteen being beaten while his coat was pulled over his head was sent by wirephoto throughout the world. The photo might have won a Pulitzer Prize, except for one thing — there was no Pulitzer award in photography at that time. The photograph played a subsequent role in Pulitzer's recognition of this phase of journalism, however. In 1942 photography was added to the Pulitzer awards. The first recipient: a *Detroit News* photographer for a photo entitled "The Picket Line."[8]

The success of the sit-down strike at GM set off a wave of strikes throughout the city and the nation. Employees of bakeries, cigar plants, five-and-tens, warehouses, laundries — all adopted the labor tactic in the hope of improving wages and work conditions. At the *News,* covering the strike hysteria was a major effort. Archie Robinson, chief labor writer, was assisted by Simmons and Asher Lauren, general assignment reporters. Looking over the massive list of striking companies, Simmons and Lauren wondered how to divide up work that could not be handled by Robinson. "Let's flip a coin," Lauren suggested. "Winner takes the west side, loser the east side." Lauren won. At the end of the year the two men counted up the strikes they had covered: Lauren's totaled eighty-seven, Simmons's eighty five.[9]

One of the new names to burst like a star-flash on the labor scene was that of James R. Hoffa, business agent for the Teamsters Union. Hoffa had made a name in the union movement as early as 1932 when, at the age of nineteen, he successfully struck a grocery warehouse, seeking a shorter work week, higher wages and improved working conditions. Working independently, he had organized a union of three hundred grocery store employees and demanded bargaining rights. The demands were ignored until a trainload of strawberries arrived.[10] The workers opened the car doors, then stood by as a warm sun beat down. Threatened with the loss of an entire shipment, the company agreed to recognize the union. Noting Hoffa's brash approach to labor relations was Bert Brennan, a power in the Teamsters Union. Soon Hoffa took his membership into the Teamsters and as a reward was made a business agent. For Hoffa it was just a beginning.

From 1936 until the outbreak of World War II in Europe in 1939, Detroit and the nation's union leaders worked to consolidate their strength. America's lend-lease program in 1940 bolstered industry with cost-plus contracts and demands for expansion. This, and the entry of the United States into the war in 1941, with its tremendous demands for production, consolidated the union movement.

On April 2, 1941, the UAW, determined to win recognition at the Ford Motor Company, massed pickets and flying squadrons of toughs in such numbers that they virtually sealed off all approaches to the Rouge plant. State police, who had by now become veterans at strike duty, assembled to maintain order. Most Ford workers decided an attempt to enter the plant would be foolhardy and either went home or lingered in the area to watch the action. On April 3, the second day of the strike, a lone Ford worker started across Miller Road, bound for a plant gate. He didn't make it. UAW pickets pounced on him and beat him unmercifully. The scene was recorded by the *News*'s Milton E. (Pete) Brooks; it won a Pulitzer Prize. How Brooks happened to be on the right spot at the right time caused other photographers covering the picketing to shake their heads in dismay.

A newspaper and newsreel photographer who had worked in Chicago and New York, Brooks, at thirty-nine, exhibited a confidence and an independence that irked his competitors. He seldom took more than one picture of any news event. A reporter's attempt to get him to hurry to a fire invariably brought the retort, "If it's a good one, it'll still be burning when we get there."

Arriving at the Rouge plant, Brooks found a place from which he figured he would be privy to the action. He took his camera, a four-by-five Graphic, out of its leather case, placed the case next to a chain link fence, sat on it and waited, resting his back against the fence. Photographers from newspapers and wire services milled around and waited for a newsworthy picture. Suddenly the word of a skirmish farther along the picket line sent the group scurrying. Brooks got up, decided that the fight, if it was worth anything, would wait his arrival. At this moment the unfortunate worker tried to cross Miller Road and union pickets descended on him — a few feet from where Brooks was standing. He simply focused his camera and clicked the shutter. Once. With the other photographers off on a futile chase, he was the only lensman to capture the scene. As inconspicuously as he took the picture, he walked to a waiting *News* car and sent the plate to the office. The film was developed by William Seiter. As soon as the figures emerged under the developing emulsion Seiter knew it belonged in the paper in a hurry and sent it quickly to the city desk. Played four columns wide, the photograph was mute evidence of the UAW's determination. Circulated by the Associated Press, it was reprinted in thousands of newspapers and eventually took its place in the history of labor-management struggles.[11]

With the nation's entry into war, the need for labor-management peace on the home front was obvious. Reuther, who had become director of the union's GM department, had made a reputation as a sound labor theorist. As the war heightened, he was named labor's representative on the War Manpower Commission and in the Office of War Production. He became the author of what was to become known as "The Reuther Plan" for using the auto industry for the mass production of war planes.

The war's end brought a new rash of demands from labor, which had watched industry grow fat on cost-plus contracts. In November 1945, Walter Reuther led 175,000 GM workers in a strike that paralyzed ninety-two plants in fifty cities. In typical Reuther fashion, his red hair a flag to bullish management, he demanded that the union be allowed to examine the corporation's books to determine how large a raise could be granted without increasing car prices and causing inflation. GM refused. The strike lasted 113 days. In a compromise settlement workers got an eighteen-and-a-half-cent-an-hour increase. GM did not open its books. A few days later, in March 1946, Reuther was elected president of the union.

The title was misleading. Torn by factionalism, the UAW had developed a powerful left wing headed by George F. Addes, secretary-treasurer. The union's left wing fought for survival with Reuther, who had toured Russia only to become an avowed anti-Communist. In a 1946 union election the Addes faction fought Reuther by backing R. J. Thomas, who had once served the union as a compromise president. Reuther won by the slim margin of 124 votes. During the next year Reuther rid the union hierarchy of opposition and consolidated his position. He won the 1947 union election by a two-to-one landslide.

His job secure, Reuther started on a planned course to surround himself with a new breed of educated labor leaders who supported his broad theories of social advancement for workers. Along the way he made enemies both within and without the union.[12]

On the evening of April 20, 1948, barely a year after his landslide victory, Reuther was standing in the kitchen of his ranch-style home on Detroit's northwest side, talking to his wife, May. Outside, lurking in the shadows, an assassin with a shotgun watched his every move. When Reuther moved away from his wife and into gunsight he fired. The charge ripped into Reuther's right arm and shoulder; Mrs. Reuther was unharmed. Hospitalized for days, Reuther soon was back on the job, this time watched over by a union guard. In his right hand he carried a small rubber ball that he squeezed incessantly in a therapy program to return his arm and hand to usefulness.[13]

Almost a year later, while police were still seeking Reuther's assailant, a similar attempt was made on the life of his brother Victor, the union's educational director. The blast struck Victor in the face. He survived, but with the loss of an eye.

Dissatisfied with the police investigation, the union hired its own investigator, a graying veteran of congressional inquiries into anti-labor practices — Ralph Winstead.

Five years later, on January 6, 1954, largely on information provided by Winstead, warrants were issued charging four men in the shooting of Walter Reuther. Three of the men — Santo (Sam) Perrone, Clarence Jacobs and Peter Lombardo — had police records. The fourth, Carl Renda, Perrone's son-in-law, who had held a lucrative scrap metal contract with the Briggs Manufacturing Company, had never been arrested. Perrone, a known labor-baiter, had risen from a laborer at the stove works to the holder of a scrap metal contract that netted him $3,000 a month. Jacobs and Lombardo were hoodlum companions.

The arrests caused a sensation for three days, when the investigation suddenly took on the aspect of a comic opera. On January 9, the chief witness, Don Ritchie, a Canadian, slipped out of a

Detroit hotel room where he was held in protective custody and crossed the Detroit River to Windsor. Police said Ritchie had named Jacobs as the man who attempted to kill the union leader.[14]

As the search for Ritchie was pressed, the UAW admitted it had given the fugitive $5,000 in reward money at the hotel, unwittingly financing his flight. The sum was in addition to $100,000 the union had posted to bring the assassin to justice. On January 13 the missing witness showed up in Preston, Ontario. There he gave himself up to one of the town's newspaper reporters. Eleven days later, after doing much talking, he declared he knew nothing of the Reuther shooting. His repudiation destroyed the case. Nobody was satisfied, not even Renda. He filed a $4.5 million damage suit against the union. The case went to trial in the winter of 1957. Winstead was ordered to produce his records in court. On the day before he was to appear he left his home near Lake St. Clair to walk on the ice of a nearby canal. When he did not return his wife called the police. A week later his body was found under the frozen lake. The UAW eventually settled the Renda suit out of court for $50,000.

Reuther had not allowed the attempted assassination to disrupt his union activity. His peak achievement came in June 1955, when the UAW reached a settlement with the Ford Motor Company, covering eighty-four thousand workers in thirty-seven plants.[15] A scoop by the *Detroit Free Press* detailed Ford's initial offer: "an income stabilization plan" under which workers would participate in stock purchases, half of the cost of which would be borne by the company. The "beat" was not received lightly by the *News*'s labor writers. Lauren discovered that the leak had come from a Ford vice president during a conversation with Lee Hills, the publisher of the *Free Press* who was then writing a column. Incensed, the labor writer threatened to phone Warren S. Booth, who had succeeded Will Scripps as publisher of the *News,* to tell him it was his fault the *News* was beaten by its morning rival. It was an unusual turnabout in employer-employee relationships, even for a newspaper. Lauren was restrained from making the call and was advised to take a two-week vacation "to cool off."

Another set of circumstances soon evened the score for the *News*. The man to do it was Simmons. Arriving at 7:30 A.M. at the Detroit-Leland Hotel, where the negotiations were being held, Simmons discovered Hank Shurmur, who contracted for news pictures with Station WWJ–TV, sipping coffee at a counter. Obviously weary from a night on the town, Shurmur muttered he had the story of the final settlement, but he was afraid no one was listening to him. His companion on a round of saloons the night before had been an old friend, a UAW official, who had given him the details of the compromise agreement between Ford and the union. At 2 that morning, Shurmur, his speech somewhat slurred by the excitement of the evening, had phoned Harvey Patton, *News* managing editor. "Patton gave me hell," Shurmur told Simmons, "for calling him in the middle of the night when I was drunk. But he told me to call back when my head cleared." Shurmur then called Allen Nieber, city editor, and got the same advice. By the time Simmons talked to Shurmur, the newsreel cameraman had slept several hours and appeared to be a fairly reliable source. He did not remember that he had called Patton a second time and was offered a bonus if the story stood up.

"Who were you with?" Simmons asked.

Shurmur gave the name of a union official.

"How can we check it?" Simmons pursued.

"Let's go over to the WWJ newsroom," Shurmur offered, "and I'll call him up."

The call was made with Simmons listening in on a second phone. "I was thinking about what you told me last night," Shurmur began. "But the details are kind of blurry."

"Wait a minute," the union leader said, hesitating while he apparently reached for some papers. Then he detailed the terms of the union demand as Simmons jotted them down.

Next Simmons scribbled a note and handed it to Shurmur. "Ask him if the union has given this to Ford?"

"We gave it to them yesterday," came back the reply. Simmons ran out of the newsroom, through the tunnel that connected WWJ and the newspaper, and wrote the story.

"You're sure of your source?" Patton asked.

The Battle of the Overpass, famous in labor history, shows Ford Motor Company servicemen in "bargaining session" with UAW's Richard Frankensteen

Pulitzer prizewinning photo, "The Picket Line"

In historic Prohibition era photo, rum-runners carry suitcases filled with Canadian whiskey to waiting cars as scout car keeps lookout for rival gangs

Gar Wood, world-famous racer, in 1921 trial heat in Miss America I

Did Ty Cobb intentionally spike "Home Run" Baker? *News* photo says he didn't

WWJ – The *Detroit News.* For first broadcast, "Roses of Picardy"

Detroit's transit wars and strikes erupted for thirty years. Here Judge James Phelan (in derby) points accusing finger at mayor

Teddy Roosevelt in Detroit for 1912 Bull Moose campaign

The city's main stem, Woodward Avenue, in 1915

The end of a brilliant pitching career: Lynwood (Schoolboy) Rowe leaves
the mound for the last time, captured by a *News* photographer

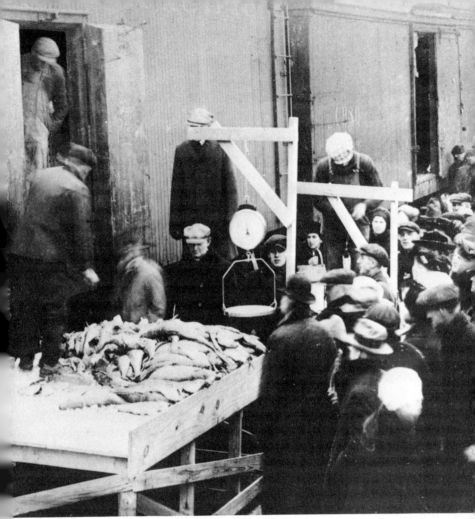

When the price of foodstuffs got too high in the opinion of the *News,* the paper imported fish and sold it at a railroad siding for ten cents a pound. Move forced down food prices 25 percent

Early aerial photography: The man with the camera is the *News*'s William Kuenzel, who photographed many of Detroit's historic moments

"Positive," Simmons replied.[16]

The story threw the negotiations into a frenzy. But before the day was out, both sides confirmed it. Among other benefits, the compromise settlement established a $55 million job security fund from which laid-off workers could draw pay for twenty-six weeks. Model changeovers no longer would create the hardships that annually wracked the industry.[17]

Nor was Hoffa idle. Rising to the top of the Teamsters Union in October 1957, he became the chief spokesman of 1,500,000 union members.

If Reuther controlled the men inside the plants, Hoffa controlled those on the outside — the men who delivered the goods. But while Reuther demanded democratic procedures in the UAW and an educated approach to problems, Hoffa was a "loner" who was accused of hiring men convicted or suspected of labor racketeering to do his bidding. Hoffa's explanation to critics was that he only offered these men "a helping hand." He explained the loyalty of teamster members by saying, "I deliver the goods. They're interested in how many bucks they can make. I get them for them."[18]

After twelve years of "getting them what they want," Hoffa reached the apex of his union career in 1964 by gaining a nationwide trucking contract for over-the-road drivers. With Teamsters hauling more than 80 percent of the nation's freight, the contract gave Hoffa incalculable power over interstate commerce. By now his every move was under scrutiny from a variety of interested agencies.

On March 13, 1957, Robert F. Kennedy, legal counsel for the Senate Rackets Committee, accused Hoffa of attempting to bribe a committee investigator. Hoffa was acquitted on July 19 of the same year. Kennedy called Hoffa's operation of union affairs "a conspiracy of evil" and assigned a large staff of investigators to search out further possible wrongdoing. On March 5, 1964, Hoffa and three co-defendants were convicted of jury tampering in Chattanooga, Tennessee. Hoffa was sentenced to eight years in prison and fined $10,000. The offense occurred during a trial charging the defendants with misuse of union funds in a trucking company operation. He was sentenced to the federal penitentiary at Lewisburg, Pennsylvana. While serving this sentence he was tried and convicted of mail fraud and conspiracy involving a Florida land venture and received an additional five-year term.

With Hoffa in prison, reportedly issuing union orders to underlings on the outside, Walter Reuther was living an almost ascetic life. Like Hoffa, he did not drink, smoke or go to nightclubs. Unlike Hoffa, whose salary was raised from $75,000 to $100,000 while he was in prison, Reuther was paid $32,907. Like Hoffa, Reuther worked tirelessly, but his goals were much broader. The UAW chief was interested in bringing about social change. While Hoffa and others were calling simply for more wages and better hours, he demanded full employment and issued programs he thought would make it possible. His belief in the necessity of an educated union leadership to bargain with big industry led him to establish the UAW Family Education Center on Black Lake, three hundred miles north of Detroit, into which he poured $14 million in union funds. Here union leaders could learn the techniques of collective bargaining while their families frolicked.

On May 9, 1970, flying in a chartered jet plane with four other persons, including his wife, Reuther headed for the camp at Black Lake and a meeting with fellow union officers. The huge investment had put the union's finances in dire straits. With the light failing, the plane dropped into a normal landing pattern. But on making the approach, flying too low, the jet clipped the tops of trees outlining the field and hurtled, a flaming ball, into the spindly forest and crusted lichen below. No one survived. Reuther was sixty-two.[19]

The spring forest where pink hepaticas and white trillium grew amid rotting leaves and pine needles was far removed from the concrete and smokestacks of the city where he had won a world-wide reputation.

Said a *News* editorial: "He lived simply and remained until his death probably the lowest paid president of a major industrial union. He was not a labor leader for the money he got out of it. He derived his satisfaction from the power his union could exert to benefit its members and, as he saw it, men and women everywhere. . . ."[20]

At the time of Reuther's death, Hoffa was working in the laundry of Lewisburg prison. Appeal after appeal had failed to lessen his sentence. On January 5, 1972, he announced he would not seek reelection to the presidency of the Teamsters Union and gave his support to his longtime associate, Frank Fitzsimmons, who replaced him. The arrangement reportedly was part of a deal that brought about the release of Hoffa on parole. While it was reported President Nixon sanctioned Hoffa's release, no proof was forthcoming. Hoffa had served fifty-eight months. He was fifty-eight years old.

On his return to Detroit Hoffa gave his first interview to a reporter he had known almost from the start of his career, the *News*'s labor editor Jack Crellin. He told Crellin that the union pension owed him amounted to $1,700,000 and he had decided to take it in a lump sum. After taxes he realized $1,200,000. Under the parole agreement he was ordered to refrain from union activity until 1980. He would then be sixty-six years old. He said he planned to spend the next few years working to improve the conditions in the nation's prisons.[21]

He meant it. His dedication to prison reform was just as great as his devotion to the labor movement. Before long he was stumping to better the lot of prisoners. He knew prison conditions firsthand.

6

We Were the First to Sing on Raaadio

THE THOUSAND DOLLARS that James E. Scripps gave Tom Clark in 1902 did not go to waste. Like every other inventor who tinkered with wireless sending devices, Clark acquired the nickname of "Sparks." Didn't sparks fly every time he tapped a transmitter and sent a sound clear across a room? Will Scripps, James's son, was fascinated by Clark's experiments. Soon Clark taught Will the Morse code. Within a few years after James's death, Will installed the best available receiving and transmitting set on the second floor of the Scripps home on Trumbull. And when Will's son, William J., born in 1905, was old enough to understand the magic, he was taught to send and receive wireless messages.

Will, whose interest in things mechanical was endless, became the first man in Michigan in 1912 to own and fly an airplane (he taught himself to fly). He also became a pioneer in night flight when he decided to fly to Harsen's Island in the St. Clair River flats after sunset in a sea plane he owned. He told caretakers at the Old Club, then the resort spa for Scripps family members, to light a barrel of oil at the end of the club pier. He made the flight without incident.

The development of radio by Guglielmo Marconi, who first sent a message via the ether waves in 1895, spurred his excitement. Will and W. J. would be front-runners in learning all about it and in putting it to practical use.

One evening in 1918 Will and his wife, Nina, were in the sitting room of their home when W. J., then thirteen years old, ran down the stairs from his second-floor transmission room. "Father, Father," he shouted, "I hear voices. Come and listen."[1]

Will and Nina ascended the stairs and slipped into the room. The atmosphere was that of a séance. No one dared to make a sound. Then two or three words squeaked through the speaker. In the excitement no one could remember what they were. The important thing was that human voices were being received by air. Radio hams had been born and Will and his son W. J. were two of the most enthusiastic. Before the evening's transmissions had ended, Will Scripps, who had taken over as publisher of the *News* from George Gough Booth, was convinced that the paper had to have a radio broadcasting station. If he could arrange it, it would be the first newspaper in the nation with a radio outlet.

A meeting of the paper's board of directors was called. Will arrived with Clark at his side and outlined his plan. At his urging the board agreed to appropriate the necessary funds to retain the services of Dr. Lee DeForest. DeForest, an early pioneer with Clark, had cleared the way for commercial broadcasting by adding the radio tube oscillator to his earlier inventions of the radio tube triode and the radio amplifier. The mechanism provided a transmitter using a two hundred meter wavelength. Convinced of its practicality, the U.S. Navy had been successfully using DeForest equipment, which provided a range of a hundred miles. Will argued that it was just a matter of moving the device from sea to land and a whole new world would be opened to every person who could afford a receiving set.

With the funds appropriated, Will wasted no time in ordering DeForest's equipment. When it arrived a quick decision had to be made where to place it. The building at Lafayette and Second, erected in 1917 "to last the paper for a lifetime," had been built for editorial expansion. There was room on the second floor and a studio was quickly improvised. Detroiters Frank Edwards, a transmission operator, and his technical aide, Keith Bernard, put the equipment in working order in a corner of the city room. It seemed a most logical place to locate a radio station emanating from a newspaper — in the hub of activity.

On the evening of August 20, 1920, Harold Trumbo, who managed an Edison Company shop in Detroit, was asked to bring a phonograph and a few records to the *News* building. The phonograph was placed close to the transmitter and Trumbo put "Roses of Picardy" on the turntable. Elton Plant, the senior office boy in the editorial room, held a cardboard megaphone up to the phonograph speaker to magnify the sound. At 8:15 Edwards leaned over the mouthpiece and announced: "This is 8MK calling." Then Trumbo started the phonograph and "Roses of Picardy" trickled forth in the night air to an estimated hundred ham operators within receiving range.[2]

When the tune ended, Edwards spoke into the transmitter again. "How did you get it?" he asked. He soon got an assuring crescendo of answers. Since ham operators could both send as well as receive, a medley of voices rumbled over 8MK's receiver. "It's coming in fine." "We're getting everything distinctly." "Loud and clear." Gratified beyond expectations, the pioneer group then played a recording of "Taps" and the first reveille for the airwaves was over. Among the listeners were Will, thirty-eight, and his son, W. J., just fifteen.[3]

The next day's newspaper carried no mention of the pioneer broadcast. Much more experimenting had to take place, more refinements made, before the station would be so bold as to advertise its capabilities. It would take just eleven days to acquire this confidence. For the remainder of the month, records were played nightly. Then, on August 31, the paper proclaimed on Page One "The *News* Radiophone to Give Vote Results." Almost matter-of-factly the article declared, "The *Detroit News* tonight will announce the results, as they may be received, of the State, Congressional and County primaries over southeastern Michigan, using, as a medium, its newly-completed wireless telephone. The messages will be carried by real 'voices of the night.' Through the Lower Peninsula, possibly, but more particularly within a radius of 100 miles of Detroit, hundreds of wireless telegraph operators and enthusiasts will listen and get the results, not in telegraphic code but by direct transmission of the human voice. So far as it is known here, this is the first time in the history of radio development that a newspaper will use a radiophone for the transmission of news."[4]

The next day the paper spoke with even greater authority: "The sending of the election returns by the *Detroit News* Radiophone Tuesday night was fraught with romance and must go down in the history of man's conquest of the elements as a gigantic step in his progress. In the four hours that the apparatus was hissing and whirring its messages into space, few realized that a dream and a prediction had come true. The news of the world was being given forth through this invisible trumpet to the waiting crowds in an unseen marketplace. With the perfection of aerials and amplifiers, the not too distant future may see the installation of regular news service."

Election eve listeners were even more enthusiastic than the hams who had picked up the first broadcast. The *News* promised to expand its radio facilities and to continue daily broadcasts. The expansion took place on the fourth floor of the *News* building dignified with a sign over a doorway stating STUDIO.

Besieged with phone calls and letters from persons who wanted to construct receiving sets, the paper began printing instructional articles and advertising radio components. Anyone, it was declared, with a modicum of skill at tinkering could put a crystal set together for a few dollars, including the primitive but effective device — a bit of galena — that was contacted intermittently by a wire, called "a cat's whisker." This tuned in the station to earphones. A few days after the election broadcast the *News* reported it had received the first want ad ever to be sent to a paper by radiophone.[5] It offered for sale a pair of twelve-power prism binoculars and came from a Detroit high school student, Albert Allen, a ham operator who eventually became an engineer for the station. The station's call numbers were to be changed first to WBL and then to WWJ. The observant insider noted that the second two letters were the initials of Will's son. But the similarity in the governmentally issued call letters was just a happy coincidence.

Dancing to music "out of the blue" first occurred on September 4, less than three weeks after the station's first furtive broadcast.

The setting was the home of Charles F. Hammond, Jr., in the city's fashionable Indian Village district. Hammond, a grandson of the builder of Detroit's first "skyscraper" (ten stories, in 1889), had hooked up a receiving set to a phonograph horn. A dozen young men and women who had gathered for the occasion waited in silence.

"It's like magic," one girl whispered to her escort. Then the strains of "The Naughty Waltz" emerged from the speaker and the dance was on.

Two days later the station sent out news flashes on a boxing match held at Benton Harbor, Michigan, between heavyweight champion Jack Dempsey and challenger Billy Misky. Sports had hit the ether waves and fans were appreciative.[6] Those with transmitters quickly "talked back" to the station.

"Hooray for Dempsey," one of them shouted into his transmitter.

"Fifteen people are here listening to you," another told the station. "Clearest we've had yet."

A fan twenty miles distant reported, "a little weak but we heard it all right." The ham then announced, "We laughed at Dad who went downtown to watch a bulletin board, when he telephoned us the news we'd already heard — that Dempsey had won 'by a knockout in the third round.'"

The era of animated bulletin boards outside of newspaper offices where people gathered to read the latest newsflashes was doomed. A few days later a wireless operator on a Great Lakes freighter reported he could pick up the station on the northernmost reaches of Lake Huron. "I find myself looking forward to your nightly concerts," he said.

When the *News*'s station broadcast the election returns in the presidential race between two Ohio editors, Warren G. Harding and James M. Cox, on November 2, 1920, it had company on the air — the Westinghouse Electric and Manufacturing Company's station at East Pittsburgh, Pennsylvania, KDKA. The Pittsburgh station made the claim that it was the first station to broadcast regularly, a claim eventually put to rest by Dr. DeForest himself. Although KDKA had been the first station in the nation to be issued call letters, the *News*'s station, he said, was the first commercial radio station "in all the world." Not until eleven weeks after its founding did WWJ share the channels with the rival KDKA.[7]

By the time KDKA began regular broadcasts in December 1920, WWJ already was confronted with a new phenomenon in the entertainment world: radio prima donnas. All had performed before live audiences and the experience of singing or talking into a cold microphone was just short of traumatic. When no applause greeted the first number in his radio debut, singer Ernest Ball looked baffled, then stuck out his tongue at the microphone. Asked to give a humorous dialogue, comedian Frank Tinney would not believe that he was being heard by anyone outside the studio. He had no faith in the eerie invention, and thought he was the victim of a practical joke. Walter Hampden, the great Shakespearean actor, refused to recite the soliloquy from *Hamlet* unless everybody — including the technicians — left the studio. A compromise was worked out and Hampden was given the solitude he demanded — alone with the mike in a locked women's rest room.

By 1922 some sixty-six commercial stations had sprouted all over the nation. Like the others, WWJ grew with each new technological breakthrough. By extending two wires 290 feet to the Fort Shelby Hotel, WWJ increased it transmission range to one thousand five hundred miles "on a clear night." A radio station erected by the navy in World War I at Bordeaux, France, sent a message that it was receiving music "loud and clear."

A quirk in timing led Herbert Hoover, then secretary of commerce in President Harding's cabinet, to make his maiden radio speech over WWJ. He made it from St. Paul's Episcopal Cathedral, where equipment had been installed to broadcast the service on Easter Sunday 1922. Hoover, in Detroit to make an address on behalf of the American Red Cross, was asked if he objected to speaking from the church. He did not.

Arriving at the church, he ascended the pulpit and delivered his address. Unfortunately, the microphone stood in the chancel where it had picked up the Easter service and Hoover was heard only in the church. Edwin G. Boyes, WWJ engineer, had been advised that on no account was Hoover to be interrupted once he began to speak. The engineer finally solved the problem by handing Hoover a note, explaining the difficulty. Hoover simply left the pulpit and walked to the chancel where, surrounded by radio equipment, he reread his speech.[8]

Other newspapers with radio outlets now included the *San Francisco Examiner,* the *Rochester* (N.Y.) *Times-Union,* and the *Richmond* (Va.) *Palladium.* The programming fell into a natural pattern at each paper's station. At the *News,* the paper's household editor presented a fifteen-minute talk, "Tonight's Dinner," the first woman's feature on the air — preceding Julia Child in the cookery department by almost a half century. Early sound effects included clapping together coconut shells to simulate horses' hooves. This announced the arrival of a program called "The Town Crier." A bell preceded each news flash. *News* reporters, such as human interest writer Rex G. White, participated in early dramatic productions. *News* humorist C. C. Bradner was pressed into radio service as a newscaster. He did not let the casting alter his disposition: He devised the technique of softening the daily boxscore of tragic world events with a bit of humor.

As stations proliferated, the back fence conversation in all of America was about "DX" — shorthand for distance. "What did you get last night?" "Cincinnati." "You don't say. Herman got Yonkers." "DX" kept America up most of the night. And kept it talking most of the day.

WWJ kept its name in the nation's conversation. William F. Holliday, its first announcer and subsequent general manager, did it by presenting programming that kept the avid listeners on the edge of their seats. After hearing a group of twelve collegians at a University of Michigan J-Hop, headed by a friend from his hometown, Tyrone, Pennsylvania, Holliday invited the group to broadcast over the *News's* station. Called the Pennsylvanians, the band made its radio debut in Detroit, conducted by Fred Waring, whose name was to become synonymous with good music throughout America for three decades. The Pennsylvanians were so popular over WWJ that the band won an eight-week engagement at a Detroit theater. And its career was launched.[9]

The success of Waring reminded Holliday of another hometown friend, Edwin L. (Ty) Tyson, who had shown some talent in minstrel shows at the Tyrone Elks Club. He wired Tyson, offering him a job as a broadcaster. Tyson's acceptance started him on a career in Detroit that was to bring him national recognition as a sportscaster, a new term in the radio dictionary.[10]

In August 1924, Tyson initiated radio coverage of the Gold Cup powerboat races in Detroit, and later the Harmsworth races, which made Detroit's Gar Wood a national motorboat hero. That fall Tyson made the first radio broadcast of a football game in the Middle West from the University of Michigan's Ferry Field in Ann Arbor. Fielding H. Yost, the legendary U. of M. coach, had successfully blocked the broadcast of games for fear that it would hurt ticket sales. He relented for the game with Wisconsin only because the stands had been sold out. Tyson's broadcast created a new interest among fans, who deluged U. of M. for tickets to future games. After that Yost acceded to regular radio coverage. On April 19, 1927, Tyson made the first broadcast of a major league baseball game.[11]

Tyson's style was distinct. He thought of himself as a reporter rather than as an entertainer and he tried to relate in simple terms what went on before him. While he became best known for his sports broadcasts, he often interviewed arriving notables, including Detroit-born Charles A. Lindbergh, who visited Detroit after his historic 1927 flight to see his schoolteacher mother; Helen Keller, the talented deaf-mute who taught all America about the intelligence and sensitivities of people who suffered her affliction; and Will Rogers, whose biting wit made the nation laugh and think twice for two generations.

The growth of radio created a new position on the *News* and on papers throughout "radioland" — the radio writer. It also created a yen on the part of many Americans to capitalize on the new entertainment medium. Among the job-seekers was a midget page boy who worked for the Fort Shelby Hotel, anchor of WWJ's antenna. Known as Colossal Boris, the page boy yearned for a career as a "Johnny" on a popular radio show that opened with a page boy singing out, "Call for Philip Morris." Boris appealed to Herschell Hart, the *News*'s radio writer, to intercede with the press agent for the cigarette company. Hart gave Boris a letter that he carried to New York, already the center of network radio. On the day Colossal Boris arrived in New York, Hart received a wire from the press agent: "Thanks for sending me a midget. Business is so bad, I ate him." The Wall Street crash of 1929 had sent the country into a deep economic depression. The nation's newspapers and its radio outlets suffered alike.[12]

As the Depression worsened, many newspaper publishers openly blamed radio for siphoning off advertising revenue. Because the *News* was the first to start a commercial station, they looked unkindly on its representatives. In 1933, W. Steele Gilmore, editor of the *News*, found himself standing alone as a defender of the rival medium at a conference of leading editors at Princeton University. The subject was radio's effect on newspapers. Gilmore reported that like Fielding Yost, who learned radio would only enhance attendance at a football game, the *News* found radio spurred the interest of listeners in the events of the day. Newspapers had the advantage, he told the editors, of telling "the whole story," and putting it in a fashion — in type — that could be read and reread. The editors went away convinced that when the economic skies cleared they would plug for radio affiliations to spur interest in world events, and consequently in their newspapers.[13]

Will Scripps, who had watched his radio child develop into robust health, was now concerned both about the station and the newspaper. With the banks closed, advertising fell off sharply. From his office as publisher, he penned a letter to Jay G. Hayden, chief of the paper's Washington Bureau. Scripps felt that under the leadership of James Couzens, then United States senator, Detroit's banks could reorganize their assets and begin paying "as much as 50 cents on the dollar." He instructed Hayden to talk to Couzens about giving up his seat in the Senate "to help out his home town."

Couzens thought about the request, then told Hayden that it was his opinion that "since Detroit went through the bank wringer first it could rest assured it would come out first."

Scripps promptly answered Hayden's letter. His advice for Couzens came out of personal experience. "The theory regarding our being put through the wringer first and for that reason being the first to come back is certainly encouraging," he wrote. Then he added " – if it were not for the fact that ordinarily when things are put through the wringer they come out pretty flat with even the buttons missing."[14]

As the Depression continued both the *News* and its radio outlet were forced to cut expenses. The first layoff in the paper's history was noted as "Black Friday." To cut costs the station resorted to such devices as reconstructed sports broadcasts. Instead of sending a crew to another city, a telegraph operator in the opponent's park would tap out coded play-by-play messages. These were typed out by an operator in the hometown studio and handed to the sportscaster. It was his task to piece out the meager data and from his own experience reconstruct the game. At WWJ it was Ty Tyson. Only his experience made the reconstructions at all palatable.

Tyson's following was such that in 1934, when the networks tried to bar "partisan" hometown announcers from broadcasting World Series' games, some six hundred thousand fans petitioned Baseball Commissioner Kenesaw Mountain Landis. The Detroit Tigers had won the American League pennant and Tyson's fans did not want to hear about their World Series play from anyone but him. Landis gave Tyson special dispensation to do the broadcasts.

Poor times kept all of America at home, ears glued to radio sets. The first President to maximize the effect of radio in winning votes was Franklin D. Roosevelt, whose Fireside Chats were heard over WWJ and other network stations beginning on March 12, 1933. They continued in an effort to carry a dispirited nation throughout the Depression and into World War II. The last Fireside Chat was written on April 11, 1945; it was not delivered. Roosevelt died the next day in Warm Springs, Georgia. The broadcast was to be given April 14, 1945.

On August 20, 1936, having surmounted the worst of the Depression, WWJ moved out of its studio in the *News* building into a newly completed structure across the street. Within sixteen years the world's first commercial radio station had reached adulthood in a building with five studios on three floors, soundproofed in a construction technique developed by Detroit's Albert Kahn.

Plaques of black granite were placed on either side of the entrance, the work of Swedish sculptor Carl Milles. One represented a group of musicians playing for dear life. The other represented radio's army of listeners — some intensely interested, some patently bored.[15]

A week of dedicatory programs brought to Detroit Walter Hampden, no longer demanding privacy in the studio; Ethel Barrymore, who starred in a play; America's foremost soprano, Jessica Dragonette; and Fred Waring and his Pennsylvanians. Dr. DeForest gave the sixteenth birthday address. The acting manager of WWJ who introduced the program was William J. Scripps, whose excitement as a boy had spurred his father toward the establishment of the pioneer station. In the audience, beaming, was Will Scripps.

In 1941, WWJ established the first FM station in Michigan, with studios at the top of Detroit's highest skyscraper, the forty-seven-story Penobscot Building. The tower studios also were used in the introduction of television. On October 23, 1946, the *News* gave Detroiters their first chance to watch TV in the city's Convention Hall. When trained bears and doves performed on a stage with comics, the audience could shift their eyes from the performers to closed-circuit black-and-white television monitors. On March 4, 1947, when there were fewer than a hundred receiving sets in Detroit, the station began daily experimental programs consisting of a mixture of test patterns and studio presentations. Within two years Detroit was linked to the East Coast by coaxial cable, bringing network television to Michigan. The fever to own a home receiving set was unstoppable.[16]

On May 10, 1950, a white-haired man visited the station to see how things were working out. It was Tom Clark, lean and wiry at eighty-one. He walked through the building, inquisitive about each man's job. When he was about to leave, the staff from the youngest recruit to the station's general manager Harry Bannister gathered around him.

"Things change fast in radio and television," he said. "I look at some television pictures and I say, 'That's the last word, it can't be improved upon.' And the next thing I know it has improved. We are just entering the field. Its limits are beyond even our imagination. Back in the old days of what they called wireless, we knew we had something — but what? Folks used to shake their heads and say, 'That Tom is a nut.' Well, I couldn't disprove it lots of times. But somehow we could just sort of feel things and know that out there in the atmosphere was sound, sound that could be controlled. But how? We'd work and work and get nowhere, and I'd tell the boys to go on home, we'd try it again another day."[17]

The "Sparks" of the 1900s was getting tired. He walked toward the exit, his listeners following. At the door he stopped to add: "No use talking about the television of tomorrow. Nobody knows what it is destined to become. All these wonderful machines I've seen here are steppingstones. I'm not retired, by the way, even if I do spend the winters in Florida. I'm still experimenting in the great science that attracted me long ago."

Tom Clark, who began in the age of wireless telegraphy, lived long enough to see the advent of color television and satellite transmission from outer space. He died at ninety-three in 1962.

Between April 12 and May 11, 1962, the newspaper and its radio outlet merged their efforts once again to keep Detroiters informed of what was going on in the world. A twenty-nine-day strike of union employees had halted production of both the *News* and the *Free Press*. During the strike *News* reporters continued to cover the city and the nation, but their production stopped on spikes of various editors' desks. The idea of capsuling the news and letting each reporter present his day's discoveries seemed a natural one. Half-hour television newscasts were held. They proved one point: that the newspaper and its air wave outlet across the street were worlds apart. Hard-bitten newsmen, accustomed to talking to the city's and the nation's top officials and the lowliest of citizens, were frigid performers, paralyzed by the microphone. They had grown up with pencils and typewriters. Their electronic comrades were a breed apart. "Never again," they vowed when their best friends began to admit to them, "you were absolutely horrible."

An exception to the general discomfort before the video cameras was Bill Matney, former magazine editor of the *Detroit Chronicle*, the city's black newspaper. Matney, a general reporter at the *News*, left the paper a year later to join the National Broadcasting Company, and later the American Broadcasting Company, as a correspondent.

Subsequent newspaper strikes in 1964 and again in 1967 failed to bring *News* reporters to the public's rescue. The television station expanded its own coverage with men who had been weaned on microphones and cameras.

7

Bullets and Beer

THE ADOPTION OF Prohibition in 1919 with the Volstead Act opened the doors to the longest, most continuous Page One headline in history.[1] Forty years after the repeal of the Eighteenth Amendment in 1933, the effects of "The Great Experiment" continue to be seen on the front pages of the nation's newspapers. Prohibition was a fertile spawning ground for organized crime in America. Gangland tactics became sophisticated in the day-to-day competition between rival mobsters and with law-enforcing agencies. But for those who claimed that the press made "a circus out of Prohibition," there is ample evidence that it did not.

It can be rightfully argued that without the floodlight played on gangs by newspapers (and during the twenties and thirties by radio), the likes of Al Capone, for years the lord of Chicago's underworld, would not have been the subject of a constant federal harassment that finally put him behind bars on the only charge for which he could not put others forward to take the rap — income tax evasion. Capone, Ma Barker, John Dillinger, Bonnie and Clyde and the rest all felt the heat. Only the most neurotic of them enjoyed it. The "professionals" shunned the limelight like they would a competing gang's executioner. While some members of the press must stand with heads bowed before the charge of "sensationalism," others may claim journalistic responsibility in a very emotional and melodramatic time. It is difficult not to sensationalize a headline when the facts themselves are sensational. The Collingwood massacre of three hired killers by members of the infamous Purple Gang on Detroit's northwest side on September 18, 1931, was comparable in gangland terrorism to Chicago's St. Valentine Day massacre of February 14, 1929, when seven were slain. The Purples were reputedly named by a robbery victim who said they were bad like bad meat — purple.

The argument and the struggle is unending. The responsible members of the nation's press continue to insist that they not only must depict the daily events of the community and the world but must mirror the public conscience; ideally they must put light into dark places, expose evil where they find it, provide the leadership to create a good society. How to do it honestly and effectively is a continuous challenge. Through the years the constant deterrent in revealing the depth of criminal involvement has been the Constitution and the Bill of Rights. Criminal attorneys resort to it rightfully to keep their clients' names and "reputations" free of public attention. The Fifth Amendment, written to safeguard Americans from forced self-incrimination, remains the refuge for criminals just as it protects law-abiding citizens from invasion of their privacy. "I'll take the Fifth," has been uttered in American courts more often than any other phrase except, perhaps, "Do you swear to tell the truth. . . ."

On August 10, 1963, Jack M. Carlisle, who joined the *Detroit News* staff in 1927 and almost immediately was assigned to crime coverage, was sitting at his desk in the rear of the newspaper's tennis court–sized city room. From thirty-five years as a reporter and later as a columnist, Carlisle had developed and maintained links with Detroit's underworld so that the *News* not only could keep abreast of its activities, but explain to its readers the extent to which criminals were participating in their everyday lives.

Facing the front of the *News*'s oak-paneled city room in his austerely furnished office, Harvey Patton, then managing editor, was pacing up and down, a telephone locked to his ear. Patton had first learned about crime from his father, who served for years as chief of the newspaper's police beat. Patton was talking to Jerry ter Horst, chief of the *News*'s Washington Bureau. In a pause in the conversation, he pressed a buzzer for his secretary and ordered Carlisle front and center. Carlisle arrived as Patton clapped down the receiver. For months Carlisle, with a team of *News* reporters, had been trying to track down organized crime members. The team knew the Mafiosa had racetrack interests, was involved in nightclubs, cleaning and dyeing establishments, car wash installations and other outlets doing business with the public every day. But the kind of evidence that would hold up in court against any kind of libel action could not be developed.[2] Now a new development, hopefully, would give the *News* a wedge by which it could legally name the kingpins of Detroit's underworld and their business enterprises. Under a legal concept called qualified privilege, a newspaper faces no jeopardy from a possible libel action if its news report is an accurate account of testimony given in court or before a legislative body. Thus, any testimony before Congress relating to Mafia penetration could be used.

Patton and Martin Hayden, who in 1959 had succeeded Harry V. Wade (the *News*'s Senator Soaper of the thirties and forties) as editor, had just read an issue of the *Saturday Evening Post* that revealed the first of what were to be commonly called "the Valachi papers."[3] In U.S. Attorney General Robert F. Kennedy's introduction to an article, "Mafia — The Inside Story," he declared that "many Americans think that organized crime doesn't involve them. . . ." He went on to explain that increased prices resulted from racketeers' involvement in business and labor and the involvement meant extortion and death to those who opposed them. Hayden, who had served ten years in the Washington Bureau, seven as its chief, knew the techniques of moving Capitol Hill. He had been informed by ter Horst that the Senate committee on organized crime and narcotics, chaired by Senator John L. McClellan, planned to convene in mid-October to probe into criminal activities in Chicago, New York and Cleveland. "Why not Detroit?" the *News* editor asked.

"Jack," Patton said to his crime reporter, "I have ordered ter Horst into town and I want you and Jerry to talk to George Edwards [then Detroit's police commissioner]. If he and Piersante [Vincent, then district detective inspector] are allowed to testify, the names and business connections of Mafia members in Detroit will be a matter of public record." When ter Horst arrived, he and Carlisle laid out the plan to Edwards.[4] The commissioner not only endorsed the idea, he gave the *News* reporters the names of the men to see in Washington. However, in Washington there was no rush to accept the proposal. Committee investigators wanted to confine the scope of the probe to New York, Chicago and Cleveland. Carlisle and ter Horst pressed for action. The final decision was left to Kennedy, the committee's former legal counsel. If the committee would establish the record, Kennedy was told, the *News* would publish the information, including Detroit's "family tree of crime." Kennedy cleared the way and shortly Edwards and Piersante were subpoenaed.

Now the work of preparing the testimony began. But when Piersante and Edwards turned to police files of the 1920s and early 1930s to draw a picture of how the seeds of organized crime were sown during Prohibition days and afterward, the records had strangely disappeared. Edwards called Carlisle. "Jack, you covered this era. Why don't you write down what you know and what you can discover in your newspaper morgue?" Carlisle spent three weeks in the paper's clipping files.[5] When he emerged he had the vital information that explained the network of organized crime in Detroit.

"In many ways," Edwards testified during the hearing, "the modern racket situation in Detroit begins with Pete Licavoli's arrival. . . ."[6]

Licavoli arrived from St. Louis in 1927, the same year Carlisle joined the *News* from the campus of the University of Detroit. In his coverage of rum-running, Carlisle got to know Licavoli intimately. They ate and drank together in Detroit blind pigs supplied by Licavoli and rival mobsters.

"Pete Licavoli's brother, Dominic," Edwards testified, "is married to Joe Zerilli's daughter, Rosalie, so there is a family tie between Zerilli and Licavoli in that fashion. Jack Lucido, son of Sam Lucido, married Pete's niece, Concetta, who is the daughter of Thomas Yonnie Licavoli. Yonnie Licavoli is Pete's brother, who is serving a life sentence for murder in Ohio. . . ."[7] Edwards produced charts and photographs and referred to them during his testimony.

" 'Long Joe' Bommarito, who is on that chart on the second level, is a brother-in-law of Pete. 'Long Joe' married Pete's sister Mamie and Pete married 'Long Joe's' sister Grace, so that the Bommarito and the Licavoli combine, as well as the Zerilli combine, is pulled together pretty well by past origin in Terrasina, Sicily, on the part of the parents, and by these marriages. . . ."

Resorting to Carlisle's research, Edwards inserted this statement in the Senate record: "There are interesting newspaper clips from that period which report police arrests of Pete in the early days, actually out in the field with a pair of spyglasses looking at rumrunner boats from Belle Isle and waiting to signal them when to land. . . ."

There certainly are. By May 27, 1929, the *New York Times* had published a full-page article about the activities in Detroit under the headline, "Our 'Rum Capital': An Amazing Picture." The business of the era was captured in this succinct paragraph: "The manufacture and the sale of automobiles in Detroit involves nearly $2,000,000,000 annually and the chemical industry is rated at about $90,000,000. Between the two stands Detroit's illegal liquor traffic, estimated at $215,000,000."[8]

That the city was wide open was no secret to anyone west of the Holland Tunnel. No candidate for mayor was elected during the Prohibition era who made a stand against alcohol. Those elected who were not "wets" got into office by staying mum about reform. At one time it was estimated there were as many as twenty-five thousand blind pigs operating in the big city and in its environs. Blind pigs and bookies were run within sight of police headquarters, city hall and other prominent buildings, vantage points from which the comings and goings of customers were viewed regularly. In 1930, while Mayor Charles Bowles was attending the Kentucky Derby, betting legally on the horse race, a *News* photographer stood at a window in his office and photographed a bookie in operation. When Bowles returned he was furious. The handbook kept operating and business improved as a result of the publicity.[9]

Harry Sahs, who joined the *News* in 1924 and served most of his years on the police beat until his retirement, frequently ate "free lunch," a carryover from the pre-Prohibition saloon days, at a blind pig above a bondsman's office across the street from police headquarters. So did William R. Muller, for years an editorial columnist for the *News*, then a reporter for the *Times* assigned to the biggest continuing story in town — Prohibition and all its ramifications. Policemen and reporters alike hailed the potato soup served there by the jovial proprietor, Nick Schaefer. Buy a beer or two and lunch was free. Blind pig operators vied at serving the best lunch in town to attract lunchtime drinkers. Houses of prostitution ran openly. Hattie Miller's was the reported payoff point between grafting police and city officials and gangs who sought to augment bootlegging with the operation of handbooks, craps and other games of chance. Hattie continued in her role of benevolent madam for nearly twenty years, long after Prohibition had passed on and the game in town was numbers.[10]

On the morning of April 11, 1929, *News* photographer Monroe D. Stroeker was standing on several boxes in an abandoned warehouse at the foot of Riopelle Street and the Detroit River, on the city's near east side. Canada was clearly visible less than a half mile across the water. Tipped off by crime reporter Sahs of an impending landing by one of Licavoli's rumrunners, Fred Gaertner, Jr., then city editor, had sent Stroeker to the scene hours before the scheduled landing, and for good reason. The photographer cleaned a spot on the grime-coated window, focused his camera on an imaginary spot next to the breakwater, and waited. The result was a photograph that is historic in the annals of bootlegging in Detroit. Played six columns wide on Page One, the picture shows a touring car, with a cloth top, at the water's edge. Four rumrunners are hurriedly loading it with suitcases in which liquor had been transported by speedboat from Riverside, Ontario, "two minutes and fifty-five seconds away." A second touring car stood by, waiting for its share of the shipment. About fifty feet away was a bootlegger's "scout car." It had arrived shortly after Stroeker had positioned himself. The role of the scout car was to reconnoiter

the scene in advance of the landing and to give the "all clear"
signal.

Said the *News* the next day:

> The daring with which Detroit rumrunners operate along the
> riverfront is demonstrated daily at the foot of Riopelle street, nine
> blocks east of Woodward avenue, where fast boats land many times
> each day to discharge their cargoes of contraband liquor into waiting
> automobiles.
>
> Despite the proximity of the Customs Border Patrol headquarters —
> four blocks east, at the foot of Dubois street — the rummers ply their
> trade. Speedboats capable of 45 to 60 miles an hour literally "run
> rings" around the slower U.S. Customs Border patrol boats, land their
> cargoes into the arms of waiting dockmen, and whisk away before
> the Federal officers are able to gain the pier.

Then came this insight to the extent of power held by the gangs:

> The only fear that the rummer has, apparently, is of the officers
> doing land duty. The Federal Government has failed to match the
> rummers' boats for speed, so that alertness on the part of the rummers
> and their lookouts is all that is necessary to protect their cargoes.
> To afford that protection, Detroit rum runners have resorted even to
> the employment of "traffic officers," who station themselves along the
> right-of-way from the foot of Riopelle street, halting cross-traffic on
> intersecting thoroughfares, at a signal from the dock which tells them
> that the automobiles are loaded and ready to go. . . .[11]

In his testimony Edwards explained to the senators: "The West
Side faction of this rum-running operation was headed by Joe
Tallman, and Tallman ultimately was suspected of having insti-
gated the arrest and the conviction of Yonnie Licavoli and Frank
Cammarato on a concealed weapons charge. The net result of that
was that a gang war developed between the East Side and the
West Side rum-running mobs. This particularly broke out over the
hijacking of 5,000 gallons of West Side liquor and the kidnapping
of a fellow named Abe Rosenberg who was held for 10 days. The

West Side mob discovered where Rosenberg was and they kidnapped the kidnappers and subsequently Rosenberg sought to im-
plicate Pete Licavoli. A warrant was issued for him, but Rosenberg
refused to prosecute and the case was subsequently dismissed.
Shortly after that Tallman and two of his henchmen were killed.
Peter Licavoli was arrested for this crime but was subsequently
discharged. . . ."[12]

Ray Girardin, Carlisle's counterpart on the Hearst-owned *Detroit
Times* who later served as Detroit's police commissioner (1963–
1968), described the era as "incomparable to any other in police
history." He found narcotics wars waged in the late 1960s and
until his death in 1971 reminiscent of the territorial battles fought
by the beer barons. During much of this period Detroit had three
daily newspapers: the evening *News* and *Times* and the morning
Free Press. But gang warfare was too good an attraction. Two
other dailies, both tabloids, joined the journalistic mix for brief
periods. The *Detroit Mirror* lasted from 1930 to 1932 and the
Detroit Daily (later the *Daily Mirror*) persisted from 1929 to 1933.
The *Mirror* was killed by its owner, the *Chicago Tribune,* in a deal
in which the *Tribune* paid $100,000 for an option to buy the *De-
troit Free Press*. Arrangements were made to transfer top features,
including the comic "Orphan Annie," to the *Free Press*. But then
the transaction fell through. Both tabloids depended on a lurid exposé of crime in Detroit for survival and both were out of business
at Prohibition's end. Boosted by the continuing story of Prohibition, *News* circulation also rose. In 1920, daily circulation was
232,852; in 1930, it was 322,835, reflecting the growth of Detroit and
the increased interest in the affairs of the day.

Girardin appraised the role of newspapers in Detroit as follows:
"Of the three [established] papers the *News* was more for crusading against vice, the *Free Press* rarely and the *Times* not at all . . .
the tabloids played cops and robbers and their reporters managed
to get deputy badges which they flashed to impress police. . . ."
It was not a very smart idea. What kept intelligent reporters from
fatal involvement with criminals were three cardinal rules: never
break a confidence (never tell police what the robbers were
doing and vice versa); never accept as much as a cup of coffee

from either contingent; and to reflect in their stories both sides of whatever happened. The trick was to convince criminal elements they ought to tell their "side of the story, it may be your last chance." Many did and stayed friends with reporters for years in and out of prison.[13]

Practiced hands and the city's largest newspaper staff bulldogged story after story. Constant pressure against slot machines resulted in a legislative act in 1925 that for the first time declared them to be illegal gambling paraphernalia. In 1930, this law was ignored along with the law against alcoholic beverages. The *News* renewed its crusade. On information that slot machines had been installed in drugstores and candy shops in the vicinity of the city's schools and were sucking up the lunch money of youngsters, the *News* sent carloads of reporters to play the machines in the vicinity of the city's biggest schools. Eventually police were prodded into driving slot machines out of town, as the *News* intoned, "out of the reach of children."[14]

The competition to get "a beat" on a rival newspaperman was fierce. Headlines sold newspapers; street sales were an important circulation factor. There were days when the presses rarely stopped printing extras as reporters vied for new leads on stories, which, in turn, would produce a fresh, salable line. Girardin said, "We resorted to all sorts of ruses to beat the other guy. I remember once when I raced from a courtroom to a nearby telephone booth but found an 'out of order' sign on the door. With minutes to go to press time, you can imagine my frustration. But, for some reason which I can't explain I decided to drop a coin in the phone, anyway; maybe it had been repaired. To my pleasant surprise I got a clear dial tone. Then it came to me: 'That damn Carlisle.' "

The purchase of an autogiro by the *News*, at the behest of Will Scripps, also gave Girardin and others fits. The autogiro, which made its first flight for the paper on February 15, 1931, lasted two and a half years when it was replaced by a single-wing Lockheed plane, called the *Early Bird*, a name harking to Will's early interest in aviation. When news stories moved from Detroit to out-state or out-of-state locations, the *News* flew reporters and photographers in its own plane. Said Girardin: "We would pray for fog — anything that would keep it grounded. Meanwhile we would beg pilots to take us up in anything — an orange crate, hoping for a break on the story."

On a trip to New York where a Detroit murderer, Merton Ward Goodrich, a child killer, had been captured, Carlisle arrived first. When Girardin and his photographer got to their midtown hotel room, they frantically sought to locate the Detroit detectives assigned to pick up the suspect. The photographer began telephoning and finally called across the room to an impatient Girardin. "I just reached Detective Sergeant George Branton's room" he said, "and Branton told me to meet him in 30 minutes at the 121st Precinct." A resigned look came over Girardin's face. "There is no 121st Precinct and you have just talked to Mr. Jack Carlisle of the *News.*"[15]

Girardin won as many of these reportorial ruses as he lost. When Len Koenecke, a Brooklyn Dodger baseball player, went berserk and was beaten to death in a private plane over Toronto on September 17, 1935, by the pilot and a passenger, again Carlisle and Girardin were flown to the scene. The crown attorney, it so happened, had been a Notre Dame classmate of Girardin. Girardin went to his home to talk over old times and incidentally to get a first look at the killers' confession. As they talked, the phone rang. "Fellow on here who says he is Jack Carlisle of the *Detroit News,*" said the crown attorney, cupping his hand over the mouthpiece. "What shall I tell him?" "Tell him you'll meet him at the 121st Precinct in 30 minutes," Girardin instructed. "Then hang up."

Sahs said that when he arrived in the "Rum Capital" he soon determined that the gangsters were organized, the police were organized and to survive he'd better get organized. He did so by cultivating key police officers on fishing and hunting trips, the theory being that people who hunt and fish together work together. Yet his sporting friends were not averse to playing pranks on the reporter. Urged to attend an autopsy, Sahs stood in the dissecting room at the morgue, determined not to falter under the test. When the examiner finished his work, he announced he could not release a finding because part of the body was missing.

Sahs, reaching for his pipe, found the missing part where a well-organized friend had planted it — in his pocket.

Journalistic survival depended on keeping the cardinal rules. Gaertner, aware of the many temptations that daily confronted his men, warned his reporters, "If you value your life (and your job) don't ever take a cent. Buy a drink, every time they buy one." Gangsters were notorious for the ways they collected on obligations. Yet despite the precautionary advice, one *News* reporter eventually was to be caught up in the web, accused of conspiring with gamblers. Although he was not prosecuted, he was fired.[16] Gilmore, managing editor before Gaertner, recalled that covering crime during the 1920s and 1930s "was set up like everything else. I suppose it was almost like having a reporter covering the diplomatic beat. He'd have to know what mob was mad at the other mob so that when there was a killing, he'd have an idea who did it, and what the motive was."[17] The "nations" to be covered included territories controlled by the Lower East Side gang whose "fortress" included Pete Licavoli, Joe Bommarito, Max Stern and Chester LaMare; the West Side gang, headed by Tallman; the Oakland Sugar House gang where Harry Fleisher divided his time when not occupied with the Purple gang, which ranged freely over the city, running booze, murdering and hijacking until the mid-1930s when gang members either were wiped out by competitors or were sent to prison. Each gang, excepting the Purples, divided up the city as neatly as geographers might draw boundary lines in settling claims. When the gangs clashed there was little public outcry unless a policeman or an innocent bystander was slain. When police arrested a suspect and took him to court, "the Texas defense" (the scoundrel deserved to die, meaning the slaying benefited society) often freed him.[18]

On July 22, 1930, voters recalled Bowles, convinced by the press and his inaction that he was incapable of handling the city's crime problem. At 1:55 the following morning, Gerald Buckley, a crusading radio commentator, was shot to death in the lobby of the LaSalle Hotel, close to downtown Detroit. The motive for the slaying was conjectured in the newspapers for years. It variously was ascribed to attempted extortion by Buckley, to a double-cross by the radio commentator of Detroit's political structure, headed by Bowles before his recall, to Buckley's repeated threats to reveal the identity of gangland overlords, and, indirectly, at least, to a mysterious woman who called him to the lobby from his hotel room just minutes before the slaying. Buckley died under a hail of eleven bullets fired by three assassins.[19] The hotel later was converted into a residence for the elderly. It still is haunted by the specter of crime, its occupants unable to leave the building after dusk, fearful of assault by street hoodlums, mostly dope addicts, who sent the city's murder statistics soaring far beyond those of the notorious years. The murder of 690 persons in 1971 compares to 326 homicides in 1926, the peak year of the twenties, and 192 in 1930, the peak of that decade.[20]

The difference between the slayings of the 1970s and forty years ago is that many of the latter-day killings occur during street muggings of people who appear to be an easy mark. The slayings during Prohibition were coupled with hijackings and kidnappings, vices that appealed to gangs specializing in booze or gambling or both. Gangs kidnapped each other's top hoodlums and held them for ransom, often finding such capers quite amusing, if costly. The prevalence of kidnapping declined sharply after March 1, 1932. On that day Charles A. Lindbergh, Jr., twenty-month-old son of the first man to solo the Atlantic, was taken from his bedroom crib in the Lindbergh home in Hopewell, New Jersey, and later found dead. A federal law — the Lindbergh Law — was rushed through Congress to stifle the rise of kidnappings. It dampened gangland's enthusiasm by providing the death penalty for convicted interstate kidnappers. The repeal of Prohibition in 1933 further altered the criminal habits of the city's hoodlums. The chief elements now turned their attention from rum-running and kidnapping to a greater preoccupation with gambling.

By 1938 the most flourishing action in Detroit was numbers, the poor man's baccarat, with the city's factories the chief target of racketeers. Handbooks and gambling houses also provided action to dispel the doldrums of the Depression for those who could afford roulette, craps and blackjack. The numbers racket was designed to suck up the nickels and dimes of players who hoped to strike it rich by playing numbers they found in dream books or during some psychic intuition.[21] Development of the art was rooted in Prohibition, its developers Pete Licavoli, Joe (Scarface) Bommarito, Joe Massei and Sam Lucido, among others.

On the evening of Saturday, August 5, 1939, Mrs. Janet McDonald drove her automobile into her garage, her daughter Pearl, eleven, apparently asleep beside her. She got out, closed the garage door, broke a small hole in one of the car's windows, put a hose through the opening, attached it to the tail pipe, and re-entered the car. When the bodies were found the next day, investigating officers discovered packets of letters addressed to Detroit newspapers and to various city, state and federal authorities. Mrs. McDonald, a divorcée, had been a woman scorned. An employee of a numbers syndicate, she had given herself for almost three years to William McBride, payoff man for the syndicate. Now he had turned to another. There was but one way to even the score and Mrs. McDonald succeeded in doing it. The letter directed to the *News* was dated Saturday, August 6. It read:

> On this night, a girl has ended her life because of the mental cruelty caused by Racketeer William McBride, ex-Great Lakes Numbers House operator. McBride is the go-between man for Lieut. John McCarthy.
>
> He arranges the fix between our dutiful Lieut. and the Racketeers.
>
> Should you care to learn more of this story, get in touch with McBride through Ryan's bookie, 222 Lafayette Street West; Phone Clifford 1572.
>
> He glories in telling lies, so don't believe everything he tells you, as I did.
>
> *Janet McDonald*[22]

To make sure she reached an honest man somewhere in a corrupt city Mrs. McDonald sent forth letters with abandon. Here and there they reached a very receptive audience.

The story was splashed on the front pages of all three Detroit newspapers. Almost immediately public officials scoffed at the woman's charges. Lieutenant McCarthy professed to be aghast. Mayor Richard W. Reading, who had been elected in 1937, said he was appalled. Fred W. Frahm, police superintendent, sent his minions charging into known bookie joints, alas, only to find they had been all but deserted. Prosecuting Attorney Duncan C. Mc-Crea, showing real moral fiber, declared he would pursue an independent investigation with vigor. Wayne County Sheriff Thomas C. Wilcox asserted that any handbooks operating in the county outside of the city limits would be raided promptly. Even Richard W. Reading, Jr., the mayor's son who served as mayoral secretary, pressed for action. And each man performed as he promised. Within two days Lieutenant McCarthy, then head of the police rackets squad, was exonerated by his superiors of any participation in graft. Within three days Prosecutor McCrea said he had turned "his independent investigation over to the police department," declaring that each time he interfered in internal police matters he had been told to mind his own business. Police Commissioner Heinrich Pickert, who had been attending a convention in San Francisco, declared on his return that he would keep a "hands-off policy," obviously indicating he thought enough investigations were underway. Already the *News* was leveling charges of "whitewash."[23]

Convinced by its own investigation and by the accumulated evidence of recent years, the *News* editorialized on August 9 on behalf of an impartial grand jury investigation — within seventy-two hours after Mrs. McDonald's letter was received. The editorial declared that the public, fully aware of the widespread gambling operations in Detroit, "will not be convinced that it is possible without police connivance." Reading, leaning back in his high-backed mayoral chair, told reporters he preferred an inquiry through "regular channels." The *News* quickly responded with an editorial asserting the mayor's response was "baffling."[24] It was indeed. The decision to demand a grand jury was made in Editor Gilmore's office. Furthermore, it was decided that only a one-man grand jury manned by a judge and a prosecutor above reproach could do the job. "We figured," Gilmore explained, "that the old twenty-three- and twenty-four-man juries were too unwieldy. When you have a twenty-three- or twenty-four-man jury, it's almost a certainty that somebody in that body will be telling secrets out of school."[25] Almost daily editorials followed. They created enough pressure on the city government so that on August 18 Reading reversed himself and said he would bow to the public's wishes. There was little else he could do.

On August 21, the *News* editorialized that it "believes that the political influences obviously involved should disqualify both the State Attorney General's Department and the [Wayne County] Prosecutor's Office from having any hand in the investigation."

There followed a petition by seven citizens, five of them members of the Detroit Citizens League, asking the Wayne County Circuit Court to authorize a grand jury and seek necessary funds. Circuit Judge Homer Ferguson was named grand juror, Chester P. O'Hara special prosecutor. Both men had established reputations for integrity. Ferguson, who often rode downtown and back with Gilmore, his neighbor, certainly was the editor's choice. The fat was now in the fire. Shortly after Ferguson was named, Gilmore drove the judge home. As they approached Ferguson's house, the entire area was suddenly bathed in floodlights. Up to that time neither Ferguson nor Gilmore knew that the judge had acquired special around-the-clock police protection.[26]

One by one suspected police officers and civic officials were called into the jury's inner sanctum while reporters waited impatiently outside. Early in the investigation the emerging witnesses were ebullient when questioned by waiting reporters. Gradually their ebullience subsided. Toward the end of the investigation reporters knew the jury had hit pay dirt from the glum expressions of emerging witnesses. In the end all those officials, including the mayor, who had professed shock and had promised thorough investigations, were slapped with indictments. Reading, top police officers, a troop of lesser policemen, Sheriff Elmer (Buff) Ryan, the great provider of the handbook racket, McCrea, the protesting prosecutor — all were convicted of accepting graft or arranging it and went to jail for varying terms. McCarthy, "the smiling Irish cop" who "protesteth too much," followed the procession to prison. In all, Ferguson indicted 360 persons, including 75 public officials and 81 racketeers. More than 150 went to jail over a four-year period.

What about McBride, whose scorn for a woman had set it all in motion? He had died during the investigation in Florida, reportedly of pneumonia. His wife, another woman he had scorned, demanded an investigation of his death, but no evidence of foul play was uncovered.

The cleansing of city government and the police department was complete. Except for a brief disruption and a quick shuffling of handbook and numbers houses, the rackets gradually reappeared. Like alcohol, the numbers racket, dealing in nickels and dimes, in itself does not excite public indignation. It is only when gambling moves so deeply into a city's administration that its corruption hurts the human condition and brings death that there is a violent reaction. On this tenet of public apathy organized crime moved from one generation to the next, perfecting its operation.

At the time Edwards and Piersante testified, there were sixty-three known members of Michigan's crime syndicate, grossing upward of $150 million a year in illegal enterprises and another $50 million from offshoot businesses operating in the legitimate marketplace. Important money meant important people in the underworld were involved. In detailing crime in Detroit Edwards testified that Licavoli, the lord of rum-running during Prohibition, "was to our belief and knowledge, very much interested in gambling affairs and acts in the sense as director or overlord over the ones who actually operate on the street." Edwards declared that in 1947, less than seven years after the clean sweep by the Ferguson-O'Hara grand jury, "there were some arguments about the handling of gambling in the Detroit area which resulted in a meeting which we subsequently were told about by Chris Scroy [a known hoodlum]. At the meeting, designed to settle the problems in relation to gambling involving Lucido and Sam Scroy, there were present Pete Licavoli, Joe 'Scarface' Bommarito, Max Stern, Frank Caputo, Sam Lucido. . . ." Whatever deal was made, it apparently was unsatisfactory. Edwards testified that "on June 12, 1948, both Sam Scroy and Pete Lucido just plain disappeared."[27] Names and tactics established in the old gang days hadn't changed very much.

Once the testimony about crime in Detroit was on the Senate

committee's record, Carlisle, who had been sent to Washington for the hearings with the team of *News* investigators, called his office and simply said, "Let it go." Since he had helped to provide historical background, he had been privy to the kind of testimony Edwards would give. On October 11, 1963, the front page of the *News* detailed the Mafia organization in the Detroit area as revealed by the McClellan committee. At the very top was a familiar name, Joe Zerilli. His left bower was aging Peter Licavoli and his right bower John Priziola. Angelo Meli, William "Black Bill" Tocco, Joe Massei, Joe Bommarito, Salvadore Lucido, Dominic "Fats" Corrado — a total of sixty-three grand old names in Detroit's underworld was published. Now that they were on the Senate record as Mafia members, each could be so identified thereafter. The syndicate members were listed as owning ninety-eight businesses in Detroit that competed with merchants who possessed none of gangland's clout.

In the hierarchy were Vita "Billy Jack" Giacalone and his brother, Anthony, whose activities had brought them before the law on charges of gambling and operating a "juice business" — loan sharking.

"There is strong evidence," Edwards testified, "that in the Detroit area, as in other of our large cities, illegal enterprises are backed by the threat of planned, carefully executed and highly professional murder." The Mafia field force was estimated at 250.

Family names familiar with these gangs have jumped the generation gap. As long as the members are connected with the rackets in Detroit, they must be exposed. But the effort is unending. Today organized crime allegedly operates more than two hundred "legitimate" businesses in the city. Exposing the criminal attachments is a greater challenge than ever.

8

Nancy (sob) Nancy

As a warming April sun brightened the street and sidewalk below, George E. Miller, who succeeded Pipp as editor, looked out his third floor office window in the *News*'s new building on Lafayette. Miller ever was conscious of reader wants, and as passersby moved along the avenue he privately wished, "If I only knew what they were thinking." The year was 1919, a year of turning from war to peace. Life and ideals were in flux and challenges great. In the business of journalism a writer or an editor is good in the popular sense to the degree that he maintains a grassroots relationship with readers. He must know their desires if the paper is to fill their wants and he must understand them if the paper is to play a role of leadership in the community. A paper fulfills this mission in varied and sometimes not too obvious ways. But it is the mix of such fulfillments that separates the newspapers from the selective reading vehicles on the market and it is this mix that reaches the majority of the people rather than a selected few.

All these thoughts were coursing through Miller's mind when into his office walked a middle-aged woman who announced herself as Mrs. J. E. Leslie. As Mrs. Leslie began talking, Miller could see how she could fill a niche in the important pattern of newspaper success. The people were thinking, Mrs. Leslie said, about very personal things. They thought of themselves, their problems and their children's problems most of the time, and big issues of the day only to the extent that the issues would eventually affect their lives. They needed a shoulder to lean on, a place to air their problems, and a few words of advice. "I think I can do that," she said. "I have always wanted to help people and I am of an age that has given me experience in a number of areas of living." Mrs. Leslie, widowed a short time before, had caught the editor's ear. The influx of immigrants and farmers to work in Detroit's booming auto industry, returning World War I veterans and the campaign for Prohibition had created a storm of personal protest that swirled like a vortex and needed calming. Miller nodded in agreement and Mrs. Leslie found herself on the payroll.[1]

The editor was aware that Mrs. Leslie was not the first woman in American journalism to discover reader appreciation for solution of personal problems. Marie Manning developed the basic idea at the turn of the century as the Beatrice Fairfax of Hearst's *New York Journal* and the spreading Hearst newspapers. Beatrice wrote "Advice to the Lovelorn" as a means of competing with Elizabeth Gilmer, who, as Dorothy Dix, was among the nation's top human interest writers. She led a pack who played so extensively on the readers' emotions and sentiments that they acquired the sobriquet of "sob sisters." Marie Manning, then twenty-three, became celebrated in such ditties as, "Just write to Beatrice Fairfax, whenever you're in doubt; Just write to Beatrice Fairfax, And she'll help you out."

Mrs. Leslie had no intention of writing an "Advice to the Lovelorn" column. She was not twenty-three but forty-nine, and she did not look on problems of the troubled lightly or with humor. Because of her age and her sincerity, her column in the *News* was entitled "Experience." She wrote under the pseudonym of Nancy Brown, Brown being her maiden name, and she guarded her identity as religiously as she did her readers' confidences. She did not want her personality to override the important problems she hoped to alleviate. Yet in the years to come, her very personality was to play an important part in soothing troubled minds.

Launched on April 19, 1919, there was nothing cute or smart aleck about the Experience column. How should a young man new to the city meet the right kind of girls? Try church. How much should a family of three be able to save on an income of $30 a week? About $2. Each reply was simple and direct. To encourage writers to express their innermost feelings, Nancy advised them to use pen names. It was soon apparent that the Experience column filled a real want in a city that hungered for neighborliness and understanding, the sort of emotional relief that had come naturally to people in the smaller settings of rural towns and farms where many Detroiters of the era were born and raised.[2]

In October of 1919, as Nancy's column was warming to her readers' hearts, the *News* looked to other means of answering reader wants. For weeks in the late summer of 1919 the prices of foodstuffs had been rising with the inflation that came at the war's end. The overtones not only were heard in Nancy's column but elsewhere in the paper. *News* editorials raged about the exorbitant profits taken by retailers, but editorials were not enough. Receiving no positive response, the paper imported tons of fish from ocean ports and sold them at the Michigan Central siding for ten cents a pound. The arrival of refrigerator cars filled with fish resulted in a near-stampede of buyers. It also brought an overall drop of 25 percent in the price of most food products.

Nancy's column rolled on. One of her early readers, who signed herself "Pat," expressed the feeling many readers had for her: "She cares about people and believes in them. And how well they know it! Only the Recording Angel, I think, knows how many she has encouraged to fight a good fight just by believing in them. Nancy Brown has proved beyond the shadow of a doubt that she believes in 'personality, its infinite worth, its endless possibilities, its ultimate victory.' She has invested in the one thing worth investing everything in, and who shall declare the dividends?" For weeks readers would write about such problems as those of Chronic Nag, whose husband bought himself a dog and gun but "cursed her the length of the driveway" because she purchased much-needed shoes; of WCTU Worker, who thought of leaving her husband because he took a drink of beer or wine now and then — her early upbringing tolerated no such imbibing; or Just Bobby, a boy-husband whose young wife was fighting tuberculosis and who felt he was a failure because he had lost his job just when she needed him most to take her to Arizona, the sun then being the only known treatment for "the cough."

The column soon acquired a host of regular contributors, including teen-agers who were called "The In-Betweens." Dancing Eyes, a little Alaskan girl, caught the fancy of readers and carried them into the atmosphere of her Eskimo home. Blossom, a long-time favorite, wrote about the Kentucky bluegrass country. Hemlock painted vivid word-pictures of her home in northern Michigan. Life stories came in over such picturesque signatures as Friend of Poets, Colleen, Cup o' Tea, Wind among the Waste, Gingham Grandma, Rolls-Royce, Sunshine, Slim of the Hills, Sad Old Man, Ann of Dixie.

Nancy was able to handle virtually every type of letter that came to her — except one. She had never developed the suspicious nature attributed to veteran newsmen that supposedly provides them with an insight that quickly detects a phony. It was inevitable that here and there a cynic would drop a letter in the mail seeking to take advantage of her seeming naiveté. One such letter was traced eventually to the offices of the *Detroit Times,* which Hearst had added to his growing chain of newspapers in 1921. Reputed to be the work of the paper's movie critic, a series of letters appeared in Nancy's column signed Trailer Wife. Her lot in life was to try to bring up six small children in cramped quarters, a thinly disguised version of the Old Woman in the Shoe who had so many kids she did not know what to do. Her offspring all seemed to be underfoot at once, and they kept falling into the suds whenever her attention was distracted momentarily from the laundry tub at which she labored incessantly.

Nancy answered these letters with patient sympathy and radiant good cheer. Finally she invited Trailer Wife to attend one of the column-sponsored events and be introduced. The affairs were Nancy's way of getting her readers to know each other; through the years they were held in a variety of public places. Caught with this invitation, the letter writer was in a quandary, but not for long. He soon sent a letter to Nancy from Trailer Wife, dispatching her westward in the trailer to begin life anew in the great open spaces. So Trailer Wife was bid a fond adieu.

Within ten years Nancy Brown was such a success that when Joseph Pulitzer, Jr., surveyed the field of writers of advice so that he could add such a column to his *St. Louis Post-Dispatch* and *New York World,* he decided Nancy's was by far the best because of its warmth and sincerity. An emissary visited the editor of the *News* to find out how to emulate the column. He was advised: "Find another Nancy Brown."[3] Of course, in the era she served there was no other Nancy Brown. Many tried to imitate the column technique but none could reflect the sincerity that brought her readers to express their affection in prose, poetry and money when Nancy cited a need for a reader or a community project.

On each anniversary of her column's founding Nancy took to the airwaves to sound a roll call of additions to the column family: ". . . Etoile and little Mah-li, French mother and her daughter by a Chinese husband, exiled because she did not bear him a son; Stout Fella and Coeur de Lion, whose physicians warned them that life was limited for them because of faulty hearts, but who are still here and active; Trudgin' Along, who wrote tenderly and understandingly of human problems; Marr'd Pot, heart-hurt and bleeding from the dereliction of a beloved wife. . . ."[4]

She talked of the excited husband who "penned a fiercely indignant Bolshevik letter on his wife's fancy, pale-blue stationery." She quoted from Bereaved, who had written that her money had been taken from her "in the infancy of my widowhood," and from the Missus who had written, "My husband is so easy to be talked into anything by anybody but me." She advised Young Bride, who had been puzzled about the problem, that "she could be sure fish was good if the eyes were clear." Then Nancy added that, taking this advice, Young Bride had paralyzed her fish merchant by requesting "two pounds of perch with bright eyes." The jest was not lost on her readers.

The paper's interest in improving the lives of its readers was not confined to Nancy's column. At times the column and other areas of the paper combined in giant community betterment programs. In 1921, the paper's conservation columnist, Albert Stoll, Jr., began a twenty-year campaign to have Isle Royale, in Lake Superior, named a national park, thus assuring for posterity a natural reserve that otherwise would be lost in the population crawl of future generations. Stoll's success is noted at the park in a bronze plaque recognizing "his untiring efforts." The plaque is embedded in a stone entrance way that marks the Albert Stoll Jr. Memorial Trail. While Stoll's campaign was proceeding, Nancy's readers decided they, too, could do something to improve the environment.

Andy, a regular contributor to Nancy's column, opened the door by suggesting that Experience readers take part in a reforestation program undertaken by the *News*. The paper hoped to start a new generation of pine trees on cut-over lands in northern Michigan despoiled by the logger's ax during five decades of intensive lumbering. Andy suggested that readers contribute toward the reforestation of one of a number of forty-acre plots the paper hoped to reseed. The first column gift arrived by telegraph within hours from reader Biddy O'Bee who wanted to head the list. Soon enough money was raised to plant two of the plots, and it continued to arrive in amounts from ten cents to twenty-five dollars. Eventually 560 acres were reclaimed. The first seedling was planted by Nancy in 1930. A picture of this event was published. But in line with Nancy's continued belief that she should not personally expose herself in the *News*, the picture carefully avoided showing her face. "At least," she told column readers of the upcoming picture, "you will see my hat and coat and have faith that I was inside them."

In compliance with the wishes of her contributors, tablets marking the plots carried this inscription: "These 40 acres planted in 1930 by the Experience Column in honor of Nancy Brown." One expert estimated that eventually enough lumber was grown and cut to put a floor one inch thick on the entire state of Michigan. The figure may have been slightly enthusiastic.

With pine trees reaching for the skies in northern Michigan, Nancy became involved in yet another discussion that was raging in the paper's columns devoted to culture. She thought her readers ought to familiarize themselves with modern art and encouraged them to visit the Detroit Institute of Arts. "The little bronze donkey in the Fountain Court" especially attracted her attention. The bronze donkey, by Renée Sitenis, insinuated "his cute self into the affections of all who view it," she wrote. The donkey figured in an Experience column project that made Page One.

Thinking she would stir greater interest in modern art by holding a reader affair at the institute, Nancy arranged with Dr. William R. Valentiner, its director, to hold a reception in the institute's Fountain Court. She told of her plan in the column and asked each reader who planned to attend to send word to her. On Friday, November 14, 1930, the date set for the affair, she began the column by apologizing that there was not room to publish all the letters of acceptance. "But I want you to know that I read your letters and want you to come," she wrote. "Your welcome is just as cordial as if there had been space to publish your letters." She then advised readers, in the column's practical approach, where to check their coats at the institute and where to find the rest rooms. The women could attend without hats, she decided. Neither Nancy, Dr. Valentiner nor the *News* had the vaguest idea of the storm of enthusiasm Nancy was generating.[5]

Column folks were invited to appear at the institute at 8:30 P.M. Nancy cautioned them not to reveal their identities, but a box was placed next to the bronze donkey where each visitor could drop a card inscribed with his or her column name so that there would be a record of all who attended. Dr. Valentiner would stand near the donkey to greet them along with Clyde H. Burroughs, secretary of the Detroit Arts Commission, and W. Steele Gilmore, managing editor of the *News*. A police quartet, the Singing Cops, would harmonize, accompanied by the orchestra of radio station WWJ, the Oleanders — named after their leader, Ole Foerch. Gilmore would introduce Burroughs, who would give a talk on "The Approach to Art," and a conducted tour of the galleries would follow. So much for the schedule.

Lines of people began to form at the museum doors at 7 P.M. By 7:45 some eight thousand were inside — the largest crowd that had ever been within the walls of the institute. The crowd surged through the halls, filled the basement, the galleries, the side rooms. With thousands more clamoring to get in, perspiring guards locked the front doors. In the Fountain Court the donkey was surrounded by a throng so dense that only those within a few feet of the sculpture could see any more than the donkey's ears. With the help of guards the principals in the ceremonies made strenuous efforts to reach the appointed spot — without success. The crowd outside now had massed around the museum's side and rear doors. The Oleanders formed a flying wedge to enter by the side door, but their leader never made it. Inside the bass viol player became immobilized in the crush of humanity around the donkey, unable to advance or retreat. Aided by their uniforms, members of the police quartet reached their goal one by one and sang to the accompaniment of those Oleanders who got through.

At last Burroughs found a place to make his speech. "In a quarter century with the museum, I have never seen anything like this. You, Nancy Brown, wherever you are, have done more in a few brief weeks to arouse interest in art and this building than we have been able to do by our united effort over the years." Nancy was close at hand. She had found a spot on a balcony overlooking the court, behind a pillar, where she could see and hear and still remain anonymous. She was highly excited, and ready to cry. Police estimated the crowd inside and out as between thirty and thirty-five thousand people. By appealing to the desires of her readers, Nancy had done much in a single event to turn Detroit around from a stolid workingman's town to one that could find an interest in culture. It simply was a matter of finding the proper line of communication.[6]

Nancy's faith that her readers represented Everyman was total. Once Blossom, her bluegrass contributor, wrote that she "saw Man-O'-War win the Kentucky Derby twice." This greatly upset George Krehbiel, the paper's turf writer, who was as devoted to his specialty as Nancy was to hers. Record book in hand, Krehbiel hurried to Nancy's office to point out that Man-O'-War never ran in the Derby, and that since it was limited to three-year-olds, no horse could win it twice. But Nancy wouldn't listen. "I don't care what your old book says," she told the sportswriter. "If Blossom says she saw it, I believe her."

For Gilmore, who succeeded Miller as editor-in-chief, the memory of Nancy's reaction to anything that might be considered criticism of her column never waned. Although he was more than aware of Nancy's following, Gilmore for a long time had thought the Experience page could be brightened with more headlines and perhaps some drawings. The editor thought the mass of type created a gray page that might discourage new subscribers, unaware of its hidden beauty and magic. Time and again he would call Nancy to his office and, after complimenting her on some recent reader coup, he would bring up the matter of typography. As he talked, seeking to explain the merits of more headlines and white space to attract readers, Nancy sat, hunched in a chair opposite his desk. Each time he got into the matter of changing the look of the page ever so slightly the columnist's lips would begin to quiver. Knowing Nancy was on the verge of crying, Gilmore would stop talking until she composed herself. Then he would pray for a telephone call to save him or he would simply say, "Well, that is all, Nancy. Keep doing the best you can." Who was he to make Nancy Brown cry?

In matters of finance, Nancy claimed no special acumen and gladly sought out Gilmore's advice. On one occasion her banker offered to help her with her investments and she told him to go ahead. Then she found he had bought brewery stock in her name and was appalled. She hurried to Gilmore's office. Knowing that Nancy occupied a pedestal in her readers' minds over the years, a goddess who also was an oracle, Gilmore saw an immediate danger to her reputation. "Sell it immediately," he told her, "before the *Times* and the *Free Press* hear about it." She did and what would have been a scandal was averted. On another occasion she brought Gilmore a letter from a couple who asked whether they should sell a valuable piece of downtown property or hang onto it for a better price. It was a revelation to Gilmore that Nancy should be asked to advise on a matter so remote from the general thrust of her column. He told her to advise the couple to consult a realty appraiser and then see a lawyer. Had she advised them to move one way or the other wrongly, her readers' faith could be shaken and the consequences to the paper embarrassing.

After the first amazing experience at the art institute, it was four years before Nancy attempted another function there. The occasion was the presentation of a painting purchased for the museum by the contributions of column folks, *Street in Brooklyn,* by an unknown artist. The canvas had been selected in a mail ballot from among a dozen works nominated by readers. This time Nancy took precautions. She pointed out in the column that the ceremony would be brief, and most of her readers would be wise to visit the museum at some later date to view their gift. Even so, eleven thousand people arrived. *Street in Brooklyn* was unveiled by the five-year-old daughter of Nancy's nephew, Leslie Brown. Dressed in a pink party frock, Nancy Brown II was photographed unveiling the painting. But Nancy Brown I remained unidentified, mingling with the throng.

The affair at the institute led to a series of even more successful column events: sunrise services on Belle Isle, the island park in the Detroit River. On June 3, 1934, A Woman Sewing wrote: "The [institute] party was great, the picture lovely, Nancy II the sweetest ever. So many suggestions are being made — may I venture to add mine? Why not a sunrise service on a June Sunday morning? There are so many who could and would conduct such a service for us. Please, Nancy, won't you consider this?"

Nancy did not hesitate long. She answered: "I think this is a great suggestion and could be a lovely, lovely thing for us to do — something that would always be a beautiful memory for us. Suppose I set a tentative day of two weeks from today, June 17, for it, providing the weather is pleasant. It seems to me the service might be held around the Belle Isle Orchestra Shell, which would serve as a speaker's platform. Oh, it sounds wonderful to me! I have just called the Weather Bureau and find the sun will rise at 4:45 A.M. on June 17."

When 4:45 arrived that Sunday morning, the largest crowd in its history was assembled at the Belle Isle shell — forty to fifty thousand people. The first seats on park benches at the front of the shell had been taken a few minutes after midnight. Through the night there was a continual flow of people across the island bridge, by car, by bus and on foot. Older column readers and younger ones, some with babies in their arms, walked across the bridge carrying picnic baskets, thermos bottles of coffee and milk, and blankets to spread on the grass. At the official moment for sunrise, clouds obscured the eastern horizon and the sky remained dark. A trumpeter sounded the clear notes of "First Call," written for the occasion by Ole Foerch. Then came the first hymn, "Nearer, My God, to Thee," Nancy's favorite. The voices from the throng at the shell, on the side of the island closest to Canada, rolled across the international boundary. Street lights from the Windsor shore shone on the water. A Great Lakes freighter, emitting a steady stream of dusty smoke, glided quietly down the channel of what has been called the busiest waterway in the world.[7]

Soon the sun broke through, and in the sudden light robins' calls joined the human voices singing, "Holy, Holy, Holy," "Lead Kindly Light," "Blessed Be the Tie That Binds," "The Morning Light Is Breaking." Dr. Edgar Dewitt Jones, a Protestant minister, and Rabbi David Cedarbaum offered prayers. A Catholic clergyman whom Nancy had invited explained his church did not permit him to participate in a union service. In later years — but before the Catholic church was to lighten its rigid liturgical rules — Nancy solved the problem by inviting Catholic laymen to represent their faith so that all her readers could be represented in appeals to the Almighty.

As Nancy had predicted in her column, it was a morning to remember. Gilmore, who acted as master of ceremonies, suggested at the close that the sunrise service should be an annual event. His suggestion became a fact. The services were repeated year after year, each time attracting Nancy's "acres of friends" to the island.

Out of the services grew yet another column project — the erection of the Peace Carillon Tower close by the site of the sunrise gatherings. Column readers made the tower possible by inundating Nancy with gifts, as she wrote, "from their cookie jars." The cornerstone was laid December 7, 1939, and a copy of the *News* of that date was placed in a copper box fitted into the stone. It carried an editorial addressed to "those who, perhaps 500 years hence, will explore the heap of stone that today takes shape as the prayer of Experience column folks for perpetual peace." The message concluded with a plea to the men of five hundred years hence not to judge twentieth-century humanity too harshly. The message was both ominous and prophetic in the light of gathering world events.

The date of the dedication, June 17, 1940, would never be forgotten by column readers, fifty thousand of whom had gathered on Belle Isle in the predawn darkness. The first ray of sunlight on the island that morning struck its tallest peak, the white limestone tower itself. The familiar notes of "First Call" were sounded. Then the tower chimes pealed out for the first time "Nearer, My God, to Thee." While the hymns, prayers and speeches continued, a small, white-haired lady sat a few benches back with the fur collar of her coat turned up, enjoying her last minutes of anonymity. Then the moment everyone was waiting for arrived. Diminutive Mrs. Leslie — Nancy Brown all these years — stepped up to the lectern. She was barely tall enough to peek over it. In a tremulous voice she spoke face to face with her readers for the first time.[8]

Great labor and sacrifice had gone into the building of the carillon, she said. This made it more than a monument of steel and stone but "a triumph woven of dreams and struggle." She thanked Will Scripps and Gilmore for their encouragement. Most of all, she said, she thanked her column folks, with whom she had "gone shoulder to shoulder, down the road of life" for twenty-one years.

There was another event at the carillon eighteen months hence on the second anniversary of the laying of the cornerstone. Its historical significance far transcended the history of Detroit and the *News*.

At 3:45, on the morning of the service, Dr. Henry Hitt Crane, a Methodist minister, was awakened by the persistent ringing of his front doorbell. Wondering what emergency so early on a Sunday morning could lead anyone to his door, Dr. Crane answered the bell in bathrobe and slippers. He was confronted by a businesslike driver for the *News*. "I've come to drive you to Belle Isle," he announced. "You're twelve hours early," protested Dr. Crane. Nancy's service is this afternoon." The driver shook his head negatively. Nancy had left word for the minister to be picked up at 3:45 "and everything she puts on at Belle Isle has always been in the middle of the night." But the driver was in error and Dr. Crane returned to his bed.

While he and much of the city slept, *News* presses were rolling the final Sunday edition with the banner headline: "Roosevelt Sends Message to Mikado."[9] An accompanying article told of mounting concern in the capital over reports that 125,000 Japanese troops were concentrated in Indo-China and that two large and heavily escorted Japanese convoys were steaming toward the Gulf of Siam.[10] Jay Hayden's Washington column talked of the need of neutrals to choose sides. Farther back in the paper was Nancy Brown's reminder to her readers: "You will not forget our broadcast from the Carillon Tower at 4:30 this afternoon, will you? I have something very important to tell you and I hope many of you will want to be at the tower to greet us." The program was to be broadcast by Station WWJ.

A column by Blair Moody, chief of the Washington Bureau and later a U.S. senator, recounted that three hours before Nancy's broadcast, President Roosevelt completed a leisurely dinner with his lend-lease administrator, Harry L. Hopkins. They were chatting in the White House study when an urgent message came for the President — in Honolulu Sunday morning sleepers were being thrown from their beds by falling bombs. Pearl Harbor was under attack.[11]

In Detroit it was bright, sunny and cool. Mr. and Mrs. Gilmore called for Nancy at 3:15 P.M. Traffic was heavy across the Belle Isle Bridge, and cars were parked bumper to bumper along the island's curbs for some distance from the tower. Nancy remarked about the coolness of the day but found pleasure in the breeze rippling the water in the moat at the foot of the tower. In the room at the base, broadcasters and participants worked quickly but quietly. Boxes and containers cluttered the area. Two microphones on tall stands stood in the center of the floor. The carillonneur sat ready at the keyboard of the organ and the chimes. A radio operator was hunched over a low table. Concerned over the news of the day, Gilmore called the radio station on the tower telephone. The station was giving all its time to news bulletins.

Station executives wanted to abandon Nancy Brown's broadcast. Gilmore looked over the gathered throng. Many had been waiting for hours for Nancy's appearance. "War or no war," he said, "we can't disappoint Nancy's fans." Then he said, "Break in with news bulletins whenever there is something important." The program went on, and Nancy revealed that the $60,000 cost of the tower had been met by column contributors. It now belonged to the people of Detroit. Dr. Crane spoke of the tower as a great gesture of faith at a time when the world was being overwhelmed by a widening war. "But it is this tower that will be of enduring significance," he said. "Its chimes will outlast the guns of war."[12]

Four days later, on her seventy-first birthday, Nancy worked on an announcement that was published on January 8, 1942. To long-time readers it would come as yet another traumatic experience. "For nearly 23 years now, you and I have worked and played shoulder to shoulder. We have sat by our column fireside and discussed every subject under the sun. But now, my folks, I find that I am no longer able to fulfill my share of the work. The years have taken their toll. I must lay down the burden."

Letters poured in, expressing sadness at her retirement. But she said good-bye in the newspaper on February 1, 1942, turning the column over to an assistant who also was to remain anonymous. In April 1944, she returned to speak on WWJ as the Experience column celebrated its silver anniversary, and in January 1945, the year the war ended, she was enrobed "Doctor of Hopefulness" in ceremonies in Dr. Jones's church. That November 29, a dispatch from Washington in the *News* was of special interest to her; it told of the death at seventy of Mrs. Marie Manning Gasch, the Beatrice Fairfax of long ago.

Mrs. Leslie died at seventy-seven on October 7, 1948. Detroit's Central Woodward Christian Church was filled for the services two days later with column folks, many of them silver-haired. "No one can know how many she helped, how many heavy hearts she lightened," Dr. Jones eulogized. As he spoke the chimes of the Nancy Brown Peace Carillon on Belle Isle tolled "Nearer, My God, to Thee."

Her death marked the end of an era in the city's and the newspaper's history. The people and the column already were appearing in a more modern dress. The concerns expressed were those of a new generation. The advice was educated and sophisticated to meet the new audience. The Nancy Brown phenomenon had hinged on Detroit's growing rate of some fifty thousand persons a year. It was a city of strangers, and Nancy Brown had done much to bring them together. The problems of the future would belong to others. They would not be solved easily.

9

Trouble in Motor City

THAT AMERICA's melting pot never was more than a myth for blacks was tragically demonstrated in two racial riots that ripped Detroit in 1943 and again in 1967. The riots claimed seventy-seven lives and gave Detroit the distinction of being the only city in the United States to which federal troops had been called twice within twenty-four years to quell killing, looting and burning by its residents. Blacks and southern whites with age-long animosities had thronged to the city before and during World War II for jobs in its defense plants, joining the broad spectrum of nationality groups that had arrived over the previous five decades to provide the backbone of the city's automotive assembly lines.

As in many American industrial communities the nationality groups gathered at first in protective clusters, then, as new generations were born, moved elsewhere. The blacks, aided by new constitutional guarantees, were the last to break out of the ghettos that earlier had been the lot of the Irish, the Jews, the Poles, the Hungarians, the Italians and others. In 1943 the city's blacks lived chiefly in Paradise Valley, a contained area on the near east side.

In 1972 a geographic study by two hundred undergraduates of Wayne State University showed that remnants of many of the old ethnic communities still existed alongside newer ones containing Albanians, Lebanese, Yemenites, Chaldeans and Koreans. Of all the groups, the blacks occupied more and varied areas of the metropolitan area as newer generations of whites fled to the suburbs. No longer locked into Paradise Valley, blacks had scattered throughout much of the city proper.

The change that occurred between 1943 and 1967 extended to black desires and expectations in all areas of living from housing to schooling. While the riot of 1967 shocked the citizenry and the city's establishment, black discontent was not unknown. The shock came in learning the extent of the discontent. Detroiters had thought civic, social and court moves had put the city in the forefront of racial accord.

Unlike the 1967 riot, the 1943 uprising came as no surprise to alert Detroiters. Early in 1942 *News* editor Gilmore assigned a reporter to take the pulse of the city on the suspicion that all was not right. The reporter talked to blacks, whites, policemen, storekeepers — people who would know what was happening on the street. He found the blacks in the midst of a "bumping campaign," nudging whites off sidewalks, jostling them in elevators and elsewhere. He wrote a memo describing what he had found and editors were warned to watch for additional signs. The unrest became alarmingly evident in February of 1942, when an attempt to install the first blacks in a public housing project resulted in an uproar that peaked in a cloud of tear gas. The project, on the city's northeast side, straddled a traditional black-white street boundary. In April a contingent of a thousand Michigan state troops, augmented by fourteen hundred Detroit and state police, were called to stand by as fourteen black families, the vanguard of two hundred such families, were moved into the project named after Sojourner Truth, a freed slave who won fame as an abolitionist. Surprisingly, very little happened. Whites picketed the project; there was name-calling. If the city relaxed, it was mistaken. For it was like the proverbial calm before the storm.

In 1943 there were two hundred thousand Negroes in Detroit, an increase of one hundred thousand in ten years. There were forty-three blacks on the three thousand four hundred-man police force. Detroit's city council was all white, led by a white mayor, Edward J. Jeffries, Jr. Early in June a hint of trouble came when twenty-five thousand workers walked off their jobs in the Packard Motor Car Company plant, then producing airplane parts, to protest the promotion of three Negro workers. But not only were blacks and whites in conflict on their jobs, their hatreds flared elsewhere.

On Sunday, July 20, 1943, Rolf Owen, working the *News*'s police beat, became increasingly disturbed by the number of reports of "trouble" on Belle Isle. He alerted Henry Zuidema, night city editor, who in turn called Arthur Hathaway, city editor, at home.[1] Hathaway instructed Zuidema to "muster the boys for action." The instruction was not premature. The day had been torrid, especially in the crowded ghetto of Paradise Valley, which had broiled in temperatures in the nineties all weekend. Blacks had poured out of the ghetto, and with gasoline and tires rationed, crowded onto streetcars for a trip to Belle Isle, once a virtually all-white playground but more and more used by blacks for recreation. The call that alerted Hathaway was ominous. While incidents between blacks and whites had been common all weekend, at midnight Sunday two hundred police had been sent to Jefferson, Detroit's main riverside thoroughfare, and the Belle Isle Bridge to block further entrance to the island and to quell fights.[2]

The trouble might have ended with this maneuver, except that blacks and whites who had been told to go home carried stories of the fights in exaggerated versions to both the black and white sections of the city. A number went to the Forest Club, a popular black dance hall and bowling alley in the heart of Paradise Valley. There were seven hundred persons inside listening to band music. Suddenly, a young man jumped onto the stage, grabbed the microphone from the orchestra leader and shouted words that sounded the death knell for thirty-four people: "There's a riot at Belle Isle. The whites have thrown a colored lady and her baby off the bridge."

The club emptied, its patrons near panic. On the street about twenty blacks stopped a streetcar, beat its white passengers, the conductor and motorman. White motorists were stoned and beaten. The first death came just before dawn when a white pedestrian who had been beaten and knocked unconscious was run over by a taxicab. Looting of predominantly white-owned stores began almost immediately. Police attempted to seal off the area to no avail. Radio stations, seeking to avoid sensationalizing the trouble, said little in newscasts. As a consequence many work-bound white motorists who took their usual routes through black areas were yanked from their cars and beaten.[3]

Disregarding a police warning not to enter the area, Dr. Joseph De Horatiis, a white physician who had many blacks as patients, entered the area to make a house call. Within moments after passing the police cordon, he was struck on the head by a rock thrown by a rioter who then reached inside the car and beat him fatally. That same morning George W. Stark, long-time *Detroit News* editor, columnist and city historian, drove his wife, Anne Campbell, for many years the paper's poet laureate, to Children's Hospital near Paradise Valley, where she did volunteer work. As Stark drove out of the area, his car was bombarded with rocks and bricks. Hospitalized briefly for his cuts and bruises, he proceeded to the *News* to write of his experience.[4]

With Paradise Valley on the east of Woodward running amok with blacks, the blocks immediately west of Woodward in midtown Detroit, inhabited by southern whites drawn to the war plants, also had been aroused by a false rumor — that blacks had raped and murdered a white woman on the Belle Isle Bridge. Woodward Avenue became a no-man's-land between the hostile factions. Like the blacks, the whites formed into gangs. They roamed the streets, stoning autos driven by blacks and beating black passengers on streetcars. Emboldened, the whites swept their vengeance into the heart of downtown Detroit.

With World War II two years underway, the guard long since had been called into federal service. Accepting a black minister's offer to attempt to quell the riot, Mayor Jeffries issued armbands and helmets to two hundred responsible blacks who sought to restore order in Paradise Valley. Their efforts were fruitless. Early Monday afternoon, with guerilla warfare accelerating, Jeffries called Governor Harry Kelly and pleaded for federal troops. As was Romney twenty-four years later, Kelly was hesitant to take the drastic step. A three-hour battle between fifty policemen and a dozen blacks firing from a six-story hotel hastened his decision.

Haggling over who had the power to send the troops, the secretary of war or President Roosevelt, delayed their arrival twelve hours. Late Monday night when the first troops rolled down Woodward, thousands of persons were massed in Grand Circus Park on the northern edge of the downtown section. Armored cars and jeeps bristled with automatic weapons. Not a shot was fired. A single challenge to the troops came from a mob of two thousand whites on the perimeter of the black ghetto. The troops, using only rifle butts, dispersed the crowd quickly. The next morning most Detroiters were back on their jobs, the charred automobiles towed away, the overturned streetcars uprighted.

Thirty-six hours of savagery left twenty-five blacks and nine whites dead, a total of six hundred injured. Seventeen of the dead blacks had fallen to police bullets. The riot involved deep-seated racial prejudices. As a result, while the death and injury toll was high, property loss was less than $2 million.

Although his men had killed seventeen rioters, Police Commissioner John H. Witherspoon subsequently had to defend his department from charges of being "soft" on looters, a paradoxical forerunner of the postriot accusations of 1967.

In the next twenty-four years, as the black population grew to more than 40 percent of the city's total, a series of high court decisions opened additional areas of the city to blacks. But as blockbusting grew, inspired by greedy real estate dealers, a new phenomenon occurred — the flight of middle-class whites to the suburbs. As white areas were vacated, blacks moved in. The alteration in the city's makeup did not lessen the plight or the expectations of blacks who stayed. Politically, the blacks grew in power, and by 1967 two blacks were serving on the city council. It was not enough to prevent the worst riot in the city's history.

At seven o'clock Sunday morning, July 23, 1967, keeping a promise he had made months before, Girardin, now police commissioner, phoned the *News*'s veteran police reporter Herb Boldt. "I'm afraid we've got a bad one brewing. You'd better come downtown," Girardin said. Thus Boldt, whose worries had caused him to lay careful plans with the commissioner, was the first reporter in Detroit to learn that something more than the growing number of black-white rumbles was tearing at the city.

Boldt immediately phoned the *News*'s city desk, dressed hurriedly and raced downtown to police headquarters. He would not sleep in a bed again or have a change of clothes until Thursday. On receiving Boldt's alert, Jack Crellin, chief assistant city editor, telephoned *News* reporter Joseph Wolff, directing him to the precinct station closest to the center of the riot. Wolff tarried only briefly at the precinct station, then with photographer Jerry Hostetler headed for the action — Detroit's long-infamous Twelfth Street. In the hours and days ahead more than forty *News* reporters and photographers were summoned to record and report what was happening. It began like a slow-burning brush fire, gaining in momentum as Detroit sweltered in a heat wave.[5]

Twelfth Street, once a prosperous commercial thoroughfare, was the main artery of the city's Tenth Police Precinct. Just four miles from downtown Detroit, it had become a street of bars, rib joints, pawnshops and empty storefronts. Hustlers worked the street under the watchful eye of their pimps. Prostitutes blatantly solicited "Johns" day and night. Thieves and muggers returning from their forays slipped silently into the adjoining black residential streets to openly peddle their loot. Even bigger traffic was narcotics. White youths from the suburbs cruised the street in late-model cars to make their buys. The street was a running sore in the middle of one of several black communities. Many of its residents had moved into older homes vacated by a predominantly Jewish population that had grown in affluence and had moved to the suburbs. When Paradise Valley was eliminated in a series of slum clearance projects, blacks descended on the Twelfth Street area simply because housing was available and relatively inexpensive. By the late summer of 1967 an estimated 145,000 persons, nearly all black, were jammed into the precinct's six and a half square miles. It had the highest crime rate in the city.

A survey shortly before the riot showed that 73 percent of the residents felt the streets unsafe; 93 percent wished they could move. Although it was like bailing out the ocean with a teaspoon, the Detroit police department cruised the avenue in a token effort to control the vice. Reminiscent of Prohibition law enforcement, police made periodic raids on the precinct's scores of after-hours drinking establishments.

But at 4 A.M. on Sunday, July 23, a routine raid at a blind pig
— operated under the impressive name of United Community
League for Civic Action — set off a chain of events that soon turned
the brush fire into a conflagration. Inside the second floor barroom
eighty-two persons were jammed — pimps, prostitutes, gamblers
and night workers dallying on their way home from their jobs.
Encounters with the law were a part of the fabric of life and
patrons accepted the raid philosophically. One factor, however,
separated this raid from many of the others — the size of the haul
and the day of the week. Because of the number, additional police
patrol wagons were summoned, creating the image of a massive
threat to an unsympathetic audience. As the police were gathering
so were onlookers, about two hundred of them. They crawled out
of the houses on the side streets and hurried from late Saturday
night parties. Unknown to arresting officers, word already was
spreading to other black communities. Soon young unemployed
blacks — many of them school dropouts, cynical of their future,
angry at the system which they felt excluded them — hurried to the
scene.

As the crowd of onlookers swelled, the mood turned ugly. Officers
were pushed and shouts of abuse were dotted with four-letter
words. Whitey was in for a hard time. Frightened shopkeepers
printed "soul brother" on their windows, hoping they would be
spared. The plea was also adopted by some white shopkeepers as a
ruse to avoid the trouble. As the last cruiser pulled away, a rock
was hurled through the car's rear window. In moments a plate glass
store window was shattered. It was 5 A.M. and the fire for all intents
and purposes may have been beyond stopping. Twelfth Street had
already become a magnet for black militants throughout the city.
They arrived from nearby cities in the hours and days ahead to
feed the blaze.[6]

The police radio crackled with reports of trouble, but scout
cars manned for Sunday duty were few. The calls arrived with
such frequency and urgency that Lieutenant Raymond Good, in
charge at the Tenth Precinct, decided to see for himself. Accompanied by a sergeant, he arrived at Twelfth and Clairmount, the
critical intersection, to find several hundred persons milling and

grumbling. Several storefront windows had been smashed. As Good surveyed the damage, a brick struck him behind the ear. Half-stunned, he staggered back to the scout car and with the sergeant headed for a nearby police call box to notify headquarters downtown that the situation was getting out of control. Alerted at the first serious sign of trouble, Commissioner Girardin had arrived at his office by 5:30 A.M. Top officers, summoned at their homes, were on their way either to the Tenth Precinct or to headquarters. Despite the ominous reports, Girardin felt he could not commit all of his slender Sunday morning force to Twelfth Street. Such a move would have stripped Detroit's heavily black near east side of police protection. It also would have left east side utility installations and several major auto factories open to sabotage. At this point no official could say that the incident was not a part of a planned citywide insurrection.

At 4 A.M. only 220 policemen were on duty in the entire city of 1,650,000 residents. Of these only 113 officers were on the street, the rest occupied in supervisory posts or in maintaining communications. The next shift to report — at 8 A.M. — was the smallest of the week. Not knowing whether the riot was spontaneous (which he later believed) or the planned work of black militants, Girardin cautiously weighed his alternatives.[7]

One was to use a plan that had worked with notable success the summer before in a black ghetto on Kercheval, one of the main east-west thoroughfares. By saturating the Kercheval area with police cars the department had been able to seal it off and prevent the arrival of outside troublemakers. But the two situations were hardly comparable. The Kercheval trouble was at its peak when he used that tactic. Also, the population density of the area was far below Twelfth Street's. He was prepared to write off two blocks of Twelfth to the rioters by sealing the area with police, but the crowd had already grown too big for that. By now it was 7 A.M. He reached for a telephone and called Boldt and other members of the press. There was no more need to maintain silence in the hope of containing the rioting. It was a matter now of reaching responsible citizens, black and white, to warn them to stay off the streets and to keep calm.

Twelfth Street was a madhouse by the time *News* reporter Wolff arrived. The milling crowd filled the street and sidewalks. Windows were being smashed and looting had begun in almost a carnival atmosphere. Soon housewives and children joined in the mayhem. The police were vastly outnumbered. At Girardin's orders they withheld firing indiscriminately at looters, which in Girardin's opinion would have raised the death toll and worsened the emotional crisis.

Although they were conspicuous as white reporters, Wolff and other newsmen were able to move up and down the street unmolested most of the morning. When a convoy of riot patrol cars stopped to quell a disturbance at one corner, a new one would break out a block away. Firemen arriving to quench the first blaze — a shoe store — were pelted with rocks, bricks and bottles. This happened again and again.

At noon a group of the city's black leaders drove along Twelfth in a motorcade and stopped a block south of the center of the rioting. Wolff and other reporters watched John Conyers, Jr., a black congressman who represented the district in Washington, climb onto the roof of a car and with a bullhorn plead with the crowd to get off the streets, "go home." The motorcade was showered with rocks and forced to flee. With growing numbers of off-duty police called from their homes and family outings, a militarylike staging area and command post was set up on the grounds of Herman Kiefer Hospital, a large publicly operated institution just east of the riot center. At a nearby church twenty leaders of the black community met.[8] Clergymen tried desperately to establish contact with leaders of the Twelfth Street hoodlums but word came back, "We don't want to talk." The mob's resentment seemed to be directed equally at black community leaders and the white establishment. Later in the day a black social worker in the precinct bitterly told a hastily assembled group of black leaders: "For six months we have been trying to get you 'leaders' here. Now you are here and want to do a lot of mouthing."

From the windows of the *Detroit News* building, about three miles distant, smoke could be seen bellowing up from the riot area as Molotov cocktails exploded in looted buildings, turning them into infernos. They were sketched by *News* artist Jack Phillips.

Before calling Boldt, Girardin had alerted Mayor Jerome P. Cavanagh, who hurried downtown to join in the decision-making. With persuasion failing at the street level, Cavanagh and Girardin sought to mobilize adequate manpower to contain the riot. In addition to summoning all available policemen, Michigan's state police posts were notified and the first of 350 state policemen began arriving. Machinery was then put into motion to call the state's National Guardsmen, most of whom were on summer maneuvers at Camp Grayling, two hundred miles north. There were misgivings about calling the guard because of its lack of riot training. But at 4:20 P.M. Cavanagh formally requested the aid of guardsmen from Governor George Romney, who had joined the Top Command at police headquarters. Like the rest Romney would stay there most of the next five days.

By 7 P.M. guardsmen began arriving. Eventually seven thousand were deployed on Detroit streets. By this time looting and arson had spread through vast areas of the west side. That evening damage was estimated into "the millions." No one really could calculate the escalating destruction. Block after block of such business streets as Twelfth, Linwood, Dexter and Grand River, all the remains of a building boom of the early 1920s, were blackened, smoking ruins. Damage mounted as bands of looters leapfrogged across the west side, smashing windows and carrying away valuable merchandise and scattering lesser items to the heat-charged winds. Fires destroyed entire blocks as firemen were routed by rioters throwing rocks and bottles. Windows of fire trucks leaving the city's stations were cross-stitched with broad bands of tape to keep the glass from shattering and cutting firemen. Yet trucks returning to the stations were often windowless and battered as if they had gone through a war zone. A log of the fire department's communications center, taking messages from fire companies, reported the chaos: "There is no police protection here at all; there isn't a policeman in the area. . . . If you have any trouble at all, pull out! . . . We're being stoned at the scene. We need help. . . . Protect yourselves, proceed away from the scene.

. . . They are throwing rocks at us and we are getting out. . . . All companies without police protection — all companies without police protection — orders are to withdraw, do not try to put out the fires. I repeat — all companies without police protection are to withdraw, do not put out the fires."

Utility crews answering electrical and natural gas emergencies carried guardsmen in their cars and trucks for protection, but there were many areas they dared not enter. Wolff reported watching a pumper truck fleeing along Twelfth with fifty feet of hose trailing behind it on the pavement. Before evening the fire department had vacated a hundred square blocks on either side of Twelfth. And by 11:05 P.M. Governor Romney declared the city in a "state of emergency."

Saying he was without power to proclaim martial law, Romney established a 9 P.M. to 5:30 A.M. curfew, banned the sale of alcoholic beverages, and forbade gatherings of five or more persons on the city's streets. Included in the order were the enclave cities of Highland Park and Hamtramck. Twenty-four hours after the riot began, the *News* observed that what was transpiring on Twelfth Street was not a riot in the traditional sense of black pitted against white. It was not a repeat of the city's earlier riot:

"In 1943, the only way a Negro leader might have been seen in police headquarters would have been under arrest. This Sunday they were all there with their white counterparts concerned with what was happening to their city, ready to do what was required to help and accepting as a matter of course their civic obligation to help restore order.

"They were there with the governor, the mayor and all the rest who make a city tick. And in this gathering of diverse and often politically antagonistic men, there was no partisanship, no recrimination, no drawing of a black-white line."⁹

Even as the National Guard rolled into the city, Romney and Cavanagh realized that only federal troops could restore order. Three deaths during the night — the forerunners of forty more during the week — moved them to a decision. The first fatality was by gunfire. A white woman was shot as her husband's car slowed down on Woodward, a mile east of the original riot area. The shot had been fired at close range. The sounds of gunfire increased as the first day wore into the second.

At 2:15 A.M. Monday, Cavanagh called Vice President Hubert Humphrey and requested federal troops. He was advised that the governor should make the request of Attorney General Ramsey Clark. The governor hesitated calling the riot "an insurrection" lest this would void insurance on damaged properties. By 9 A.M., with the disturbances spreading, Romney and Cavanagh renewed the request for federal troops. By noon, President Johnson authorized a task force of paratroopers to go to Selfridge Air Force Base, thirty miles east of Detroit. He also ordered his personal representative, Cyrus Vance, former deputy secretary of defense, to appraise the situation.

Following a tour of the riot area Vance concluded there was no need for federal troops. But a new day of rioting was just warming up. Almost as he made his announcement, fresh clouds of smoke mushroomed into the sky and the screech of fire and police sirens grew into a hellish crescendo. More menacing was the increase in rifle fire and the occasional staccato bursts of machine guns as police and the guard fought a guerilla war with "snipers." Nine persons died Monday in such encounters. Black revolutionaries were rumored to be in greater number than they were known to exist in the city. In retrospect, students of the riot doubted that any snipers ever existed. At least none was ever identified.

By the second night of the riot *News* photographers, notably Duane Belanger, who at six feet two made a sizable target, arrived at the *News* ready for riot assignment, dressed from head to toe in black. *News* reporters and photographers who moved onto the scene used whatever protection available to stay out of the line of fire. Many lay prone under parked cars to observe what was happening. What they saw in many instances were jittery guardsmen who blazed away at the sound of a gunshot. The gunshots often were coming from other guardsmen who were firing at suspected snipers. The crossfire was deadly.

With shooting incidents and arson mounting Monday night, Vance advised President Johnson that only federal troops could restore order. In a midnight television appearance the President described Detroit as a "city out of control" and ordered the 101st Airborne Division to Detroit. Then he said: "I am sure that the American people will realize that I take this action with the greatest regret — and only because of the clear, unmistakable and undisputed evidence that Gov. Romney and the local officials have been unable to bring the situation under control."[10]

The next day the *News* leaped on Johnson's statement with an editorial charging he was using a civic tragedy to play politics:

. . . The President seemed intent on pinning the blame for the breakdown in law and order on Gov. Romney, who is regarded as a leading candidate for the 1968 GOP nomination [which the paper subsequently was to oppose].

It is true that the President acted under statutes which permit federal intervention only after the governor of a state certifies "conditions of domestic violence and disorder." But Mr. Johnson went far beyond the requirements of the occasion to make it appear it was Romney's fault, or the result of Romney's weakness, that the riots were continuing and federal troops were needed.

. . . In this matter of life and death, with the safety of thousands of people at stake and hundreds of millions of dollars in property value going up in flames, it was inexcusable for the President of the United States to indulge in partisan politics. Yet the record is clear that Mr. Johnson did just that.[11]

Under the command of General John Throckmorton, the federal troops arrived to find Detroit a city of fear. Throckmorton's first order was to forbid guardsmen to fire unless they could see that the person they were shooting at was committing an overt act. As the federal troops, many of them Vietnam veterans, moved in, the mood of the city visibly changed. The paratroopers, 20 percent of them black, exerted a calming influence. Seeing this, Throckmorton ordered all weapons to be carried unloaded, but *News* reporters and utility repairmen reported this order was not always carried out. The earlier indiscriminate firing by police and guardsmen had produced tragic results.

In one instance a four-year-old black girl looking out the window of an apartment in an area of reported sniper fire was killed by a blast of a guardsman's machine gun. An investigation showed that the "flash" he had reported seeing in the window was the match being lit by the child's uncle to light a cigarette. The gunfire also wounded the girl's aunt.

On the night of Tuesday, July 25, police entered a motel on the fringes of the riot area on Woodward, two miles north of the downtown district. When they left, three young blacks were dead — killed, the first report declared, "in a gunfight with police." The place was the Algiers Motel annex. An attempt to state what happened there subsequently became the subject of a book, *The Algiers Motel Incident*, by John Hersey, author of *Hiroshima* and other best-selling books. The book became as controversial as conflicting police reports.[12]

News reporter Richard A. Ryan was the first newsman to arrive at the scene. Since there had been no suspicion of foul play, he was instructed to search out the sniper or snipers who were thought to have precipitated police reaction. Hayden had been urging Paul Poorman, then assistant managing editor, to gather the facts needed for an article giving "the anatomy of a sniper." When Ryan returned, saying he could not find supportive information, Hayden ordered the paper's Joseph Strickland, a black reporter, to the motel to investigate.

Strickland visited the establishment on three occasions in an effort to find witnesses. Reports were circulating in the black community that at least two or three youths had been shot to death in cold blood after being beaten and terrorized by police. Police entering the building had been particularly infuriated, the reports said, to discover two young white prostitutes had been consorting with a half dozen black youths in the motel.

During the investigation Strickland learned that a recently discharged black army veteran, Robert L. Greene, had been staying at the motel and had fled to his native Kentucky immediately after the incident. Strickland located Greene by telephone and the ex-paratrooper said he had been beaten by police and that he had been present when officers shot two of the youths. Strickland soon was on his way to Kentucky in a chartered airplane, accompanied by an assistant prosecuting attorney and a homicide detective. There, Greene reiterated his charges. Strickland's exclusive interview with Greene in the *News* was the first inkling that most Detroiters had that something terribly sinister had occurred in the Algiers Motel.[13]

During the week more than seven thousand two hundred persons were arrested in a mass attempt to halt arson and sniping. When the Wayne County Jail, which serves the city, was overflowing, prisoners were shipped to county jails throughout southern Michigan, to the state prison at Jackson and to the federal penitentiary at Milan, Michigan. Some prisoners were quartered in seven city buses parked under guard near police headquarters. City laborers worked day and night transforming the women's bathhouse on Belle Isle into a detention facility, installing floodlights, guard towers, kitchen and dormitory facilities.

Judges, determined to keep troublemakers in custody, set bonds on suspected snipers and arsonists as high as $200,000. On Friday, July 28, Governor Romney appealed to the city and state bar associations to provide volunteer counsel for the hundreds arraigned daily in twenty-four-hour round-the-clock court sessions.

By Saturday calm had been restored, and that night federal troops began to pull out. The following Tuesday the curfew was lifted and National Guardsmen and state police left.

The week's toll of fires numbered 1,304. The prime target had been white-owned businesses, but in the process scores of establishments that had carried window pleas of "soul brother" fell to the flames. Of the forty-three persons killed in the riot, thirty-three were black, ten white. Seventeen, including two whites, had been shot while looting. A number of other deaths were caused by stray bullets during "sniper" gunfights. The biggest merchandise loss consisted of color television sets, which were carried away on fenders of cars, and smaller appliances which were carried on foot. Much of the loot was taken by professional thieves taking advantage of the confusion. Days later it showed up in Chicago, Cleveland and elsewhere, in pawnshops and during police raids on caches of stolen property. The ultimate damage to property was $60 million, held down because of the age and the poor condition of the housing and commercial establishments destroyed.[14]

In the aftermath, one Detroit police officer was indicted and brought to trial for murder as a result of the shooting in the Algiers Motel. The trial was moved to Mason, Michigan, a small town near the state's capital. The officer was acquitted by an all-white jury. A subsequent trial, charging three Detroit policemen involved in the Algiers incident with conspiracy to violate the civil rights of the three dead youths, seven other motel residents, and a private guard, was held in Flint, Michigan. All were acquitted by an all-white jury. Testimony showed that the only thing resembling a firearm found in the motel was a starter's gun, used at track meets, which fired only blank cartridges.

As the smoke and the trials settled, police and civic leaders who for years had been publicly optimistic about the city's racial relations questioned what happened. With no evidence that the riot was the planned device of a nationally organized black group, most fell back to the belief expressed by Mayor Cavanagh that "it is obvious that what we did [to lessen tensions over the years] could not prevent a large percentage of our population from feeling alienated. . . ." The realization that many of Detroit's black residents considered themselves second-class citizens provided the impetus for civic action in several important directions.

As the smoke was literally still rising from the ravaged riot areas, thirty-nine of the city's most influential citizens banded together in "The New Detroit Committee," designed to keep channels of communication open between blacks and whites, between the haves and the have-nots. It included the heads of the Big Three auto companies, other leading businessmen and nine blacks, some representing the city's most extreme black militant organizations. The committee immediately set out to encourage job training for the ghetto's hard-core unemployed and also moved into areas of housing, education and a wide range of social and welfare services.

At the moment of the riot, only 5 percent of Detroit's police force of 4,356 was made up of blacks. (The force itself was four hundred below authorized strength.) The black with the highest position, that of inspector, had been promoted to the post just before the riot. With a strong recruitment drive and a program to improve the police image among blacks, the department raised the number of blacks in its ranks to 15 percent over the next four years. Its announced goal was to increase the percentage of blacks on the force to equal the percentage of blacks in the city — 45 percent in 1972. By the end of 1971 nine blacks had risen to the rank of inspector.[15]

If the riot had caught the city by surprise, its complacence was understandable. When it was over civic groups worked to lessen tensions, yet the magic elixir of brotherhood still was missing. The issue of busing put it in sharp focus.

An attempt to improve schooling for blacks resulted in several controversial plans for transporting students both within and across district lines. As busing became an issue in urban areas across the nation, it soon was obvious in Detroit, at least, that it was not desirable to the majority of blacks or whites. Where unemployment, poor housing and expectancy to succeed far beyond educational means had fermented into the 1967 riots, busing now became a focal point of irritation.

A citywide survey of blacks by the *News* in 1972, aimed at pinpointing areas of discontent, indicated that less than half believed the quality of life in the city had improved or would improve. Compared to the discontent on Twelfth Street in 1967 (73 percent), the figure was optimistic but still disconcerting. Among the complaints cited were poor housing and inferior educational and job opportunities — grievances heard many times before.

Topping the list of problems present and expected to increase was crime. Since 1945, two years after the city's first major riot, murders had increased almost sevenfold — from 101 in 1945 to 690 in 1971. Rape had increased nearly one-third, from 638 to 913, and aggravated assault (basic in street crime) had quadrupled from 2,068 to more than 8,000.

The survey showed: a significant distrust among blacks of policemen — particularly white policemen; a belief by 75 percent of those polled that a black has to have money to get justice in the courts; a significant feeling in the followup interviews that police make too-aggressive use of search and seizure procedures against blacks; a widespread belief, strongest among the young, that police fail to enforce the law fairly; a strong feeling that police are not active enough in shutting down dope houses, going after top operatives in the heroin trade or raiding the fences who sell stolen goods, and anger at what many feel is frequent police discourtesy and verbal abuse of black citizens.

Unlike the racial conflict of the 1943 riot or the assault on the establishment, black and white, in 1967, the irritant of crime was pervasive and difficult to focus on. But its importance was not underestimated by the community or the *News*. Nineteen *News* reporters, supervised by Poorman (now managing editor), augmented a scientific analysis by a professional survey company with interviews and background stories that supported the study.[16]

10

The Crime of It

DESPITE THE TRAGEDY in lost lives and the heavy property destruction, the real damage of Detroit's riot in the last days of July 1967 was not immediately evident. The lawlessness, the defiance of enforcement officials, the interference with the city's fire department as it answered numerous alarms was symbolic of a moral sickness that had been growing like a malignant tumor. Even before the July rampage, the incidence of dope usage had notably increased. It was to peak in the months to follow, centering first in the inner city, then spreading to the suburbs. Young people, who in the early stages traveled to the inner city to procure various narcotics, were to become pushers in the classic vicious circle created by the awful demands of addiction. Schools in the suburban areas soon had their own underground supply. Where money-shy inner-city addicts fought desperately to get much-needed fixes, the affluent young people in the suburbs had ready cash to foster their addiction.

The lack of affluence in the inner city increased the problem of street crime to proportions far exceeding the city's gang-ridden days of Prohibition. Addicts desperate for money to buy the temporary solace that narcotics bring to dope-tortured minds and bodies quickly gave birth to a form of crime which was given the name of "ripoff." The victims of ripoffs are women, old people, crippled persons, the blind walking with white canes. The attacks are sudden, the mugger and his accomplices striking the prey to the ground, taking money and valuables and fleeing before help can

arrive. Addiction on dope and racial hatreds add to the vicious-
ness of ripoffs. A resident of a home for the aged on Woodward
Avenue, close to the downtown shopping district, is accosted by
several youths within a block of his residence. The assault leaves
him unconscious, partially blinded, confused — and hospitalized for
weeks. The success of such attacks brings more and more ripoffs.

As they increased, top editors of the *News* who gathered daily
in the offices of the editor to mull over editorial problems presented
possible solutions. The city's downtown streets were rapidly turning into a jungle. A plan in which the newspaper would offer rewards for the arrest and conviction of criminals involved in
serious crimes seemed to have merit and was begun under the
name, Secret Witness. But before the program could reach its
potential effectiveness, the *News* and the *Free Press* were shut
down by a strike of unionized employees on November 16, 1967.
The strike lasted until August 8, 1968.

During the strike of Detroit's major metropolitan dailies, crime
on the street soared. By August, homicides had nearly doubled
from an October total of 23, rape had increased from 70 to 90,
robbery from 1,306 to 1,531. Simple larceny rose steadily from 1,530
to 1,662.[1] Coupled with street crimes was a startling increase in
shoplifting and holdups of downtown businesses. Merchandisers
of such valuables as jewelry and furs who occupied upper floors
of downtown buildings began locking their doors and admitting
customers only after they had rung a doorbell and were adjudged
safe. Blacks often were denied admittance simply because of their
color. Whites were examined for dilated pupils or disjointed behavior, each a sign of drug addiction and desperation. Even
architecture was altered to eliminate windows that could be
broken for entry. The large windows exposing the *News*'s pressroom were enclosed in slate.

With the dailies struck and unable to shed light on the problem, neighborhood weeklies and the *Detroit American,* a daily
created by the strike, attacked the growing crime problem. The
American, printed by Detroit's *Polish Daily News,* was published
by the Pol-American Publishing Company, whose president
was Arthur J. Wierzbicki, at times a Detroit councilman repre-

senting the city's extremely conservative and reactionary elements. The *American* not only attacked street crime but its articles were pointed at blacks.[2] The use of such epithets as "roving packs of jackals" to describe the perpetrators of street crimes added an intense emotional element to the fear that gripped persons who shopped or worked in the downtown area. With attacks occurring close to the entrances of business establishments, including that of the *News,* businessmen called for action. When it failed to develop, a number of large concerns announced plans of moving to the suburbs. While a variety of reasons was given for departing Detroit, street crime was foremost. Some firms were having difficulty recruiting employees to work in the central city. During its campaign against street crime, the *American's* circulation, by its own figures, soared to 185,000, exhibiting the interest of Detroiters in stopping the attacks. It dropped to 30,000 shortly after the *Free Press* and the *News* resumed publication. Although the *American* had been launched as a permanent publication, it soon folded once the strike had ended.[3]

On December 30, 1968, Ray R. Eppert, sixty-six, former board chairman of the Burroughs Corporation who had been honored the year before as the city's outstanding citizen, left a civic meeting in midafternoon and walked to his car, parked in the garage under the city's newly developed Kennedy Square. Before reaching his car, Eppert stopped in the men's room. There he was robbed and severely beaten by three black youths. A blow on the head partially paralyzed him. He was able to give only a vague description of his assailants. The attack on Eppert, who had been involved for twenty years in civic groups dedicated to fostering better human relations in Detroit, provoked Francis A. Kornegay, executive director of the Detroit Urban League, to call for a united effort by both blacks and whites.[4] Five days after the attack, Kornegay proposed the creation of block clubs and neighborhood associations to work "vigorously" with police. He also asked for the formation of voluntary groups to patrol neighborhoods, reporting suspicious persons and actions to authorities.

At the time of Kornegay's call for action, the *News,* which had attacked street crime as soon as it resumed publication by printing the Police Department's daily record of crimes, was operating behind a picket line. Because the crime roundup included descriptions of suspects, most of whom were black, the *News* was accused of racism. In the city's deep black areas the paper was boycotted. Reports on the effect of the paper's printing of "the police blotter" were the subject of the daily editorial conferences. When black leaders complained that the listings painted all blacks with the same brush, the *News* broadened its boxscore so that it not only listed the race of the fugitives but the race of those persons attacked. The addition showed that many blacks as well as whites were the victims of ripoffs. Yet, the objection of many blacks and whites to the paper's determined attempt to stymie street crime continued to mount.

On May 8, 1969, *Time* magazine, picking up the chant of civil rights' advocates, reported that the *News* had published Page One stories for six days when a white policeman's son had been fatally stabbed by a black. But when a black was killed, seeking to defend his wife against an attack by a group of whites intent on raping her, the paper published only one story.[5] A *News* salvo was quick in coming. The record showed that the *News* had published twenty-two stories about the black man's murder, including a Page One article printed within four hours after the crime was discovered. Within twelve hours, on a Sunday, the paper published an extensive story on Page Three, its second news-feature page, including photographs of the victim's family.

The *News* reported it had published thirteen articles about the death of the policeman's son at Cobo Hall. The paper argued the killing was an unusually brazen attack during the daylight hours when the convention center was crowded with visitors. The black victim was slain after dark in a city park after he and his wife had spent some time drinking with the youths who attacked him.[6] The large elements of any newspaper story — place and circumstance — favored greater attention for the Cobo Hall murder. So it was printed on Page One at the start.

Answering criticism of its campaign to curtail street crimes in Detroit, the *News* declared, "Yes we do identify the race of the suspect. In doing so, we follow what we believe to be a realistic and completely nonracist policy which has been in effect on this paper much longer than charges of racism have been popular. We identify race only when we have some other descriptive detail and the suspected criminal is still being sought. . . ." The paper concluded: "True we have aroused criticism. Now when will we arouse the inner city to forget fear, reject apathy and actively join the effort to catch criminals and help to stop crime in Detroit?"[7]

When the paper was criticized by the city's mayor, Cavanagh, for its efforts to curb street crime, it editorialized: "Sweeping crime under the rug won't banish it. But reporting of crime as it occurs will help inform citizens and persuade them to demand action that will bring results. That's what we intend to do. If that's over-emphasizing crime, Mr. Mayor, the *News* pleads guilty. But we do not apologize for alerting the public to what has been going on through our efforts to 'Tell it like it is.' The results, we believe, speak for themselves."[8]

The results eventually included better lighting in city parks and the recruitment of more police officers, including blacks, who were assigned to fighting crime on the streets.

While the *News* campaigned to reduce crime on the streets in the face of strong criticism, the paper also resumed its Secret Witness program. Secret Witness was the brainchild of William L. Finstad of Chicago, who first introduced it in 1949 to the *Chicago Sun-Times* without significant success. Chicago's failure can be traced directly to gangster warfare, which often defies police solution. The *News* introduced the plan in 1967 in the hope of inducing the public to help in the arrest and conviction of suspects in serious crimes. And it was called Secret Witness to emphasize the fact that the names of witnesses who came forth would be held inviolate. A simple system in which the witness writes a number of his own making on his tip, then keeps a copy of the number, provides all the identification needed to collect a reward. To start it off the *News* created a reward fund of $100,000.[9]

At a breakfast meeting with top police officials *News* editors agreed that all tips would be reported to the Police Department, that the paper would not investigate any case until the police had time to pore over the clues provided. Secret Witness was an almost instant success. Crime had reached such proportions in the city that the broad mass of people recognized that "looking the other way" could no longer be justified in a safe society.

As Secret Witness produced results, the paper followed its daily coverage of the police blotter with a series "Crime: A Search for Solutions." The paper's determination to maintain law and order, letting the chips fall where they may, was soon obvious. In the midst of cries from the left the *News* excoriated Recorder's Court Judge George W. Crockett, Jr., a black judge, for "abuse of power." Detroit's Recorder's Courts (municipal) have criminal jurisdiction. In an editorial on April 1, 1969, it criticized him for "wholesale and indiscriminate" releases of suspects arrested in a shootout with police at a church rally of black militants. Blacks and some white civil rights leaders again cried "racist." The deeper issue, the paper insisted, was law and order.[10] About this time the *News* hired June Brown Garner, a columnist for the black *Michigan Chronicle*, to write a weekly column of her own direction in the *News Sunday Magazine*. Other black columnists were appearing elsewhere in the paper, including Roy Wilkins, executive director of the National Association for the Advancement of Colored People, Lawrence Carter and Carl T. Rowan. Rowan wrote from a background of a reporter and government official, Carter as a local businessman.

Because Secret Witness carefully protected the anonymity of the tipster and maintained a balanced selection of crimes for which rewards were offered, the campaign steered clear of racial objection from the outset. Secret Witness also had to establish its legal credibility, and it did so in the trial of the first suspect arrested as the result of one of its tips. In late 1966 and early 1967, a series of holdups — thirteen in all — were committed along Michigan Avenue, one of Detroit's main thoroughfares. The robber's modus operandi never deviated. He would enter a store, order a suit, shirts, a hat, shoes or a watch, and when the merchant turned to get the article, he would hold him up. Because the robber always "purchased" articles of clothing that fit him, police knew all his measurements, including his hat and shirt size. They knew he was over six feet tall and exceptionally thin.[11]

On February 15, 1967, Boldt, chief of the *New*'s police beat, turned in a story that ran across the top of Page One. From the description provided by police, Boldt tagged the sought-for robber as "Michigan Avenue Slim." The *News,* through its Secret Witness program, offered $1,000 for his arrest and conviction. While the paper was on the newsstands, "Michigan Avenue Slim" entered a jewelry store on Michigan Avenue, in suburban Dearborn, and wounded the owner in an exchange of shots. On February 17 "Slim" entered a gun shop to buy ammunition for his gun and was recognized by a "Secret Witness." He was arrested thirty-six hours after the reward offer was made. To safeguard the Police Department's case, the *News* withheld the information that the colorful bandit had been apprehended.

On June 16, 1967, three months after the arrest, the paper ran the first of a series of articles about the armed robbery trial of a Walter Reynolds Fleming, twenty-three. The reporter covering the trial was Robert D. Kirk. Kirk, a veteran of the circuit court beat, knew the rules of evidence, that any revelation during the case on trial that Fleming was the notorious "Michigan Avenue Slim" might cause a mistrial. Not until Fleming was convicted was he identified as "Michigan Avenue Slim" in the newspaper.

Secret Witness now was well established in the minds of readers. On August 20, 1967, Mrs. Nola Puyear, who operated a restaurant in Marshall, Michigan, received a package in the mail. When she opened it, it exploded, instantly killing her. Shortly afterwards a tipster told the *News* that Mrs. Puyear earlier had received a package of pills in the mail. After her death police found they contained poison. She had not taken any, however. An investigation showed that the combination of printing and handwriting on the pill package was similar to that on the remnants of the box that contained the bomb. When the paper published this information it offered a reward of $3,000. The reward and a photograph of the writing sample solved the case. A man who had been arrested and cleared earlier in the investigation was rearrested on a Secret

Witness tip. The tipster who knew the bomber provided samples of the suspect's handwriting, which the suspect had been able to disguise during his early interrogation. The bomber was convicted although no motive for the crime was ever established. The *News* paid the reward through an attorney who forwarded the torn corner of the Secret Witness numbered letter.

By now Secret Witness tips proliferated with nearly each *News* reward. The task of taking charge of the program fell to Boyd Simmons, the labor reporter who had moved on to become assistant managing editor. Simmons tackled the challenge with the zest he exhibited as a labor and a crime reporter. It soon became more of a task than responding to tips. At times he would become personally involved in assisting tipsters in substantiating their claims.

On March 26, 1971, the body of Fred Bodnar, twenty-two, a railroad brakeman, was found in his burning car on a freeway service drive. An autopsy showed he had been shot. The *News* story of the crime brought a phone call to Simmons. The caller wondered if there would be a reward? Simmons informed him it would be offered the following morning. The man hung up. At 8 A.M. the next day, a man was waiting at the editor's door. He stated he was a cab driver in the inner city and that he had picked up a white man near the murder scene a few minutes after fire trucks had extinguished the burning car. Since the area was virtually all black, the cabbie, also black, wondered about his passenger's presence there. The fare told the cabbie to drive to a west side suburb. While en route the cabbie watched him in a rear view mirror as he counted a thick roll of bills. In the suburb, the fare entered a bar where, he later told the cabbie, he paid off a gambling debt. Then the cabbie was asked to drive to a trailer camp where, the man said he had to pay his rent. The final trip was back to the murder scene. There, the fare told the cab driver, he had killed a man. He handed the driver $75 to keep quiet. "He showed me the gun and told me he had committed other murders," the tipster told Simmons.[12]

It was obvious to Simmons that the tip could not be turned over to police without giving away the tipster's identity. "I don't mind talking to police," the cab driver said. "But, first I want to find out where I went that night so I can prove that I'm telling the truth." For the next week the cab driver and Simmons scouted for the places the cab driver remembered taking his passenger. Finally the pieces fell together. In the only instance in five years of the Secret Witness program, the tipster revealed himself to police. The story not only was substantiated but police eventually tied the suspect to three other murders, including that of a barmaid committed the night before he was picked up on information provided by the *News*'s witness.

The *News*'s insistence on withholding the identity of its tipsters is based on Michigan law, which declares a newspaperman cannot be forced to disclose his sources of information. The issue was tested in a college bombing case involving two young men and a young girl, whose defense attorney subpoenaed Simmons to reveal the name of the tipster. Simmons refused, the paper's lawyers arguing successfully that that portion of the criminal code safeguarding a newspaperman from disclosing his news sources had been enacted more than twenty years before.

The law and its significance was uncovered by John B. Weaver, a member of the *News*'s law firm of Butzel, Long, Gust, Klein and Van Zile. It had been enacted in 1949 by a legislature intent on making it a felony for any sworn member of a one-man grand jury staff to disclose any information that transpired inside a grand jury chamber. Slipped in as part of Michigan's Code of Criminal Procedures, it had lain dormant for twenty years until Weaver was assigned to Simmons's defense. Weaver reported he only did what any attorney would do: "I looked up the statute." His authority was section 767.5a of *Michigan Compiled Laws Annotated*. He found the language to his liking. It said the law "covered any inquiry authorized by this act. . . ." Although the original act was passed in an attempt to keep jury staff members and witnesses from talking to newsmen, Weaver found it also could be interpreted to help safeguard a newspaperman. He cited the "shield" provisions in a suburban municipal court and was upheld. The case set a precedent that gave the paper's Secret Witness program strong support for its stand on protecting its tipsters.

In an article in the *Reader's Digest* in November 1971, the *News* was hailed for adding a new "dimension to law enforcement." In the five years Secret Witness had been in effect, the paper had paid $50,000 in rewards. Another $30,000 had been paid by outside concerns who joined in the effort to control crime. Since its inception, more than forty daily newspapers in the United States have adopted the Secret Witness method as a continuing program or for use in specific crimes.[13] Among them are such widely separated papers as the *Houston Post*, the *New Orleans Times-Picayune*, the *Denver Post*, the *Sacramento Bee*, the *Seattle Post-Intelligencer*, the *Dallas Morning News*, the *Philadelphia News*, the *Washington Star*, the *New York Daily News*, the *Salt Lake City Tribune* and the *Baltimore News-American*.

In the first five years of operation the *News*'s Secret Witness produced information directly responsible for solving twenty-eight murders and an array of rapes, holdups, bombings and other crimes. While it struck out at major crime, the incidental result of the program — a broad variety of miscellaneous tips — was to help deter the city's nagging street crimes. The rewards, the *News* discovered, are not solely responsible for the success of Secret Witness. An important factor is the guarantee of secrecy, often more important than the money when the witness is fearful of revenge by the criminal or any of his accomplices. But money goes a long way. And the *News* had gone a long way to hand it out in utmost privacy.

Told when she phoned that she had a reward due her, one woman, declaring she was too ill to pick up the money at the newspaper, whispered into the receiver: "Mail it in cash in a plain envelope." She provided an address. The *News*, with trepidation, placed $2,000 in bills in a white envelope and entrusted it to the post office. When no further word came from the tipster, the case was marked "paid in full." Thoughts of giving the envelope to the mailman on the beat and watching the delivery had been put aside out of fear attention would be drawn to the tipster.

In a cloak-and-dagger payoff, Simmons and John H. Worthington, administrative assistant to the paper's executive vice president, handed $5,000 in cash to a man who felt his closeness to the crime he reported would eventually bring his death. The payoff occurred in the Detroit FBI office at the tipster's request. The tipster had told police the whereabouts of three men who had been involved in holding up a bar and slaying a barmaid and a policeman. Police learned the suspects' car license number and issued a general alert. When the car was spotted, a scout car gave chase. As police closed in, the bandits' car came to a crashing halt. The three men tumbled out. In the rush to reach for his pistol to fire at police, one man accidentally shot and killed himself. The other two escaped. One arrived at police headquarters the next day and surrendered. He was tried and convicted of first degree murder. The day the story of the conviction appeared in the *News*, Simmons received a call. The caller declared it was his information that led police to the trio. Although one man was still missing, the tipster felt entitled to the reward. Simmons told him to call back the next day. Then the editor talked with homicide detectives. They had gotten the information as the tipster had indicated. What worried the tipster was that not only might the convicted man in prison suspect him of tipping police, but so might the man on the loose.

"You meet me at my room," he told Simmons. "I'll scram right after our meeting." Simmons talked to Worthington, who was to join him in the payoff. Both men suspected a trap. When they refused to go to the tipster, he suggested the FBI office. He was afraid the bandit on the loose might spot him entering the *News* building. He felt he had a better chance of slipping into the city's large Federal Building. On prior agreement, agents of the FBI escorted the tipster, carrying $5,000 in cash, to Detroit's Metropolitan Airport, the last anyone heard of him.

Underpinning the *News*'s concern about collapsing law and order was a general belief in a decline in morals that was evident since the end of World War II. The breakdown in obedience to flag and country appeared but symbolic of other disintegrations — a youthful disrespect for formal religion, a growing disenchantment with everything old, a disdain by militants and activists of the establishment. The country was unprepared to thwart the resultant violence and disrespect of law and order. Worse, the moral collapse arrived at a time when liberal intellectuals, many on college campuses, had paved the way for the arriving generations by seriously challenging the old order in its entirety.

The *News* learned early that the majority of its readership was not buying the newly espoused religion of the streets. It was a lesson that was both costly and enlightening to a concerned management that had prided itself with staying abreast of changing times.

The growth and popularity of so-called underground newspapers in the late 1960s was of major interest to the *News* staff. Was it possible that these papers, for all their lack of objectivity and disrespect of accepted standards, were fulfilling a readership desire among young people that major newspapers were missing?

With this in mind the newspaper inaugurated "The Other Section," something of an overground-underground special weekly section that bridged, without the use of four-letter words, this reading gap in a responsible way. Ten young people worked on the experiment in journalism under Robert E. Lubeck, associate editor, features. Their results intrigued the journalistic world, but as Lubeck was detailing this editorial venture to newspaper groups throughout the country, the financial facts were spelling out its demise. While surveys showed that readership was growing with each issue, interestingly enough even in the over-thirty-five-year-old group, the section could attract little advertising for its unique concept. "The Other Section" lost $500,000 in its first year of operation and was discontinued.[14]

On March 19, 1972, the paper's philosophy concerning declining morals was never more bluntly stated. A few days earlier, Lubeck met with John Finlayson, amusement editor, to discuss their growing concern over X-rated movies. So blatant was movie advertising and promotion of X-rated films that such sellers of sex as *Playboy* magazine were being furnished with special "still" photographs to further exploit the most sensational scenes from such so-called meaningful films as *A Clockwork Orange*. Lubeck and Finlayson drafted their thoughts in a memo to Hayden, who wholeheartedly subscribed to their concern. With the concurrence of the publisher and executive vice president, Hayden wrote an editorial that appeared on Page One of the Sunday paper. The

News would no longer accept display advertising of X-rated films, and would no longer carry reviews or publicity stories of X-rated films on its entertainment pages.

"In our view," the paper said,

> a sick motion picture industry is using pornography and an appeal to prurience to bolster theater attendance; quite simply we do not wish to assist them in this process. . . .
>
> We anticipate no movie industry cleanup as the result of our decision. . . . Perhaps the only result will be in our own satisfaction in a modest declaration against the theory that makes hardcore sex, voyeurism and sadistic violence the prime ingredients of art and entertainment in the 1970s.

The declaration may have been modest. But the response was overwhelming. Hundreds of letters poured into the *News* from readers. All but a handful supported the stand. Most letters began with the thought, "Thank God someone has shown enough independence to make a stand."[15]

Because the *News* was the nation's largest evening newspaper and the largest anywhere in the country to adopt such a policy, the movie industry was quick to respond.

Jack Valenti, president of the Motion Picture Association of America, flew into Detroit to hold an angry press conference in which he challenged the newspaper's right to turn down such advertising. But, he concluded, "the *News* may start an avalanche going."

Equally upset was movie producer Stanley Kubrick, whose film *A Clockwork Orange* was being shown in the Detroit area. With its X rating, it was the first movie of any major proportion to be affected by the advertising ban. From London he wrote Hayden a blistering letter, charging censorship and comparing the newspaper's action to a 1937 speech by Hitler banning "degenerate art."

In a month's time at least thirty other newspapers had followed the *News*'s lead, civic groups concerned with motion picture fare had honored the *News*, hundreds of inches of space was devoted to the controversy by newspapers and journals across the country. A few, including the *New York Times*, were against the ban. But these newspapers were in the minority. Most echoed the editorial line of the *Trenton* (N.J.) *Monitor,* a weekly newspaper that called it the "Start of a Decency Avalanche." Added a group of small Ohio papers, "With almost unanimous endorsement of the *News*'s position, society doesn't seem to be as sick as reported."

Even Kubrick was to take a second look at *A Clockwork Orange.* Six months after the *News*'s ban, he eliminated some of the film's scenes in order to receive the less objectionable R rating. Said the *New York Times* on its September 3 editorial page: "Mr. Kubrick's decision to place profits ahead of principle is a matter between him and his artistic conscience."[16]

11

Sports Heroes We've Had

In 1905, as Detroit was planting the seed of its industrial future, a wiry young man dressed in striped knicker pants that ended just under the knees strolled onto the baseball diamond at Detroit's Bennett Field (eventually Tiger Stadium). The man was Tyrus Raymond Cobb — the immortal Ty.

He made his appearance at the time when immigrants, escaping oppression and depression in foreign lands, were arriving in large numbers to work in the city's growing industrial establishments. Though they lived in ghettos of their own making, they sat, seat to seat, untroubled by biases, to watch this man who was described as "the greatest of the great, a fiery genius and the game's outstanding individualist" by H. G. Salsinger, for fifty years the *News*'s sports columnist and eventually dean of the nation's sportswriters.

Wrote Salsinger:

> Brilliant and unorthodox, he made baseball history for more than two decades. He dominated the game. He gained his preeminence not because he was the fastest base runner, nor the best base stealer, nor the fleetest fielder, nor the leading hitter, but because he had the nimblest brain that baseball has known. He had the ability to perceive a situation and take full advantage of it before his opponents became aware of it. He was a keener student of the game than his contemporaries and he understood the game better than they did. What is more, he understood them better than they understood themselves.

He knew their playing faults and weaknesses and he also knew their strength. His wide edge over the field was mental. He thought more quickly than any rival and he put his mechanical skill to more uses than they did. Many of his hits were attributed to superior speed, but the explanation does not hold since several others were as fast.[1]

Cobb's dash and daring on the bases — he perfected the slide as an offensive weapon — his flying spikes and his determination to succeed epitomized the spirit of a city that often was written about erroneously as a "drab workingman's town," when in fact its underlying vigor was yet to be discovered. Cobb was to help draw Detroit's spirit to the surface and put it in the national limelight. Detroit and the nation hailed him as "The Georgia Peach."[2]

When Cobb first arrived at the Tigers' training camp, he expressed the desire to be a pitcher. Although as a youth he had been a shortstop, he wanted this additional challenge and began pitching to anyone who would catch him. All he could exhibit was a dinky hook and other players told him, "You'll never make it as a pitcher." Cobb only tried harder. He tried so hard that he wore out his arm and had to switch to the outfield.

Edgar "Doc" Greene, who followed his father, Sam, into the *News's* sports department, added to the Cobb legend by recounting the baseball player's fights off the field, which were as notorious as those on the field. "Once," Greene wrote, "Cobb got into a fight with a night watchman at the Euclid Hotel in Cleveland and used a knife on him. The case went to the grand jury. The Detroit club spent more than $1,000 to get Cobb out of that one." On another occasion "Cobb entered a meat market in Detroit and waved a loaded .32 caliber revolver, declaring: 'Someone has insulted my wife.' The hassle was over a purchase of 20 cents worth of perch. A boy tried to protect the proprietor and Cobb went outside with him. Cobb handed the revolver to a bystander, his hat to another and proceeded to beat up the youngster. This time Cobb pleaded guilty to a charge of disturbing the peace and was fined $50. His attorney, James O. Murfin, said, in entering the guilty plea: 'Cobb regrets this incident to the bottom of his being. He has promised to control his temper in the future. He has had his lesson.' "

Detroiters familiar with such differences of opinion in their neighborhood groceries and saloons could understand. They understood the *News*'s Salsinger when he later wrote that Cobb's competitive instinct was his best asset. "Without this temperament Cobb could never have been the player he was. The trouble with most ballplayers is that they are too phlegmatic, taking matters as they come. Cobb never did. He created his own situations. Cobb had his faults as all mortals have, but he had virtues as well. Physical courage was one of them. His enemies were many and bitter, but nobody ever called him a coward."

From 1905 to 1921 Cobb's exploits were solely as a player. From 1921 to 1926 he continued as both player and manager of the team. At one time during his managing days, Ban Johnson, president of the American League, wanted Cobb to resign as manager because of the way he treated the players. Said Johnson: "Cobb ought to be training the Marines at Parris Island."

Charges of intentional spiking piled up every year. The most notable case occurred in 1909 when he slid hard into third base in a crucial game in Detroit against the Philadelphia Athletics. Frank "Home Run" Baker, the A's third baseman, was spiked on the arm while making the tag on Cobb. Philadelphia players charged that Cobb had spiked Baker intentionally and started a ruckus.[3] In the press section Philadelphia sportswriters relayed the incident back home by telegraphic wire. Philadelphians began writing letters of complaint as soon as the game ended. Cobb got several threats on his life. One writer said he would be sitting in the center field seats when the Tigers next played in Philadelphia, and he would shoot Cobb as soon as he trotted out to his position. The flap was unnecessary.

Covering the disputed game for the *News* photographic department was William Kuenzel, the paper's pioneer photographer. After the game, Kuenzel returned to the *News,* unaware of the controversy that was brewing over the play at third base. Kuenzel had printed several pictures of various plays in the game when the sports department called him to ask if he had a picture of the sliding action at third base. Kuenzel had none developed. Later he retrieved a plate he had discarded because it had a scratch on it, and developed the picture.

The photo eventually cleared Cobb of going out of his way to injure Baker. Explaining it, Cobb said, "Baker was in a strictly offensive attitude. The base path was mine by the rules. Baker's arms were extended to tag me." The photo showed that Cobb was pulling away from Baker in order to hook the bag. In the dangerous slide, Cobb was risking a serious leg injury to evade the third baseman. Eventually Philadelphia fans were mollified. Nothing happened when Cobb appeared there except that he played one of his best series of the year, offensively and defensively.

The years softened Cobb's approach to his fellow man. In 1958 he returned to Detroit for an appearance in uniform at an Old-Timer game. He had not lost his competitive spirit, but he apologized that at seventy-one he was "old and tired." The *News's* Watson Spoelstra sat with Cobb at a night game before the Saturday afternoon Old-Timer affair. Cobb watched with club owners of the Tigers from a box seat. He could not resist a habit of old: He gestured with a rolled-up scorecard as Detroit rallied to beat the Red Sox.

After the game Cobb sipped Scotch with the owners in the Tiger Stadium offices. He stayed until midnight, when Spoelstra traveled with him in a *News* car to a downtown hotel where the baseball immortal was staying. The two decided to have a nightcap. One followed another and after an hour, Spoelstra apologized that he would have to break up the conversation to return to the *News* and write the next day's story.

"I've had a long day myself," Cobb responded, "I got up at 5:30, then drove 90 miles from Cornelia, Georgia [where he lived] to the Atlanta airport. When I got to my hotel in Detroit the phone was ringing. A lot of people knew I was coming back and wanted to talk. I was on the phone all afternoon and didn't get a chance to take a nap." He had endured a nineteen-hour day.[4] The following afternoon he played ball with the Old-Timers.

Cobb died in 1961. Ralph McGill, columnist and publisher of the *Atlanta Constitution,* observed:

> All his days Ty Cobb was in competition with life, but chiefly with himself. For perhaps a dozen illness-plagued years he had been trying to get home again. Try as he would, he could not find the old dream and the old days of his youth in the hills of north Georgia where he was born. But he made it at last. He went to the mysterious eternal home yesterday afternoon just about the time players of his day would have been taking batting practice.[5]

Cobb brought to the hospital more than a million dollars worth of negotiable bonds that he placed on a table by his bed. He put a pistol on top of them. He was "eventually" convinced the valuables would be equally secure in the hospital safe.

Much of the material used in obituaries on Cobb throughout the country recounted stories that had been written earlier in a series of articles by Salsinger, who preceded Cobb in death by three years.

The *News* eulogy was written by Sam Greene, who quoted Salsinger in appraising Cobb as "the player's player just as was Christy Mathewson."

"I wouldn't want to be remembered as a doddering old man," said Cobb, the line Greene used to end his story.

At the time of Spoelstra's interview with Cobb, the *News* sportswriter knew that Cobb was a sick man. He had no idea just how sick until news of the former player's death was sent over the wires.

The debate then raged over whether Cobb, Babe Ruth or somebody else was the greatest baseball player of all time. Detroit was satisfied in letting Cobb's records speak for themselves. He broke 90 records. His lifetime batting average was .367. He batted over .400 three times. Said the *New York Herald-Tribune,* after comparing New York's own Sultan of Swat — Babe Ruth — with Cobb: "Of Ty Cobb, let it be said simply that he was the world's greatest ballplayer." As an all-around player he had no equal.

Cobb's career coincided with the city's growth as the automobile capital of the world. While his playing days had run out before baseball salaries had zoomed to $100,000 and higher for superstars, part of his wealth was to come from an investment in the "Motor City." One of his earlier stock purchases was in United Motors, which subsequently was acquired by General Motors Corporation. This and his Coca-Cola stock was to make him a fortune. He left an estate of $11,780,000.

That Detroit truly has been stirred by its athletic teams may be found by rereading what, possibly, may be the most reprinted editorial in the world, the inspirational classic, "Don't Die on Third" by William J. Cameron, the *News*'s editorial writer for fifteen years who later became a spokesman for Henry Ford. It first appeared in the *News* following a game played at old Bennett Park on May 28, 1909, between Detroit and Cleveland, which the Tigers won, 3 to 2.

Written as a moral lesson, its most poignant lines were recited for years in the city's schools.

Moriarty was at third.

Much as it meant to have advanced that far, nothing had been accomplished by it. Three-quarter runs are not marked up on the score boards. Third base runs never raised a pennant. Third base is not a destination, but the last little way station on the road home. It is better not to run at all than to run to third and "die." . . .

It is 90 feet from third to home. Sometimes that 90 feet is a leaden mile, sometimes a mere patter of lightning-like steps. If it is a mile to you, you are a failure, and the great circle of spectators groan for your incompetency; if it is but a lightning streak, you are the great man of the baseball day. . . .

Now the Cleveland pitcher is "winding up" his arm — round and round and round it swings — he poises himself — there is yet a fraction of a second in which he can recall his intended throw — Moriarty is crouched like a tiger about to spring — Now! Now!

There is a white streak across the field!

A cloud of dust at the home plate!

The umpire stands with his hands extended, palms downward.

A bursting roar of acclaim echoes and re-echoes across the space of the park. Again and again it bursts forth in thrilling electric power. Thirty-six thousand eyes strain toward the man who is slapping at the dust from his white uniform.

MORIARTY IS HOME!

All the world's a baseball diamond. You are one of the players. Perhaps you have reached first by your own efforts. It may be that the sacrifices of your parents and friends have enabled you to reach second. Then on someone's "long fly" into the business world — a "fly" that was not "long" enough to prevent him going out — or someone's fluke on the rules of simple morality and square dealing, you have advanced to third. The opposition against you at third is stronger than at either first or second. At third you are to be reckoned with. Your opponents converge all their attention on you. Pitchers and catcher, coaches and opposing fans, are watching to tip off your plans and frustrate them. From third you become either a splendid success or a dismal failure.

Don't die on third. . . .

Any fool could have led off spectacularly, but only a trained body and an alert mind could have stolen home right under the nose of the catcher whose hands were closing over the ball. Even a game means work. Work itself is a game and has its rules as its sudden openings. So, don't die on third. Bring to third every bit of your honest strength; study conditions; postpone thinking of your luck until you hear the umpire call "safe."

Then you'll score all right.[6]

As the city dipped into the Great Depression, the news of financial woes was softened by the successes of its growing sports greats. By 1935, in the depth of economic despair, Detroit could honestly hail itself as the "City of Champions." Among its champs were the Detroit Tigers, who had won the American League pennant in 1934, and in 1935 went on to win both the pennant and the World Series under Mickey "Black Mike" Cochrane. Cochrane had a temperament and fire reminiscent of Cobb. Winning the pennant was an elixir for the city's economic doldrums.[7] The celebration on October 7, 1935, was hailed by the News as greater "than the frenzy that followed the armistice of 1918." A man named Goose Goslin had singled home Cochrane to give the city its first World Series title since 1887. Almost instantly ticker tape rained down from towering office buildings. One million people, in the words of a traffic policeman, "Plain went wild."

That same year the city's champions included the Detroit Lions professional football team, struggling for recognition under coach George "Potsy" Clark.[8] By coincidence the team was quarterbacked by another Clark — Earl "Dutch" Clark — whose helmeted head gave him the appearance of a Roman gladiator. The Detroit Red Wings were still eleven years away from enjoying the services of Gordie Howe, for twenty-five years the greatest Wing of them all. But it had Jack Adams, who coached the team to the National Hockey League championship. Adams was so partial to the Wings that sportswriters had to avoid him whenever they had written something uncomplimentary about the team. "How dare you write something like that," he'd say. "Aren't you a loyal Detroiter?"

Walter Hagen, a star golfer for twenty years thereafter, was captain of the victorious 1935 Ryder Cup team. Hagen, who was born in Rochester, New York, made Detroit his home in 1918, when, after reaching early golf heights, he joined world-renowned Oakland Hills Country Club as its first professional. Although Hagen soon went on tour — the first golfer to do so — he kept Detroit as his home. He won the British Open four times, the Professional Golf Association championship five times — more than any other golfer — the United States Open twice. John Walter, who covered golf for forty-two years for the News, beginning in 1929, was closer to Hagen than any other golf writer. Walter's stories about "The Haig" have been repeated the world over. In 1967, as Hagen was dying of cancer in Traverse City, Michigan, the nation's professionals flocked to pay him homage. Fresh from winning his fiftieth golf tournament, Arnold Palmer arrived in his private jet. He said he would not miss the affair, for "Hagen has done more for golf than any other man." He paved the way to adulation for professional golfers in a world that considered pros almost like lackeys. He moved from a bench in the locker room to sit with the high and the mighty, including the Prince of Wales, a thing that shocked staid English country clubs but which America learned to love. Among the pallbearers was the News's golf writer.

Gar Wood, who had turned back a series of challengers to his line of *Miss America* motorboats, including Englishmen Kaye Don and Hubert Scott-Paine and Englishwoman Barbara "Betty" Carstairs, was the undisputed holder of the Harmsworth Trophy. He defeated Kaye Don with what the British called "a Yankee trick." Angered that Don had won the first heat, Wood sent his *Miss America X* screaming toward the starting line in the second heat in a bow-to-bow battle with the Englishman. Wood's brother, George, driving *Miss America VIII,* trailed the two over the line. Gar had led Kaye Don over the starting line two seconds ahead of the gun. Both boats were disqualified, and with Wood's brother finishing the race, the cup stayed in America.[9] On the day of the race, September 8, 1931, Gar Wood told the *News:* "When they told me I couldn't have it [a forty-five-minute delay] I made up my mind I would show Don a trick or two. I planned the start. I said I would be over that line first if I were a minute ahead of the gun, and if Don wanted to follow me that was his business. George [Wood's brother] was to stay back in *Miss America VIII* and made a fair start. Everything went off as we had planned." The next day, in an effort to calm a British uproar, Gar Wood denied in the *News* that the caper was planned. It happened, he said, only because he had given Orlin Johnson, his mechanic, orders to beat Kaye Don over the line. That he beat the gun and the Briton followed him was just one of those things. The maneuver inspired Harry LeDuc, *News* sports editor, into hailing Gar Wood as "The Gray Fox of Algonac." Ever after he was "The Gray Fox."

The year also marked a new record for Eddie Tolan, Olympics medal winner, who won the pro sprint title in Melbourne, Australia.

And there was a fellow named Joe (Barrow) Louis. Born in Alabama, Louis moved with his family to Detroit to live in the city's black belt on the lower east side. One day he walked into the Brewster Recreation Center and looked around. There he saw a young fighter, Thurston McKinney, with a small golden glove pinned to his sweater.

"Where did you get it?" Louis asked.

"I won it with the boxing team," McKinney replied.

"I got to get me one of them," mumbled Louis.[10]

At his mother's insistence Louis had been learning to play the violin. He began to skip his lessons to appear at the recreation center. Almost as soon as he donned boxing gloves he was recognized as a natural. He was strong from working summers on an ice truck. Entering Detroit's Golden Gloves tournament, then sponsored by the *Free Press,* he moved quickly to the top. *Free Press* sports editor Charles Ward dubbed him "The Brown Bomber," a name that in its day offended no one.

Louis's first professional fight lasted one round on July 4, 1934, in Chicago. His victim was an obscure heavyweight, Jack Kracken, who went down in a flurry of Louis punches that was to mark his style for fights to come. And come they did. He fought seventy-one matches, losing only three. Kracken was the first victim of fifty-four knockouts. As Louis battled to the top, the *News* noted editorially that "The World Loves a Winner." Said the paper:

> A year ago Joe Louis had so few friends in Detroit and so little money that he had to borrow money from the *Chicago Tribune* to go to Chicago for a fight. Now Louis has $215,000 as his share of the Max Baer fight gate and tens of thousands of friends who insist they "knew him when." Truly, the world loves a winner.[11]

A year later Salsinger, who had seen them all since he joined the *News* in 1907, predicted that Louis would be the best fighter of all time:

> Louis, a boxer still two years removed from his peak, is being pronounced as a greater fighter than John Lawrence Sullivan, James J. Corbett, Robert Fitzsimmons, James J. Jeffries and Jack Dempsey. Nothing like this has ever happened before. No heavyweight champion in history was ever considered as anything more than a good prospect after 18 months of professional boxing. Louis should continue flattening the heavyweights of the world and by the time he retires he undoubtedly will be nominated the greatest fighter of all time by acclamation.[12]

Each Louis victory made Detroit delirious. The city's blacks never were more enthralled and the whites couldn't have felt better about having a Brown Bomber as the premier heavyweight of

James E. Scripps

George G. Booth

W. E. Scripps

Warren S. Booth

Peter B. Clark

The paper's first building

The second building

Home editorial and business offices

New North plant serving metropolitan, suburban circulation

A wild celebration in the midst of Depression — Detroit wins the World
Series

The Brown Bomber: Joe Louis giving Bob Pastor the "one-two"

Nancy Brown, a contemporary of Beatrice Fairfax, and 50,000 Detroiters at sunrise service at Nancy Brown Peace Carillon

The funeral of Gerald Buckley, radio commentator slain in gangland fashion, drew a crowd of former listeners who never learned the names of the real killers

The Real Victim of Racial Discord

Bobby Layne, hailed by many as one of the first "superstar" quarterbacks, turned the corner for professional football in Detroit. With Layne came the first season ticket sales of 40,000 and more

Mickey Lolich, popular for his pitching and his potbelly

the world. The city mourned when, on June 19, 1936, Louis was defeated by Max Schmeling, a product of Nazi Germany, in the twelfth round. But the return match on June 22, 1938, bolstered the ego of the city and the nation. Louis pummeled the German heavyweight unmercifully, stalking him around the ring, and nailing him to the canvas in 2:04 minutes of the first round.

After retiring from the ring a champion, Louis, pinched financially, attempted to return to the throne in a fight with Rocky Marciano, in New York, in 1951. Louis was thirty-seven, long past his peak, and Marciano a vibrant twenty-eight. Marciano won the fight in eight rounds. In his corner, his nose bleeding, the winner explained, "Joe caught me with a few left jabs but he didn't have much on the right." The left, right — one, two — punch, which had carried Louis to the top, no longer had its zing. A year later Louis returned to Detroit to visit friends and to perform. He was touring the country as a comedian and a tap dancer. A photographer wanted one more picture of Louis, the fighter. "I don't have any boxing trunks," Louis explained. "I don't even know where I can find a pair."

This was Salsinger's appraisal:

Louis did for boxing what Babe Ruth did for baseball, only more so. Joe came into the fight game when it was controlled by the survivors of the bootleg wars. Fixed bouts were the order of the day. Boxing had reached its lowest level and Louis pulled the game out of the gutter. Louis set a standard for ring conduct and boxing decency. He came closer to being the perfect champion than any man before him. He always did the right thing, instinctively and not by design.

While Cobb had helped immensely in building baseball into a national pastime, Babe Ruth gave it a transfusion — the home run ball — when it was beginning to waver. Louis did much the same thing for boxing, which had known its heyday, had slipped into near oblivion, and was brought leaping to life with his bombing fists.

The fortune Louis earned in the ring was dissipated in bad

management, sapped away by would-be friends. In 1970 a group was organized in Detroit to help him straighten out his financial affairs by tossing a civic dinner. Prices for the affair were rated much as they are at boxing matches. The closer to "ringside," the speaker's table, the higher the cost — from $5 to $1,000. For years Louis had been in hock to the Internal Revenue Service, and sickness added to his travail. The champ did not show up for the celebration although it had been announced he would. Mental illness kept him away. It would have been a traumatic homecoming for even a healthy man who had hit such heroic heights, only to topple to the nadir of accepting charity. Among the guests was Thurston McKinney whose golden glove had inspired Louis's career.[13]

Hitler's invasion of Poland on September 1, 1939, and the increasingly obvious German moves toward world conquest gradually changed the City of Champions into the Arsenal of Democracy. On July 15, 1940, France surrendered and Der Führer snapped his fingers, chuckled and did a goose step. In America there was a division of thought between "America Firsters" and those who thought the nation should enter the war before it was too late. On September 23, 1940, conscription was signed into law in the United States. And that month the Detroit Tigers were heading down the stretch to the American League pennant, only to falter in the World Series. On March 11, 1941, the Lend-Lease Act was signed into law and the city's industrialists turned to making armaments for the allied nations. The attack by the Japanese on Pearl Harbor on December 7, 1941, and America's declaration of war had a direct effect on professional sports.

Reflecting the drain of the draft, the caliber of the nation's sports teams deteriorated. That sports were allowed to continue at all was a decision in the interest of providing war workers with some alleviating diversion from news flowing from the war zones. Sports events also were piped by Armed Forces Radio as a morale booster to men doing the fighting. By the fall of 1945, the Tigers again led the American League. Why shouldn't they? critics asked. The St. Louis Browns had been reduced to using a one-armed ballplayer, and the other players were so infirm they often tripped over their own feet rounding the bases. The critique was not entirely accurate. Pete Gray, who lost his right arm in a childhood accident, had proven himself an adept player in the minors. A number of top athletes suffered handicaps that excused them from the war but did not deter them from playing baseball.[14] Among them were Hal Newhouser and Dizzy Trout, both 4-F as soldiers but A-1 as pitchers. With Newhouser, a 25-and-7 pitcher in 1945, and Trout, 18-and-15, the Tigers won the pennant and defeated the Chicago Cubs in the World Series (4 to 3). The city was doubly joyous. It was the first time the Tigers had won a pennant in a decade. And the war had ended a few weeks earlier when the Japanese surrendered in a rite aboard the battleship *Missouri*, on September 2.

Now the city went to work to reconvert its factories from producing war goods to automobiles. And its athletic teams, with men returning from service, set about to find new heroes.

But Detroit was not to have a superstar it could admire with the intensity it loved Louis until the arrival of Bobby Layne, a blond Texan, whose antics off the field nearly excelled those on the gridiron. With Layne at quarterback, the Detroit Lions won National Football League championships in 1952 and 1953. After defeating the Cleveland Browns in the 1952 season, the Lions found themselves in a championship match with the same opponent the following year. With less than three minutes left to go, the Lions trailed, 16 to 10.

"Give me a little time, boys," Layne said with a throat made scratchy from the activities of the night before. "Do a little blocking and I'll have you in the Chicago All-Star game." In less than sixty seconds Layne advanced the team the length of the field for a 17 to 16 victory and the title. The victory marked the turning point for professional football in Detroit. The Lions never again had to worry about empty seats in the stadium. The tradition of selling over forty thousand season tickets every year was born. The time would come when the club could arbitrate where it would play, in downtown Detroit or in the suburbs. Its future was a foregone conclusion.

In 1954 the Browns and the Lions were at it again, this time in Cleveland. The *News* published the following dialogue between Nick Kerbawy, the Lions' general manager, and Layne. Kerbawy had met Layne in the Lions' hotel lobby in Cleveland as the team prepared to board a bus for the stadium.

"How do you feel, Bobby?" Kerbawy asked.

"Super," replied Layne. "I had just about ten hours in the sack."

Kerbawy frowned. He turned away and muttered, "We're in trouble — Bobby had a good night's sleep."

He was right. In a touted air battle, Layne was outmaneuvered by the Brown's Otto Graham who carried his team to a lopsided victory. The night's sleep — or the loss — was Layne's eventual undoing. The next season Lions' Coach Buddy Parker obtained passer Tobin Rote, whom he planned to alternate with Layne when Layne came up flat. The formula did not work. The Lions had been Layne's team; he could not share the players with a newcomer. When Parker discovered in spring practice that the plan would not work, he stood before a fan club dinner in Detroit and shocked the gathering by abruptly announcing, "I quit. I can't handle this team anymore."

Layne stayed with the Lions until 1958, when he was traded to the Pittsburgh Steelers. But his memory lingered on as the Detroit team tried quarterback after quarterback, hoping to find one with Layne's passing ability, ball-handling finesse, and crowd-pleasing charm. In fifteen years in the NFL Layne surpassed his boyhood hero, Sammy Baugh, another Texan, in many record areas. When he was asked about this, Layne sighed: "Records don't mean much. They only remind you you're getting old."[15]

The player's night-owling antics were legend. Players who tried to keep up with Layne in his nightly rounds shortened their careers considerably. "I may feel pretty bad a lot of times at practice," he was quoted as saying. "But I work just as hard as anybody. I don't baby myself."

Layne's humor seldom wavered in adverse situations. In 1957, when he broke his right leg in a game with the Browns, Edgar "Doc" Greene, the *News* sports columnist, visited him at the Detroit Osteopathic Hospital where Layne was holding court, his leg in a cast. "A guy from another team called this morning," he told Greene, "and asked how I felt. I told him, 'I feel terrible, I got in all kinds of trouble last night. I've been drinking cold milk all morning.'"

Other stories were spun. Layne recounted that when he was in Texas he was arrested after an all-night spree and haled into court. The prosecutor argued that when the police officer arrested Layne he was unable to understand him. "Mr. Layne had a case of laryngitis," his lawyer retorted.

To which the prosecutor's rejoinder was: "What? A whole case?"[16]

Greene's own life-style was quite apart from most newsmen and he sympathized with Layne's plight. Greene emerged from World War II, scarred from a raking-over by Japanese marksmen, and determined to live the rest of his life to the full. With a Hemingway interpretation of life, he lived with sports figures and wrote about them as they really were. He painted no artificial heroes. Toward the end of his life, he joined in a syndicate, unknown to *News* editor Martin Hayden, to promote a heavyweight fight in Detroit featuring Cassius Clay (Muhammad Ali) when Clay was in disfavor for seeking to dodge the draft on religious principles. The first Hayden heard about Greene's efforts came when Poorman, the assistant managing editor, saw an Associated Press telegraph story out of Philadelphia, quoting Greene as saying he was among the sponsors of a Clay fight in Detroit. Poorman took the story to Hayden and asked if there was any truth to it. Since the story mentioned an appearance of the fight sponsors before Michigan's Governor William G. Milliken, Hayden telephoned Milliken and asked him if he had talked to Greene. "Sure," Milliken said, "the *News* sent him to see me, didn't it?" Hayden assured Milliken the paper had not. The editor then called Greene to his office. Had Greene cleared the proposal with anyone in authority at the paper? Greene said he met Edwin K. Wheeler, the paper's executive vice president in a *News* restroom one day and mentioned that Clay might fight in Detroit. There was no request or permission. Hayden said the *News* did not care to sponsor such a fight in view of the feelings of many people in the nation about Clay's antidraft actions.

He fired Greene after the columnist admitted his part in the promotion.[17] On his way out of Hayden's office, he mumbled to Mrs. Dorothea Ryan, assistant to the editor, "Nothing's sacred around here anymore." The remark could be interpreted in many ways.

Layne's impact on Detroit was summed up in a quotation by Lion Joe Schmidt. "I'm sick," moaned Schmidt, a linebacker who later took over as head coach. "They've just traded the guy who made pro football in this town."[18]

Layne continued to play with the Steelers without singular success until 1962, when he rested on his laurels.

After the city's 1967 riot, the need for something to heal the wounds was obvious to blacks and whites. The Detroit Tigers again played a large role in reviving the city's spirit. Two players who took a leading role were Dennis McLain, a hellion of the stripe of Layne, and Mickey Lolich, two white pitchers. With the support of black players, including Willie Horton, slugging left fielder, and Gates Brown, a leading pinch hitter in the league for several seasons, the team was able to "put it all together" to take the American League pennant. The disharmony on the streets visibly ebbed as the ball club moved into the World Series.

While the blacks and whites joined in the team effort, McLain and Lolich did little to hide their personal feelings toward each other as they vied for public acclaim. McLain played the organ in nightclubs, flew his own airplane and got special clubhouse privileges that were overlooked in the drive for the championship. He would end the season a thirty-one-game winner. Lolich, who frowned on McLain's off-field behavior, saw himself suffering in the publicity department by his exemplary behavior. While McLain left games early and circled the field in his plane, Lolich simply popped aboard his motorcycle and went home.

McLain was trim of body, a determined pitcher who seldom lost his concentration on the mound. Lolich's potbelly was the object of concern of everyone on the ball club but Lolich. He told Spoelstra that the potbelly really was a thing of economic value to the Tigers: "I'm a hero to the guy watching television," he said. "He sees me strike out the side and hollers to his wife: 'See the fat guy, hon. That's Mickey Lolich and he just struck out Frank Howard. Get me another beer.' "

While McLain involved himself with the gambling fraternity, which eventually was to bring about his fall from the pinnacle, Lolich felt he got where he was and stayed there because his "guardian angel was working overtime." To Spoelstra he said, "Remember when Danny Cater's line drive hit me on the left arm in Oakland? The doctor said the elbow would have been shattered if I had been hit an inch lower." When he still was in the minors, he recalled, he had been struck in the face by a line drive. "My cheekbone was broken and I lost two teeth. An inch higher and it would have gotten my eye." Then Lolich paused, his eyes twinkling, and told Spoelstra: "I always did say baseball was a game of inches." And guardian angels.

In the 1968 season, Lolich won seventeen games but the mass of publicity went to McLain.[19] McLain had excited the city more than any athlete since Lynwood "Schoolboy" Rowe had arrived from El Dorado, Arkansas, talked about his Edna, pitched sixteen consecutive victories while running up a 24 and 8 record in 1934 to help the Tigers to the first of two straight pennants. The romance hit high key when Rowe appeared on the Eddie Cantor radio show in 1934, said he aspired to be an announcer, spoke a few lines, then whispered into the microphone, "How'm I doin', Edna?" The line became famous. For the 1934 World Series the News brought Edna Mary Skinner to Detroit to write on baseball, cooking or whatever. The move sent the romance to a fever pitch and after the series the couple married. Detroit and much of the nation was enraptured. His arm weary, Rowe was optioned to the minor leagues in 1938.

Before he left, News photographer Rolland R. Ransom was sent to the stadium to get a parting photograph. The photo made sports history, winning Ransom thirty-one awards. He pictured the fallen hero in street clothes, walking off the mound toward the stands he had filled so many times. No photo of the back of a man ever said so much.

Lolich was a different breed. When St. Louis sportswriters ridiculed his paunch and his stance on the mound, Lolich retorted that his build was a family trait. When someone asked him why he didn't pull up his pants, which let his belt ride on his hips, he declared, "I'm a gunslinger from the West. We wear our pants low out there." He was not to be perturbed by ridicule. If he was to get angry at anyone it would be Lolich. Lolich had to show the part he played in the Tigers' pennant surge. And show it he did.[20]

The series ran the full seven games. McLain, the recognized superstar, lost the opener. Lolich slipped in a victory before Earl Wilson and McLain lost two more, making the series one and three. Then Lolich won his second game, followed by McLain's first win. When the seventh game arrived, it was not McLain but Lolich whose job it was to clinch the flag.

As he paused in his windup, his pitching hand holding the ball in his glove, resting on his potbelly, the Cardinals did not know whether to laugh or cry. When Lolich's fast ball outsped the heralded blue streak of Cardinal Bob Gibson, the Tiger who had played second fiddle all season suddenly was given a new appraisal. Lolich was ready for the newspapermen and television reporters who rushed to the winning team's locker room after the game.

"What did you have for breakfast?" gushed one reporter.

"Tiger juice," Lolich promptly replied.

On the charter flight to Detroit after the series windup, Lolich confided to Pete Waldmeir, *News* sports columnist: "I guess I'm an unlikely hero. Potbelly, big ears. Just a steady guy who shows up every day and gets the job done as well as he knows how." Again, Detroiters could understand such thinking.

The final game of the series stopped normal work in Detroit. Workers were either glued to transistor radios or, where possible, to a television screen. As if on signal, as soon as the final pitch had been delivered, horns began to blow on Detroit streets and public sirens wailed. A group of reporters and editors climbed to the roof of the *News* building to watch the city celebrate. Already the streets were bedlam. Ticker tape flowed from the top floors of office buildings and, blessed by a soft, wafting updraft, floated for blocks, undulating all the way from Griswold, the center of the financial district, to Third Street where it drifted onto the roof of the paper's nine-level garage.

After the first few moments traffic was hopelessly snarled. The town that just fifteen months before had witnessed its worst race riot was in the mood for love. Whites riding in open cars were greeted by blacks on street corners, shouting, "We did it, brothers. We did it." Blacks got out of their cars and danced in the streets with celebrating whites. The festivities lasted throughout the night. At dawn's early light streetsweepers went to work to brush up the debris. What they would not sweep away was the feeling that brotherhood could result from mutual endeavor and mutual victory. A sports team had shown the way. It was up to others to build a firmer foundation.

12

We Helped Give the City a Face-Lift

GRACING THE SOUTHERLY SIDE of the city's downtown area, Detroit's Civic Center stretches along the river that links Lakes Erie and St. Clair. An integral part of the St. Lawrence Seaway, the river is an artery in the lifeline of middle America to the sea. Lake freighters and ocean-going cargo vessels pass by with a frequency that makes the river the busiest waterway in the world, busier than the Panama and Suez canals ever were. As the sun sets, the city's skyline reflects in the water, the elongated shadows of its skyscrapers slicing nearly to the shore of Windsor, Detroit's Canadian neighbor. The Civic Center buildings include Cobo Hall and Arena. Cobo Hall is the nation's second largest convention center, next to Chicago's McCormick Place. The arena, which houses sports and entertainment events, lies adjacent to the Henry and Edsel Ford Auditorium. With a blocked, ebony face, the auditorium has the shape of a curved, rectangular phonograph speaker. It houses Detroit's symphony orchestra. There is a ten-story Veterans Memorial Building; the beginning of a hotel, restaurant and apartment complex and a gigantic fountain designed so that its multicolored waters would flow in mechanical rhythm symbolic of the city's thumping industry. At the eastern terminus is Mariner's Church, built in 1848, where windjammer sailors and those who frequented Billy Boushaw's saloon sought spiritual succor. The Civic Center, the freighters passing by, the saving of the old limestone and mortar church — and much more — is not just an accident of history. The part the *News* played in giving the city this heart that pumps blood into the cold industrial skeleton has continued virtually without pause since the paper's beginning.

In late February 1911, George E. Miller was sitting in the paper's Washington Bureau when he was visited by Michigan Senator-elect Charles E. Townsend. The two got to chatting about Townsend's future on Capitol Hill.

"George," Townsend said after some reflection, "what I need is some program, some campaign, that is popular with my constituents and which I can fight for whenever the opportunity presents itself."

Miller stroked his chin, then said, "I think I've got just the thing for you. Just last night I was listening to a speech by a power lobbyist who was arguing that we ought to deepen the St. Lawrence River system, enlarge the locks to let bigger, deep-drafted ocean vessels into the Great Lakes. By giving farmers and industrialists a water route to world markets, business would grow. There'd be more jobs. Lake ports would become sea ports."[1]

It was a fresh idea to Townsend, but after considering the implications he patted Miller on the knee and, using an expression later popularized in song, declared, "By George, I think you've got it."

Townsend spent the next days preparing a bill. The night before he introduced it he showed it to President Taft, winning his approval. It was presented in Congress on March 3, 1911. That same day the *News* headlined the story by Miller on Page One. The first paragraph read: "Senator-elect Townsend, of Michigan, sprung a tremendous surprise on the country today. . . ." His bill calling for a reciprocity with Canada proposed "a project of such magnitude that once understood by the people of the United States and Canada, all opposition to the agreement will be compelled to yield."[2]

Told ahead of time of the upcoming bill, the *News* was ready to give the recommendation full editorial support. On the same day the bill was introduced, the paper devoted nearly a column of its editorial page to extolling the merits of the plan. The *News* said the seaway would make Detroit a port of call for Liverpool, Glasgow and Hamburg steamships, and make the swish of the lake at the docks of Duluth and Fort William "tidewater." The editorial cited possible eastern opposition, and said, "This nation does not consist of New York City nor of New England. What if their docks do not see an increase of trade so long as the traffic of this nation which makes and unmakes ports, finds its way with the greatest economy to its market?"[3] A second editorial followed the next day. And more were to come — a stream of thought that continued for almost fifty years.

The legislator pounded away at the proposal so often that by the time he left office in 1917 he had picked up the nickname of "Seaway Townsend."

Urged by the *News* and Michigan congressmen, each successive U.S. President endorsed the seaway for its economic potential to middle America. Each renewed resolution was fought vigorously by eastern seaport cities and railroads who foresaw a loss of revenue they currently derived from hauling grain and cargo from middle America to eastern ports and Europe.

Among the *News* editorial writers assigned to extolling the benefits of a new seaway was Karl Miller, whose father was the Washington Bureau chief and later editor of the *News* who gave the idea for the waterway to Senator Townsend. As Karl Miller wrote, he would utter his sentences aloud in a quirk that amused his compatriots.

In the 1940s, W. K. Kelsey, the paper's "Commentator" for twenty-five years, stopped Miller in the heat of editorial inspiration by asking, "Karl, don't you get tired of talking to yourself?"

Miller replied: "Not at all. It goes in one ear and out the other."

Of Kelsey, whose articles often ran counter to the paper's editorial policy, George Miller, his early editor, said: "If Sousa's band played 'Stars and Stripes Forever,' marching down Woodward Avenue, Kelsey would say it was the most unpatriotic thing he had ever seen or heard." As an editorial writer Kelsey would write memos to the editor "to educate him." Some were so good George Miller signed them with phony names and published them in the Public Letter Box.[4] When Gilmore became editor, his discussions with editorial writers also were memoed by Kelsey. But instead of publishing the contrary opinion in the Public Letter Box,

Gilmore made Kelsey a columnist, reasoning that the writer's independence of thought gave the paper's editorial pages a balance of opinion. Kelsey's opinions often were more highly commented upon than the *News*'s own. Yet, when the paper supported the seaway, Kelsey gave it his full endorsement.

Editorial support arrived all the way from France and England where Russell Barnes, foreign affairs writer, headed a *Detroit News* bureau in the late 1920s. Barnes discovered European shippers saw the immediate economic value of carrying goods directly to their destination in middle America. The new seaway proved them right by avoiding the costs of transshipping goods from eastern ports by rail. The paper's Washington Bureau kept pace with the campaign by importuning legislators and successive Presidents.

In the spring of 1953 the *News*'s editor-in-chief Harry V. Wade met one of the paper's feature writers on the sidewalk outside the *News* building. He tapped the young man on the shoulder and said, "How are your sea legs?" The writer confessed he had never been to sea. Wade smiled enigmatically, and said, "You'll find out pretty soon," then walked on.

The conversation resulted in the first trip by a midwestern newspaperman from the port of Detroit in an ocean freighter constructed small enough — a maximum of 250 feet in length — to negotiate the antique St. Lawrence Seaway locks. The old seaway had been built in the 1800s to accommodate sailing vessels. The reporter's trip from Detroit to Quebec took six days. At the Long Sault Rapids, on the St. Lawrence, the vessel was shot along, without steerage, at twelve to fifteen miles an hour. A dam and a lock were needed to eliminate this navigational hazard. At existing canals, lockmasters handcranked the gates that opened and released Great Lakes water as it fell some six hundred feet in its twelve-hundred-mile journey from the head of the lakes to the sea. The trip across the Atlantic took nine days. What the *News* succeeded in doing through the trip was to dramatize for Detroit and the nation a seaway that long ago had become obsolete. Since the 1930s European shipping companies had gotten minimal use out of the old seaway by using specially designed small ships. How much greater the traffic would be with a seaway that would allow bigger ships to call at Great Lakes ports.

Articles were published daily for fourteen weeks.[5] In the months and years to follow, the paper's arguments increased. In 1954 Congress passed the bill that authorized construction of a new waterway. Among the reporters to make the historic maiden trip over the new seaway, which was opened in April 1959, was Stoddard White, *News* marine writer, whose father Lee A White was the paper's first public relations director. The vessel White rode was more than twice the length of the ships that traversed the old seaway and it carried twice the cargo. Under *News* pressure for a public port facility, private shipping interests enlarged their terminals to handle increased trade once it had arrived. Cities throughout the Great Lakes system were quick to take advantage of the economic value of the new seaway. Milwaukee, with a public terminal, was ready for the traffic long before it was a fact.

Newspapers in the port cities of Cleveland, Toledo, Chicago and Duluth had added their editorial support in beating down the opposition to the seaway. The *News* campaign, lasting forty-eight years, was the longest in the paper's history of crusades.

Just as the seaway produced critics, the paper's campaign for riverfront development was under persistent attack. George Gough Booth, the *News*'s second publisher, was bombarded first by the *Detroit Journal,* in 1912, and in 1924 and thereafter by the *Detroit Times.* The *Journal* called Booth the "Baron of Cranbrook," a pseudonym that referred to Booth's purchase in 1905 of three hundred acres of farmland in Bloomfield Hills, Michigan, where he had established a farm estate. The *Times* was even less kind. In 1924 it picked up the chant of mayoral candidate John W. Smith, who was angered by the *News*'s opposition to his candidacy.[6] Smith called Booth the "Duke of Cranbrook," giving him a royal title more commensurate with the publisher's development of Cranbrook as a world-renowned cultural and educational center. Cranbrook eventually came under the guidance of Booth's son Henry and Eliel Saarinen, the famed architect. But on October 29, 1924, the *Times* quoted Smith as saying, "George Booth, who lives on his great estate of Cranbrook, in Oakland County, which is patrolled by armed guards — for the very good reason that he fears the hundreds of men he has wronged through his newspaper — this Duke of Cranbrook tries to tell voters of Detroit that I am not fit to be mayor."[7]

Elected mayor, Smith continued his vendetta against the *News* and Booth. When John Lodge, serving as council president, was supported by the *News* for a proposed new riverfront development, Smith charged on November 3, 1927, that the paper owned eleven pieces of property on the site, assessed at $1,140,230, and hoped to prosper by their resale. The *News* responded three days later with a map of the proposed development site showing none of the property was owned by the *News* or any of its directors.[8] Smith then admitted that the parcels were not on the site but declared they were close enough to appreciate in value. Lodge came to the paper's defense ten days later and listed the ownership of the eleven pieces.[9] The owners were the W. A. Scripps Company, founded by a brother of the paper's founder, who had no connection with the paper, Clarence A. Booth, cousin of George Booth, and J. E. Scripps Company, an independent investment company begun by the paper's founder. Lodge declared that in any event no property owner on the site or near it would benefit because the proposal included a clause that would elevate the taxes of all surrounding property commensurate with the appreciated value. In the midst of the hassle, the *Times* disclosed that several of the eleven properties owned by kin of the *News*'s owners were occupied by whorehouses.[10] This much, at least, was fact.

Undaunted by the attack, the *News* continued an unabated campaign for riverfront development. As Lodge's proposal reached the planning stage, the 1929 Crash knocked it into oblivion. Only when the city and the nation began to climb out of the Depression did the *News* return to the fight. On June 8, 1937, the paper ran an opening editorial of a new campaign, headlined "Build It on the River." The editorial decried Detroit's lack of a hall that could compete for business with convention centers in Cleveland, Kansas City, St. Louis and Atlantic City.[11] A ten-year campaign was hailed on June 4, 1947, in an editorial familiarly entitled

"Return to the River." The editorial hailed the breaking of ground for the first unit of the Civic Center, a war memorial building. It said:

> Too long has this city, founded by lakefarers and nourished to greatness by lake navigation, turned its back on the sparkling blue strait from which it took its name. . . . All that is to change now. Detroit is to face about and enjoy the beauty of its river where its past began and where, too, its future largely lies . . . with the St. Lawrence Seaway at long last nearing realization. . . .[12]

The development of the city culturally had the steadiness of childbirth and sometimes the pain. When the Detroit Institute of Arts commissioned Mexican artist Diego Rivera to paint murals on the walls of its garden court, the city waited anxiously to view the result of his genius. The viewing created a furore. The controversial artist had been in and out of the Communist party several times and his murals appeared to many Detroiters to reflect his politics. They depicted man and machine in a montage that critics said robbed the workingman of his dignity. In the heat of the controversy, the *News* editorialized that "owing to the criticism of so many . . . perhaps the best thing to do would be to whitewash the entire work completely and return the court to its original beauty." It was an editorial that enlightened editors in a later day would rue with dismay. The murals stayed.

A gift of 2.5 million by the Ford Motor Company Fund and by individual Ford and Lincoln-Mercury dealers made the second Civic Center building a possibility — a symphonic auditorium. Next to follow in 1960 was the $54 million Cobo Hall and Arena, named after Mayor Albert E. Cobo, who had the acumen necessary to put together the financial package while serving for years as the city's treasurer. While the Civic Center buildings were underway, Robert L. Wells, City-County Building reporter, was assigned to plunk for other downtown improvements. On April 10, 1958, Wells reported that five plans were under consideration for the construction of underground parking facilities to alleviate a critical parking shortage created largely by new expressway and building construction.[13] One of the plans called for the razing of Detroit's historic yellow sandstone city hall and the erection of an underground garage on the site, topped off by a park and a pool. The paper's own "Town Talk" columnist George W. Stark, a former city editor, gave vent editorially to a citizen campaign to "Save Old City Hall."[14] At the same time the paper editorially supported its removal for the sake of progress. The old city hall, the *News's* William Tremblay wrote, cost the city $100,000 a year to preserve as a shrine. Its purpose had died when a new City-County Building arose in the Civic Center area. The old structure was razed in 1961 and the garage and park completed six years later.

In 1963, four years after he became editor-in-chief, Martin Hayden lunched with Cavanagh, the new mayor. The conversation naturally gravitated to the Civic Center.

"The one thing missing in the whole plan is a great fountain," Cavanagh said. "But fountains are costly."

The number of Detroiters who could afford to give the city such a gift ran through Hayden's mind. "How about Mrs. Horace E. Dodge?" he asked.

Cavanagh liked the suggestion but both men wondered how they could approach Mrs. Dodge, then ninety-six and living a secluded life in her Lake Shore mansion.[15] The solution was soon forthcoming. An article by Eleanor Breitmeyer, *News* society editor, accompanied by color photographs that appeared in the Sunday Magazine turned the trick. Seeing the magazine, Mrs. Dodge instructed her social secretary to phone Hayden and relate her delight. Could Mrs. Dodge have a set of the photographs taken of her mansion? Of course. Not only could she have them but Hayden would see to it personally. With the package of photographs the editor included this letter:

Dear Mrs. Dodge: Let me apologize in advance for what you will consider a most presumptuous letter. I am writing, however, because I know of no other than this direct way to present to you some thoughts and a suggestion.

Let me say first that many years ago my father, who wrote from Washington for the *News,* was a friend and admirer of the two

Dodge brothers. As a youngster, and since, I have heard him describe those days of Mayors Thompson, Marx and Couzens, of the Russell House and the old Pontchartrain Hotel, of the infant auto industry and of the Dodges who had so much to do with its growth and benefits to all of us who were born in Detroit.

This was the background against which I returned to Detroit from the Washington Bureau to become editor of the *News*. Full of it, I was interested in the expressways, auditoriums and buildings by which the names of most of the greats of the automotive birth years — Ford, Couzens, Fisher, Chrysler, were memorialized. I was also struck by the fact that the Dodge name was prominent in just one place — the John and Horace Dodge Memorial Hall of Industry — at the Historical Museum. It is a fine memorial for those who see it and recognize it. Unfortunately, the great mass of Detroiters is unaware of its existence.

As you already have probably assumed, I have an idea in which I would hope you might be interested.

You may already be aware that the Master Plan for the riverfront development calls for a reflection pool and fountain to be built on the riverfront below Woodward avenue and between Ford Auditorium and the Veterans Memorial Building.

Hayden related further plans for the fountain, then said, "To me it seems appropriate that it be the 'Horace Dodge Fountain.' "[16] If the idea remotely interested her, Hayden said, he would be happy to pay her a visit, accompanied by the mayor. The idea did interest the widow of Horace E. Dodge, and she sent word to Hayden that she would discuss the proposal. Because of her advanced years and ailments the visit was restricted to fifteen minutes. To bolster their proposal, Cavanagh and Hayden took a film clip of a world-famous fountain in Barcelona, Spain, to show to Mrs. Dodge.

She saw her visitors in the Music Room of her home, Rose Terrace, in Grosse Pointe Farms. The fifteen-minute visit limitation lengthened into over an hour as Mrs. Dodge's interest grew. After the film was shown, she expressed interest in the idea and told her callers she would let them know her decision. Hayden returned to the *News* office and wrote a short letter thanking Mrs. Dodge for her kindness. There the matter stood for a year. Then, while

Hayden was in Washington, conferring with Jerry ter Horst, chief of the paper's capital bureau, he received a phone call from Mrs. Dodge's attorney, who had called the *News* and learned his whereabouts.

"What about this fountain?" the attorney asked.

"What fountain?" Hayden replied.

"The fountain Mrs. Dodge intends to leave the city of Detroit in her will," the attorney explained. "How much will it cost?" he persisted.

Hayden paused a moment, then thought a million dollars would build it. The conversation ended and Hayden went about his business. Shortly, there was a second call from the attorney.

"Mrs. Dodge is leaving $2,000,000," he said. "She said costs have gone up."

Hayden returned to Detroit assured that the jewel had been set in the Civic Center Plaza. Sunday Magazine writer Jane Schermerhorn, whose uncle James Schermerhorn had published the *Detroit Times* before the Hearst era, wrote the story. It told how the fountain was conceived by the editor and the mayor, how Mrs. Dodge's will would make it a reality. Under specific orders the bequest was not to be publicized until after Mrs. Dodge's death. She was to live six more years. When she died, at the age of 103, the article, which had been set in type years before, was published in the magazine.[17] The fountain was designed by Isamu Noguchi, a Japanese-American sculptor. Arguments over its design and exact location brought litigation that stalled construction until early 1973.

The Historical Museum to which Hayden had referred in the letter to Mrs. Dodge had also been a project of the *News*. Funds for erection of the building were contributed during World War II through a campaign conducted by Stark through his column. By now Stark, a former city editor, had become the city's official historiographer. The museum, built north of the downtown section, was dedicated on July 24, 1951, the city's 250th birthday. Pennants of the three nations that ruled Detroit from its founding — the French Royal Banner, the British Ensign and the American flag of George Washington — fly from flagstaffs donated by the *News*.

Stark, whose wife, Anne, was the paper's poet laureate for almost a half century, also was responsible for the relocating of the 103-year-old Mariner's Church. Stark's columns about the landmark induced city fathers to save it from razing and move it easterly from Woodward Avenue, where it stood in the way of progress. There it was restored in 1954 and serves as a contrast with Detroit's present and a reminder of its past.

An interview with Henry Ford II on November 24, 1971, by the paper's Robert Popa resulted in the revelation of yet another new development in the city's Civic Center program. A fifty-three-acre strip of land, much of it occupied by railroads that no longer needed it, had been the object of envy of city planners. Redeveloped, the land held the key to a further revitalization of downtown Detroit. Hurt by the suburban sprawl of both business and residents, the central city was looking for an additional attraction to bring suburbanites back downtown. Ford popped the information that he had taken a personal interest in the redevelopment area. It was just such backing that was needed to get the project off dead center. Ford had retained John C. Portman, the architect who designed Peachtree Center in Atlanta, Georgia, and a new ocean face for San Francisco. It was Portman's task to give the city's Civic Center another shining facet that would attract visitors and Detroiters living in the suburbs. The *News*, which had pushed the Civic Center project for so many years, was obviously delighted. "Ford Has a Better Idea," the paper chortled, picking up a Ford Motor Company advertising slogan. The project was planned as a crowning touch. A hotel, restaurants, riverside apartments, office complexes were designed to give the historic riverfront an even greater role in the city's future. Coincidentally, the *News* was the largest single landowner in the area. A 9.8-acre parcel had been purchased years before by the paper as a possible site for a new plant, but the suburban sprawl had made the location obsolete.[18]

Coincidentally, while Henry Ford pushed to revitalize downtown Detroit, his brother, William C. Ford, owner of the Detroit Lions, was seeking to move the team out of town to a proposed stadium in suburban Pontiac. William Ford's move pulled the props from under a downtown stadium plan that was part of a total revitalization project. The two brothers kept their private and civic projects separate entities, with neither publicly seeking to influence the other. Led by Henry Ford, eventually forty Detroit businessmen and industrialists raised $35 million to make the project financially possible. Ford refused any credit. A contest was held to select a name for the development; there was one stipulation: don't use the name of Ford.

The paper's own contributions to changing the face of the city have been many. Occasionally they have taken strange twists. Before the paper was twenty years old, its founder provided the funds to build the Trinity Protestant Episcopal Church. Modeled after gothic churches James Scripps had seen in Europe, the edifice was erected in 1892 at Trumbull and Myrtle, near Scripps's home. It did not serve the Scripps family for long, however. A change in ministers shortly after it was dedicated resulted in reforms in doxology that irritated Scripps. Angered, he left the services one Sunday and took his family to another Episcopal church nearby. He never returned to Trinity. On March 17, 1935, the hundredth anniversary of his birth, the church remembered him with a memorial service.[19]

Scripps, a member of the city's first art commission in 1885, gave the city paintings he had collected in two years of travel abroad. It was one of the Detroit Art Institute's first gifts. Scripps estimated their worth at between $75,000 and $80,000. There were eighty paintings; he presented them in 1889 with the proviso that only fifty would be retained. In this manner, he explained, the city's art curator would not feel obliged to accept something he might feel was "bad art." He asked that "the cullings" be left in his hands so that the walls of the museum would not be "cumbered" with undesirable objects.[20]

Like his predecessor, George Booth also was interested in cultural advancement. Early in his tenure as publisher he recommended that the News support a charter amendment that would enable further development of the art institute. The first time the issue was placed on the ballot it lost. In the first ward, controlled by Boushaw, the wardheeler saloonkeeper, not a vote was cast for or against. Jay Hayden was sent to see Boushaw. He asked the saloonkeeper why no votes were cast in "the foist of the foist" on the *News*'s art institute amendment.

"Oh, Christ, Jay," Boushaw declared. "Was that amendment yours? Why the hell didn't you tell us about it? We got to looking at the amendment the night before the election and I said, 'What the hell's this?' Nobody knew, so we threw it in the river."[21]

The paper and members of the Scripps and Booth families continued their interest with gifts and editorial support. The main section of a new museum was built in 1927 and north and south wings were added in subsequent years.

Booth's purchase of the Cranbrook estate developed after a picnic in the country in 1904 with his wife, Ellen Scripps Booth, and their children, Henry, James, Warren, Grace and Florence. The picnic was held on a farm owned by Samuel Alexander, a naturalist.[22] The rolling hills, meandering streams and scattering of farm buildings was reminiscent of the Booth ancestral village, Cranbrook, England. It was purchased the next year and called Cranbrook. The first activity at Cranbrook was a Sunday school class held in a tent. In the ensuing years, a Greek theater was constructed, then a meetinghouse — the eventual birthplace of nationally known Brookside School and Christ Church Cranbrook. Beginning in 1924, with Saarinen's arrival, the institution grew rapidly. For his Cranbrook School for Boys Saarinen was awarded an Architectural League of New York Gold Medal. The school opened in 1927 and that year the Booths formed a foundation to help perpetuate the institution. Typical of George G. Booth's philosophy, which dictated that others should share in the pleasure of such philanthropy, he left a relatively small endowment. To objecting trustees he said, "Let those who follow me take up some of the burden."[23] Years later sales of valuable Cranbrook artifacts and masterpieces were necessary to enrich the endowment, thus assuring the continuance of the art and educational center. In 1930 Kingswood School Cranbrook and the Cranbrook Institute of Science were founded. A Cranbrook Academy of Art also was formed. The Booths lived to see Cranbrook institutions win international recognition for improving and extending education and cultural facilities.

While the Scripps and the Booth families extended their philan-
thropies, the newspaper appealed to the broad mass of its readers
through a variety of educational, recreational, and community
service programs — sixty-six in all, by survey, the most offered by
any paper in the United States. By far the broadest program is the
News-sponsored Metropolitan Spelling Bee, begun in 1921 by
Malcolm Bingay, who later was fired (by his own admission "for
drunkenness and other derelictions") and moved easterly on Lafayette to the *Free Press*.[24] The spelling bee has made readers of young
people years before they could become self-sustaining subscribers.

The appeal to the average reader — James Scripps's early formula for success — continues to be threaded throughout the paper's
service programs. For years, participation in a national Soapbox
Derby appealed to young boys (and in recent years, young girls);
a garden and flower show reaches a wide span of backyard
gardeners; there's an annual bridge tournament; forensic awards;
a patrol boy safety program and a juvenile law program. Hundreds
of thousands of copies of the paper are used annually in the class-
room as a teaching tool. Recreation programs range from a father
and son bowling tournament and a hole-in-one golf tournament
through events in most areas of sports. As interests change, programs are varied. A hiking club and a birdhouse contest gave way
in recent years to such things as a ski meet and a young hunters
safety clinic. To bring the National Collegiate Athletic Association
annual track and field meet to Detroit, the paper donated a $31,-
000 track, built to meet the specifications of Cobo Arena. When
its Soapbox Derby outgrew existing facilities, the paper erected
Derby Hill, a manmade nine-hundred-foot incline that is a year-
round attraction to racers and tobogganists. When an aquarium
on Belle Isle suffered from a lack of life, the paper donated four
seals, and to entertain children near their homes the paper bought
four ponies and carts that are taken by Detroit's Department of
Parks and Recreation into residential areas in summer, offering
rides free of charge. When the Detroit Zoo was constructed in
1928 in suburban Royal Oak it was one of the few barless animal
exhibits in the world. Because of the large area required in the
open, moated construction, the *News* donated a miniature railroad

to carry visitors on two and one half miles of rail around the park. In 1933 the *News*, noting something important was missing from the city's smaller Belle Isle Zoo — an elephant — conducted a campaign that started pennies pouring from a hundred thousand piggy banks of Detroit children. Writer Rex G. White was sent to New York to escort the animal to Detroit. The Washington Bureau was alerted to smooth any customs and immigration problems. When the elephant was swung off the freighter that carried it to the United States from Africa, White fell into a fit of depression. Instead of the two-ton Goliath he had promised to deliver, the animal was a 1,275-pound baby. Undaunted, White began the trip from the east by truck. In each town, the truck was stopped while the curious admired the animal and fed it candy, ice cream and pop. An elephant-sized stomachache was solved when White, with the help of a druggist who guessed the dosage, poured one quart of cathartic into the beast's mouth. By the time Sheba, the name given to the new attraction, reached Detroit, the animal was well, White ill from observing the "cure." Thousands of youngsters gathered for her debut.[25] The pet of the zoo, Sheba lived until 1959. When she died, the paper repeated the campaign. The new baby was named Kita — also by the children of the city.

A "Questions of General Public Interest" column, begun December 19, 1917, continued through the years, resulting today in a question-and-answer column, "Ask The News." The service handles a hundred thousand telephoned questions and twelve thousand letters annually. A wise decision of more than a half century ago continues to exclude answers to any questions dealing with legal, medical or religious subjects.

In recent years the paper extended its editorial public service programs to include special supplements that would be of especial interest to readers. These sections have been produced with no advertising. Remarkable among these was a special roto magazine section folded into the newspapers shortly after the assassination of President John F. Kennedy. The supplement's cover, a portrait of the President, had no type whatsoever, no newspaper identification that would detract from the seriousness of the presentation. The supplement was so popular that circulation spurted dramatically.

The *News* printed 150,000 additional newspapers to handle the demand, which continued for days. Special sections also were produced to recapitulate the tragedy of the city's 1967 riot, to mark man's quest of the moon, and the deaths of Presidents Eisenhower, Truman and Johnson. When the city's freeways neared completion, presenting a confusing driving situation to motorists, the feature department produced a freeway guide. The war in Vietnam was explained by a four-page color section not only telling Detroiters where the action was occurring, but also showing the locations of the units where their sons were stationed.

On August 9, 1968, the day the *News* resumed publication after the nine-month strike, the paper displayed a new reader service column, "Contact 10." The decision to publish such a column was under consideration for two years while the paper's rival, the *Detroit Free Press*, was showing readership gains with its "Action Line" column. The first reader service column of this kind was published by the *Houston Chronicle* and called "Watchem." When the *News* finally moved, it was with characteristic thoroughness. Using the strike period, its feature department organized a ten-man team — thus the name of the column — headed by James M. Lycett, a former *News* Sunday supplement editor. The *News*'s column was strongly oriented to consumer problems, one of the few reader service columns in the country to take on the challenge of reader concerns without regard to advertisers who might be named. The strength of the column was soon shown by the faith its readers expressed in it. Among its questioners have been readers disgruntled with the *News* itself for some reason or another. In a new day of journalism, Contact 10 fulfilled some of the early reader needs expressed in Nancy Brown's Experience column. Typical of the letters received by the column was the suffering consumer who could not get a new toaster fixed on warranty: "I never thought I'd be writing to you for help, but. . . ." Where Nancy Brown answered the personal cries of readers, Contact 10 stepped in to solve more practical problems created by a sometimes faulty system of free enterprise.

When "Miss Ellen" left Detroit in 1878 to help her stepbrother, Edward Wyllis Scripps, develop the struggling *Cleveland Penny*

Press, she left behind a small bequest (less than $1,000) that she said should be used through the years to purchase a box of candy at Christmastime for every woman employee of the paper. When she left, only four or five women were in the paper's employ. She had no way of knowing that soon the growth of the *News* and the increased number of career women would place the number of its employees in the hundreds. The chocolate fund soon ran out. The paper continued to present its women employees with boxes of candy until the late 1950s when the idea went out of fashion.[26]

While the *Detroit News* was growing in power and prominence, the early investment in the Cleveland paper grew under the direction of Edward Wyllis Scripps. Today the Scripps-Howard Newspapers headed by Charles Scripps, a grandson of Edward Wyllis, operate eighteen daily newspapers in as many cities. A news syndicate begun by Edward and an early partner, Milton McRae, developed into the United Press and finally, in 1960, the United Press International. Other Scripps newspapers include thirty-one papers in the Scripps League, headed by E. W. Scripps, and eleven papers in the John P. Scripps Newspapers, all on the West Coast. Both E. W. and John P. are grandsons of Edward Wyllis, the young stepbrother of the founder of the *News.*

In 1890, with the earnings already mounting, Miss Ellen moved to Miramar, California, a few miles north of San Diego, to join Edward and other family members. There Edward had built a rambling mansion on a twenty-one-hundred-acre estate from which he issued orders to the expanding E. W. Scripps newspaper enterprises. Eventually Ellen established her own home at La Jolla, where her philanthropy is sharply visible.

With Edward she endowed the Scripps Institute of Oceanography, the largest marine research institute in the world, now a branch of the University of California. The Scripps Memorial Hospital and a metabolic clinic at La Jolla also resulted from her philanthropy.[27] In 1924 Miss Ellen gave the land to enlarge the campus of Pomona College, the next year she proposed the establishment of a college for women at Claremont, California, which bears her name.

"My present stockholding in The Evening News Association is

4,000 shares," she wrote in her bequest.[28] Of this she gave the college a thousand shares. Her early efforts at the *Detroit News* had reached to the Pacific in enhancing education and culture. She lived to the age of ninety-five. Before her death in 1932 she conveyed to the town of Rushville, Illinois, land she had inherited from her father and converted it into a park that bears the Scripps name. Miss Ellen was eighteen when Edward Wyllis was born. After the death of her father, James Mogg Scripps, in 1873, the year the *News* was founded, she became Edward Wyllis's mother and mentor. But Ellen's interest in culture was not shared wholeheartedly by her stepbrother. Soon after the *News* built its own plant on Lafayette in 1917, then considered the most up-to-date newspaper facility in the nation, Edward Wyllis returned to Detroit to look over the newspaper he had left to strike out on his own. George Booth escorted the fiery member of the Scripps clan on a tour of the pressroom, the composing room, the editorial rooms and business offices. He then took him through the paper's George B. Catlin Memorial Library, named after a staff member who helped write early Detroit history. The library, with twenty-six thousand volumes and millions of newspaper clippings, received a careful inspection. Edward Wyllis walked down the aisle separating the cubical offices of editorial writers and oaken nooks housing the library's tomes of information. He did not utter a word. His red hair had begun to grow thin. Finally, Booth said the obvious: "This is one of the finest newspaper libraries in the country." Edward Wyllis looked at Booth, one eye cast as it had since birth, and muttered, "This is the most wasteful extravagance in the history of American journalism."[29]

The difference in philosophy between James E. Scripps, the cultured, businesslike newspaperman, and his stepbrother, Edward Wyllis, shrewd, called "Lusty" by his own biographer, had not been bridged. Yet, each was to emerge as one of the most important men in American journalism.

Epilogue

In 1873, after the early months of struggle had passed, James E. Scripps confided to his wife, Hattie, that he would be pleased if the paper he founded eventually netted a profit of $25,000. A hundred years ago it seemed to be the impossible dream. There was no way of foreseeing that the philosophy which guided him in starting the *News* and the business principles that the paper followed would, in a few years, cause the growth of the newspaper far beyond his expectations. The careful wedding of a strongly independent editorial vehicle with sound business practices created a structure whose strength has given the *News* freedom of action the weak do not enjoy. The survival of the founder's early beliefs may be directly related to the paper's steadily increasing economic independence. In times of attempted influence over its editorial ethics, when it faced the threats of libel action for speaking out, the strength of the paper's financial structure gave its decision-makers the ability to act forthrightly and in the community's interest.

In a century of publishing in which it was to become the largest evening newspaper circulated in the United States, five men were largely responsible for building this structure and guiding the paper's business fortunes. After the paper's early beginnings — when the editorial and business offices were one — the business affairs fell to a succession of Canadians, Hereward S. Scott, who joined the *News* in 1890 and stayed for forty-seven years; Herbert Ponting, from 1896 to 1944; and D. Roy Merrill, from 1905 to

1958. The Canadian line was broken with Edwin K. Wheeler, a member of the Evening News Association since 1937, who at intervals directed the business operations of stations WWJ, WWJ-FM and WWJ-TV and the *News*. In 1963 Wheeler became executive vice president and general manager of the paper. In 1969 James T. Dorris was promoted to the post of general manager and vice president. When Scott retired in 1937 he declared that he had only two bosses in his life — the *News* and Queen Victoria, both monarchs.

From a small shop in old downtown Detroit, at Shelby and Julius Alley, and an original capital investment of approximately $21,000, the *News* survived a panic, the Great Depression, the financial crimping that resulted from two world wars and a series of smaller conflicts that disrupted the nation, to become a major voice of opinion in America. Its success was notably remarkable in 1971 when it became the foremost evening newspaper in the nation while serving the fifth-largest city.

The paper that began with James E. Scripps, a few newsmen he could interest in taking the gamble, and family members who arrived to help in the enterprise, is today a part of a broad corporation — the Evening News Association — with gross sales in excess of $100 million. The Evening News Association, which consists of the *News* and the stations of WWJ, employs more than three thousand persons. Two wholly owned subsidiaries of the Association are the Universal Communications Corporation, which owns Station WALA-TV, Mobile, Alabama, and Station KOLD-TV, in Tucson, Arizona, and the Commercial Marine Terminal, Inc., Detroit, a warehouse for storing newsprint.[1]

At the time James Scripps bequeathed the paper in a thirty-year trust administered by George G. Booth, William E. Scripps and Edgar Bancroft Whitcomb, its shares of stock totaled fifty. Since the expiration of the trust in 1936, the number of shares has grown to five hundred thousand. There are two hundred stockholders, among them colleges, foundations and trusts, which represent bequests of inheritors over the years.[2] While maintaining the creed of independence for the newspapers, the Evening News Association announced plans in 1972 to further strengthen its financial base by actively seeking newspapers in other areas of the nation, each to be operated independently of the Detroit newspaper. William Borglund, vice president of Newspaper Enterprise Association, a feature syndicate that sprang from Miss Ellen's early columns, was hired to pinpoint possible acquisitions. That the Booth-Scripps families remain an integral part of the paper's operation is evident in the corporation's high echelon. All but one director, Wheeler, is related to the founder, James E. Scripps. Among the founder's grandsons on the board of directors are Henry S. Booth and Robert W. Scripps. Among the great-grandsons on the board are James S. Whitcomb, Jr., Warren S. Wilkinson and John B. Beresford. Besides Clark, the president and publisher, another great-grandson who holds a corporate office is Richard B. Wallace, treasurer and assistant secretary. Richard M. Spitzley, senior vice president and secretary, is the husband of a granddaughter of the founder.

On the morning of November 22, 1963, Warren S. Booth, publisher, told Martin Hayden, editor, that the Evening News board of directors was meeting at noon to select his (Booth's) successor. Two years before the board had looked over the family's new generation and had made Peter B. Clark, an assistant professor of political science at Yale University, secretary of the corporation. Clark, then thirty-two, great-grandson of the founder, now was moving up to publisher.

Booth, who detested personal publicity, told Hayden to "write a small article about it."

Hayden's eyebrows shot up. "Small? Why, Mr. Booth, this will be only the fifth publisher in the history of the paper. We have to give it proper treatment."

"No," Booth demurred. "Keep it short."

The article did not appear that day at all. At 1:30 P.M. Detroit time President John F. Kennedy was assassinated in Dallas, Texas. On his way to the city room, Hayden met Clark on a stairway. "I guess we'd better wait with our announcement," Clark told Hayden. The editor nodded. The story, slightly longer than Booth had ordered, appeared the following Sunday on Page One.[3]

In Detroit, the "Home Newspaper," a name given the *News* by the founder, maintains a four-story, block-square central editorial and business office, a Times Square plant, housing high-speed production and distribution equipment and a nine-level garage for a *News*-owned fleet of cars and trucks. In suburban Sterling Heights, a $40 million North plant, opening in the paper's centennial year, gave the *News* for the second time in its history the most modern newspaper printing plant in the nation. Utilizing specially developed electronic computer equipment, the North facility is tied to the home office like an umbilical cord. Every day the *News* has the capability of transmitting for printing as many words as are contained in several full-length novels, and at a speed literally as fast as sound.

The newspaper that once measured the worth of its stories by the yardstick, "How close is it to Woodward Avenue?" today has editorial offices throughout the city's sprawling metropolitan area. These offices provide the news and feature stories that fill sections of the paper zoned with articles of interest close to each reader's home. Woodward has become Maple Lane, Elm, Pine or Bonnie Brae Drive, miles from Detroit's main thoroughfare. The home newspaper continues to fill a century-old, successful editorial appeal while fulfilling a later-day demand for world-wide news and articles of human interest and entertainment.

From the provincial newspaper of a hundred years ago, the *News* blankets the major stories of the world with its reporters and feature writers. *News* reporter Anthony Ripley was standing within an arm's length of Jack Ruby when he shot Lee Harvey Oswald, the assassin of John Kennedy. The *News* Washington Bureau chief, Jerry ter Horst, was in the caravan in Dallas, Texas, the day Kennedy was shot and killed by a gunman watching the passing cars through the sight of a high-powered rifle. Reporter Palmer Hutchinson was killed by an airplane propeller while accompanying Sir Hubert Wilkins, an explorer, on a *News*-sponsored expedition in the Arctic in 1926. Foreign analyst Philip Adler died in an airplane crash in 1947 near Tokyo while on assignment in the Far East. Edwin G. Pipp, grandson of the pre–World War I editor, covered the air war in Vietnam after becoming the dean of the nation's aerospace writers by covering every U.S. "shot" since Sputnik, the Soviet rocket that started the race to the moon.

In 1971, after negotiating a three-year contract with unions representing mechanical trades, the *News* announced that in concert with its agreement made at the bargaining table, nonunion employees would benefit equally. For higher bracketed personnel, it meant across-the-board increases of $42 a week. It was as much money as was paid per week to many older employees when they entered the newspaper business twenty-five or thirty-five years before. Sylvia Rumpa, secretary, asked Paul Poorman, managing editor, if the "rumor" was true. Assured that it was no rumor, Miss Rumpa innocently remarked, "I certainly hope they know what they are doing."[4]

They did.

Acknowledgments

THE AUTHOR acknowledges the help and research assistance of members and former members of the *Detroit News* staff and of persons outside of the newspaper who were close to events that figured importantly in the paper's history.

Foremost among these are W. Steele Gilmore, who served the newspaper from 1909 to 1953, from reporter to editor-in-chief. His reminiscences at the age of eighty-five fleshed out many of the skeletal stories found in the normal course of historical search.

Special mention is given to Don Lochbiler, reporter, feature writer and assistant city editor beginning in 1929; to E. A. Batchelor, Jr., who worked at the *News* before World War II, then at the *Times* from 1945 until 1960, and again at the *News* as a rewriteman; to Boyd Simmons, who got his first taste of the newspaper business as a sit-down striker, "stringing" for the paper in 1935; and to Watson Spoelstra, a sportswriter for the *Free Press* and the Associated Press before closing his career at the *News*.

These men not only researched the areas of *News* history in which they personally played a part, but added recollections of others that brought these periods dramatically to life.

Mr. Lochbiler knew Nancy Brown (Mrs. J. E. Leslie) personally. He also was at the *News* when radio station WWJ was in its infancy and operating out of the *News* building.

Mr. Batchelor served as a writer at the *News* during the 1967 riot and his contribution to the story of that phase of the city's and the paper's history went beyond the newspaper's files to the people who worked during those tragic days.

Mr. Simmons handed notes out of a window of the Cadillac plant to waiting *News* reporters during the early sit-down strikes. After joining the paper in 1937 he served as a labor reporter, then as city editor and assistant managing editor. His personal knowledge of the Reuther brothers and James P. Hoffa added credence to the telling of the important role labor played in the city's history.

Mr. Simmons's work in the area of crime reporting in later years figured importantly in the paper's Secret Witness program, which has been copied widely.

Mr. Spoelstra, who joined the *News* in 1944, was personally involved in a great part of the city's sports history of note. It was on Mr. Spoelstra's head that pitcher Denny McLain dumped a bucket of ice water, creating an incident that eventually led to the banishment of the thirty-one-game winner from the Detroit Tigers baseball team.

Research that delved beyond the recall of persons living was eased by the efforts of Mrs. Ruth P. Braun, librarian of the Catlin Memorial Library, the *Detroit News;* Robert A. Diehl, reference department head, and library assistant Vivian Buc. The chapter dealing with Henry Ford and the beginnings of the auto industry was helpfully put in perspective by Owen W. Bombard, public relations manager, Lincoln-Mercury division, the Ford Motor Company.

Others who contributed insights to particular events were the *News's* Harry V. Wade, former editor-in-chief; Ray Girardin, former *Detroit Times* reporter and police commissioner; Harry Sahs, for years chief of the *News's* police beat; and John M. Carlisle, member of the staff from 1927 to 1971.

The recollections of Girardin, Sahs and Carlisle comprise much of the editorial history of the newspaper during the lurid 1930s and early 1940s.

An unpublished manuscript by Cyril Arthur Player, former staff member, contributed heavily to the chronology of corporate events as they figured in the city's history.

The book was written at the request of Peter B. Clark, president and publisher, and Martin S. Hayden, vice president and editor, both of whom refused to exert editorial judgment over the material selected. Mention is made of James T. Dorris, vice president and general manager; Richard M. Spitzley, senior vice president; Richard B. Wallace, treasurer; Edwin K. Wheeler, executive vice president; Robert E. Lubeck, associate editor, features; and John H. O'Brien, associate editor, for their continuing support. Jane Schermerhorn, for many years a writer at the *Times* and the *News*, and Nora Griesbeck, editorial assistant, greatly assisted in the editorial preparation.

Appreciation also is extended to Dr. George A. Hough III, Professor John Murray and Dr. W. Cameron Meyers, all of the Michigan State University School of Journalism, and Professor Frank Senger, chairman of the MSU journalism school, for their able assistance.

Chapter Notes

PROLOGUE

1. *Detroit News,* June 14, 1971, pp. 1, 8–A.
2. Ibid., June 15, 1971, pp. 1, 4–A.
3. Ibid., June 16, 1971, pp. 1, 19–A, 4–C.
4. Ibid., June 17, 1971, pp. 1, 22–A, 23–A (three articles), 24A (three).
5. Ibid., June 18, 1971, pp. 1 (two), 19–A, 8–C (five).
6. Ibid., June 19, 1971, p. 1 (two).
7. Ibid., June 27, 1971, p. 1.

CHAPTER 1

1. *Detroit News,* March 8, 1933, p. 2.
2. Cyril Arthur Player, "The Story of James Edmund Scripps," p. 129.
3. *News,* May 29, 1906, p. 1.
4. Ibid., August 23, 1873, p. 1.
5. Player, pps. 133–134.
6. Arthur Pound, *The Only Thing Worth Finding,* pp. 103–108.
7. Player, p. 136.
8. Ibid., pp. 137–148.
9. *News,* March 8, 1933, p. 1.
10. Player, p. 146.
11. Ibid., p. 159.
12. *Time* magazine, October 19, 1962, p. 45.
13. W. Steele Gilmore, an interview, November 21, 1971.

14. Player, p. 167.
15. Lee A White, *The Detroit News 1873–1917*, p. 17.
16. Ibid., p. 19.
17. Paul Leake, *History of Detroit*, pp. 239–242.

CHAPTER 2

1. Louis L. Richards, *Detroit News*, March 30, 1931, p. 24.
2. Melvin G. Holli, *Reform in Detroit*, p. 43.
3. Hazen S. Pingree, *Facts and Opinion*, p. 72.
4. William P. Lovett, *Detroit Rules Itself*, p. 189.
5. *Detroit News*, November 6, 1889, p. 1.
6. George B. Catlin, *The Story of Detroit*, pps. 593–594.
7. Cyril Arthur Player, "The Story of James Edmund Scripps," p. 288. Pingree called Detroit a "Boodle City," a name that quickly caught the public's fancy.
8. *News*, August 16, 1894, p. 1.
9. Jere C. Hutchins, *A Personal Story*, pp. 197–198.
10. *News*, June 13, 1894, p. 1.
11. Ibid., October 19, 1892, p. 1.
12. Holli, p. 100.
13. Malcolm W. Bingay, *Of Me I Sing*, p. 239.
14. Player, pp. 303–308.
15. *News*, May 5, 1903.
16. Player, p. 339.
17. Ibid., pp. 688–722.
18. *News*, November 20, 1962, p. 11–B.

CHAPTER 3

1. *Detroit Free Press*, July 26, 1912. Stories discussed the mayoralty campaign, a boat race and Belle Isle, the island park.
2. John C. Lodge, *I Remember Detroit*, p. 98.
3. Martin S. Hayden, an interview, 1971.
4. Gilmore, an interview, November 21, 1971.
5. *Detroit News*, July 27, 1912, p. 1.
6. Malcolm W. Bingay, *Of Me I Sing*, p. 181.
7. *News*, July and August, 1912.

8. Ibid., June 25, 1918, p. 1.
9. Lodge, *I Remember Detroit*, p. 94.
10. Gilmore, an interview, November 21, 1971.
11. White, corporate correspondence, November 15, 1947.
12. *News*, January 12, 1912, p. 9.
13. Martin S. Hayden, an interview, 1971.
14. Jay G. Hayden, "James Couzens."
15. Ibid.

CHAPTER 4

1. Richard Crabb, *Birth of a Giant*, pp. 248–250.
2. *Detroit News*, June 5, 1950, Question and Answer Column.
3. Ibid., July 16, 1899, p. 22.
4. Gilmore, an interview, November 21, 1971.
5. *News-Tribune*, July 30, 1918, p. 4.
6. Crabb, p. 57.
7. Ibid., see index for Buick, Olds, Chevrolet and others.
8. Floyd Clymer, *Historical Motor Scrapbook*, p. 103.
9. Crabb, p. 265.
10. *News*, January 5, 1941, p. 1.
11. Ford Motor Company Archives.
12. Crabb, pp. 398–407.
13. *News*, August 31, 1916, p. 1.
14. Ibid., May 26, 1927, p. 1.
15. Allan Nevins, *Henry Ford: Decline and Rebirth, 1933–1962*, p. 138.
16. Bob Considine, *The Fabulous Henry Ford II*, p. 1.
17. William Serrin, New York Times Magazine, October 19, 1968.
18. Ibid.
19. *News*, April 8, 1947, p. 1.
20. Ibid., April 9, 1947, p. 22.

CHAPTER 5

1. *Detroit News*, December 10, 1936, p. 21.
2. Martin Hayden, an interview, 1971.

3. *News*, December 30, 1936, p. 1.
4. Boyd Simmons, an interview, February 25, 1972.
5. *News*, February 17, 1937.
6. Simmons, an interview, February 25, 1971.
7. James E. Kilpatrick, an interview.
8. Ibid.
9. Asher Lauren, in a talk to the *News* advertising staff, Aug. 8, 1960.
10. *News*, March 14, 1957, p. 1.
11. Simmons, an interview regarding the photographer, William L. Seiter, who processed Brooks's prize winning photographs.
12. Ibid., an interview, February 25, 1971.
13. *News*, April 21, 1948, p. 1.
14. Ibid., January 6, 1954, p. 1.
15. Ibid., May 27, 1955, p. 1.
16. Simmons, an interview, Feb. 25, 1971.
17. *News*, June 6, 1955, p. 1.
18. *New York Times*, March 5, 1964.
19. *News*, May 10, 1970, p. 1.
20. Ibid., May 11, 1970, p. 18–A.
21. Simmons, an interview, February 25, 1972.

CHAPTER 6

1. William E. Scripps, an address given at the tenth anniversary of station WWJ, August 29, 1930.
2. Cynthia Boyes Young, "WWJ — Pioneer in Broadcasting," pp. 413–425.
3. *Detroit News*, August 20, 1930.
4. Ibid., August 31, 1920, p. 1.
5. Ibid., September 3, 1930, p. 1.
6. Ibid., September 6, 1920, p. 1.
7. Ibid., August 20, 1936, p. 1.
8. Ibid., February 5, 1933, p. 14.
9. Ibid., October 15, 1932, p. 4.
10. Ibid., August 22, 1941, p. 12.
11. Ibid., August 20, 1930, p. 15.
12. Gilmore, an interview, November 21, 1970, with Don Lochbiler.

13. The talk by Gilmore to the nation's editors is available in the Catlin Library.
14. Corporate correspondence, letters exchanged by Jay G. Hayden and William E. Scripps, discussing James Couzens and Detroit's bank failures.
15. *News*, December 12, 1968, p. 1.
16. Young, pp. 413–425.
17. *News*, May 11, 1950, p. 7.

CHAPTER 7

1. Ernest S. Dewey, "Crime and the Press," *Commonweal*, December 30, 1971.
2. Harvey Patton, an interview, November 16, 1971.
3. Peter Maas, "Crime in America," *Saturday Evening Post*, August 10, 1963.
4. Jack Carlisle, an interview, October 19, 1971.
5. Ibid.
6. *Organized Crime and Illicit Traffic in Narcotics*, pp. 424–425.
7. All subsequent chapter quotations from Senate hearings are quoted from the above source.
8. Charles A. Selden, New York *Times*, May 27, 1929, Section 9, p. 1.
9. Ray Girardin, an interview, November 5, 1971.
10. Harry Sahs, an interview, October 4, 1971.
11. *Detroit News*, April 12, 1929, p. 1.
12. *Organized Crime*, p. 425.
13. Girardin, an interview, November 5, 1971.
14. *News*, November 17, 1928, p. 1.
15. Girardin, an interview, November 5, 1971.
16. *News*, February 22, 1940, p. 1.
17. Gilmore, an interview, November 21, 1970.
18. *Organized Crime*, p. 428.
19. *News*, July 23, 1930, p. 1.
20. Detroit Police Department, homicide records.
21. Stoddard White, *News*, March 16, 1954, p. 1.
22. *News*, August 7, 1939, p. 1.
23. Ibid., August 7–9, 1939, p. 1.
24. Ibid., August 10, 1939, p. 1.

25. Gilmore, an interview, November 21, 1970.
26. Ibid.
27. *Organized Crime*, p. 430.

CHAPTER 8

1. Gilmore, an interview, November 21, 1970.
2. *Detroit News*, April 19, 1919, p. 15.
3. Gilmore, November 21, 1970.
4. See Experience columns in Catlin Library.
5. *News*, November 14, 1930, p. 42.
6. Ibid., November 15, 1930, p. 1.
7. Ibid., June 18, 1934, p. 1.
8. Ibid., June 18, 1940, p. 18.
9. Ibid., December 7, 1941, p. 1.
10. Ibid., December 8, 1941, pgs. 11, 23.
11. Ibid., December 8, 1941, p. 1.
12. Ibid.

CHAPTER 9

1. Rolf Owen, an interview, January 8, 1972.
2. Sahs, an interview, October 14, 1971.
3. *Detroit News*, July 21, 1943, p. 1.
4. See *News* articles for July 22–25, 1943.
5. E. A. Batchelor, Jr., an interview with Herb Boldt relating start of 1967 riot, in December 1971.
6. *News*, July 24, 1967, p. 1.
7. Batchelor, an interview with Girardin in October 1971.
8. *News*, August 1, 1967, p. 1–B.
9. Ibid., July 24, 1967, p. 1.
10. Ibid., July 25, 1967, p. 19–A.
11. Ibid., July 26, 1967, p. 14–B.
12. John Hersey, *The Algiers Motel Incident*.
13. *News*, July 31, 1967, p. 1. Also, August 1, p. 1, August 2, 12–B.
14. Ibid., November 3, 1967, p. 10–C.

15. Ibid., *Sunday Magazine,* November 28, 1971.
16. *News,* February 6, 1972, p. 1.

CHAPTER 10

1. Detroit Police Department Record Bureau.
2. *Detroit American,* December 1967 to August 1968.
3. *Detroit News,* October 2, 1968, p. 12–A.
4. Ibid., January 14, 1969, p. 4–A.
5. *Time* magazine, May 8, 1969. "Press" section.
6. *News,* December 27, 1968, p. 13–A.
7. Ibid., October 20, 1968, p. 16–B.
8. Ibid., February 13, 1969, p. 6–B.
9. Martin Hayden, an interview, February 17, 1972.
10. *News,* April 1, 1969, p. 18–A.
11. Ibid., February 15, 1967, p. 1.
12. Simmons, an interview, February 25, 1971.
13. *Reader's Digest,* November 1971.
14. *News,* Other Section, October 22, 1970, p. 2–F.
15. Ibid., March 19, 1972, p. 1.
16. *New York Times,* September 3, 1972, Editorial Page.

CHAPTER 11

1. H. G. Salsinger, *Detroit News,* July 18, 1961, p. 1–C.
2. *Time* magazine, July 28, 1961.
3. *News,* August 27, 1909.
4. Watson N. Spoelstra, an interview, December 15, 1971.
5. *News,* Ralph McGill, July 18, 1961, p. 1.
6. Ibid., May 19, 1909, p. 4.
7. Ibid., March 30, 1935, p. 17.
8. Ibid., August 18, 1963, 90th Anniversary Magazine Section, p. 72.
9. Ibid., June 20, 1971, George Van, p. 1–D.
10. Spoelstra, December 15, 1971, an interview.
11. *News,* September 26, 1935, p. 26.
12. Ibid., August 18, 1963, 90th Anniversary Magazine Section, p. 61.
13. Ibid., August 20, 1970, p. 8–D.

14. Ibid., August 15, 1971, p. 1–D.
15. Ibid., August 25, 1958, p. 1–C.
16. Ibid., December 10, 1957, p. 29.
17. Greene's tenure at the *News* was severed on June 24, 1970.
18. Spoelstra, an interview, December 15, 1971.
19. *News*, October 11, 1968, p. 3–D.
20. Spoelstra, an interview, December 15, 1971.

CHAPTER 12

1. Gilmore, an interview, 1971.
2. *Detroit News*, March 3, 1911, p. 1.
3. Ibid., March 3, 1911, p. 4.
4. Gilmore, 1971, an interview.
5. *News*, April 5 to June 30, 1953.
6. Ibid., September 3, 1924, p. 1.
7. *Detroit Times*, October 30, 1924, p. 1.
8. *News*, November 7, 1927, pp. 1–2.
9. *Free Press*, November 7, 1927, p. 1.
10. *Times*, November 18, 1926, p. 1.
11. *News*, July 8, 1937, p. 22.
12. Ibid., June 4, 1947, p. 22.
13. Ibid., December 21, 1943, p. 32.
14. Ibid., April 10, 1958, p. 1.
15. Martin Hayden, an interview, 1971.
16. Corporate correspondence.
17. *News*, Sunday Magazine, June 21, 1970.
18. *News*, November 24, 1971, p. 1.
19. Ibid., May 17, 1925, p. 6.
20. Ibid., March 17, 1935. Sec. 3, p. 17.
21. Martin Hayden, an interview, 1971.
22. *Cranbrook Magazine*, Summer, vol. 2, no. 4, 1971.
23. Henry Booth, an interview, May 15, 1972.
24. Malcolm W. Bingay, *Of Me I Sing*, p. 239.
25. *News*, 90th Anniversary Magazine Section, August 18, 1963, p. 50.
26. Ruth P. Braun, an interview, February 14, 1972.
27. Albert Britt, *Ellen Browning Scripps*, pp. 37, 43, 49, 53, 55, 61, 63, 65.

28.   F. W. Kellogg, an address at the dedication of the Ellen Browning residence hall, Scripps College, September 1929. Also see "The College at the Crossroads," an address by William Bennett Munro, Pomona College, June 15, 1925.
29.   Gilmore, an interview, 1971.

EPILOGUE

1.   Corporate records, The Evening News Association.
2.   Edwin K. Wheeler, an interview, March 2, 1971.
3.   Martin Hayden, an interview, August 15, 1972.
4.   Paul A. Poorman, an interview, May 21, 1971.

Bibliography

BOOKS

Bingay, Malcolm W. *Of Me I Sing*. Indianapolis: Bobbs-Merrill Co., 1949.

Britt, Albert. *Ellen Browning Scripps*. New York: Oxford University Press, 1960.

Burton, Clarence M. *The City of Detroit, 1701–1922*. Detroit: S. J. Clarke Publishing Co., 1922.

Catlin, George B. *The Story of Detroit*. Chicago: Lakeside Press, 1926.

Chidsey, Donald Barr. *On and Off the Wagon*. New York: Cowles Book Co., 1969.

Clymer, Floyd. *Henry's Wonderful Model T*. New York: McGraw-Hill Book Co., 1955.

Crabb, Richard. *Birth of a Giant*. Philadelphia: Chilton Book Co., 1969.

Carlson, Oliver, and Bates, Ernest S. *Hearst, Lord of San Simeon*. New York. The Viking Press, 1937.

Emery, Edwin, and Smith, Henry Ladd. *The Press and America*. New York: Prentice-Hall, 1954.

Ford, Edwin H. *Selected Reading in the History of American Journalism*. Minneapolis: University of Minnesota, 1939.

Gardner, Gilson. *Lusty Scripps*. New York: Vanguard Press, 1932.

Goddard, Morrill. *What Pleases People and Why*. New York: The American Weekly, 1935.

Grambling, Oliver. *AP: The Story of News*. New York: Farrar and Rinehart, 1940.

Hanna, Mark. *Moral Cranks and Others*. Brooklyn: George E. Spinney Co., 1900.

Hersey, John. *The Algiers Motel Incident*. New York: Alfred A. Knopf, 1968.

Holli, Melvin G. *Reform in Detroit*. New York: Oxford University Press, 1969.

Hutchins, Jere C. *A Personal Story*. Norwood, Mass.: Plimpton Press, 1938.

Jardin, Anne. *The First Henry Ford*. Cambridge, Mass.: MIT Press, 1970.

Leake, Paul. *History of Detroit*. Chicago: Lewis Publishing Co., 1912.

Lodge, John C. *I Remember Detroit*. Detroit: Wayne University Press, 1949.

Lovett, William B. *Detroit Rules Itself*. Boston: Richard G. Badger, The Gorham Press, 1930.

Mencken, H. L. *Heathen Days*. New York: Alfred A. Knopf, 1943.

Nevins, Allan. *Ford: Decline and Rebirth, 1933–1962*. New York: Charles Scribner's Sons, 1962–1963.

Olson, Sidney. *Young Henry Ford*. Detroit: Wayne University Press, 1963.

Pingree, Hazen S. *Facts and Opinions*. Detroit: F. B. Dickerson Co., 1895.

Pound, Arthur. *The Only Thing Worth Finding*. Detroit: Wayne University Press, 1964.

Reid, Ed. *The Grim Reapers*. Chicago: Henry Regnery Co., 1969.

Slosson, William Preston. *The Great Crusade and After*. New York: Macmillan Co., 1930.

White, Lee A. *The Detroit News, 1873–1917*. Detroit: Evening News Association, 1918.

Woodford, Frank B. *Alex J. Groesbeck*. Detroit: Wayne University Press, 1962.

REPORTS

Organized Crime and Illicit Traffic in Narcotics. Hearings before the Permanent Subcommittee on Investigations of the Committee on Government Operations, United States Senate, Eighty-eighth Congress, First Session, Part 2. Washington: U.S. Government Printing Office, 1963.

ARTICLES

Catlin, George B. "Adventures in Journalism: Detroit Newspapers Since 1850." *Michigan History Magazine,* vol. 29, 1945.

Considine, Bob. "The Fabulous Henry Ford II." *Hearst Newspapers,* November 29–December 6, 1964.

Dewey, Ernest A. "Crime and the Press." *Commonweal,* December 30, 1931.

Durand, Will. "The American Newspaper." *Collier's,* February 18, 1911.

Kellogg, Mrs. F. W. "The Character and Influence of Ellen Browning Scripps." Claremont, Calif.: booklet of addresses published by Scripps College, 1929.

Lovett, William P. "Pingree of Detroit – Demagogue or Statesman." *National Municipal Review,* vol. 8, no. 9, November 1919.

Maas, Peter. "Crime in America." *Saturday Evening Post,* August 10, 1963.

New York Times, March 5, 1964, "Man in the News" column.

Richards, Louis L. "Tabloid Tales of an Old Reporter." *Detroit News,* March 30, 1931.

Selden, Charles A. "Our 'Rum Capital': An Amazing Picture." *New York Times,* May 27, 1929.

Serrin, William. "At Ford Everyone Knows Who Is the Boss." *New York Times Magazine,* October 19, 1968.

Young, Cynthia Boyes. "WWJ – Pioneer in Broadcasting." *Michigan History Magazine,* vol. 44, no. 4, 1960.

INTERVIEWS

Abbott, Albert L., assistant managing editor of the *News,* an interview, February 7, 1972.

Booth, Henry S., an interview, May 15, 1972.

Carlisle, Jack, an interview, October 29, 1971.

Carlson, Kenneth T., advertising director, the *News,* interviews, 1971 and 1972.

Gilmore, W. Steele, interviews in 1970 and 1971.

Girardin, Ray, an interview, November 5, 1971.

Grofer, Edward J., promotion and research director, the *News*, interviews in 1971.

Hayden, Martin S., interviews in 1971, 1972.

List, Glenn P., circulation manager, the *News*, interviews in January and February, 1972.

Owen, Rolf, *News*, an interview, January 8, 1972.

Patton, Harvey, an interview, November 16, 1971.

Sahs, Harry, an interview, October 14, 1971.

Sieger, Robert R., sports editor, the *News*, interviews in 1970–1972.

Simmons, Boyd, an interview, February 25, 1972.

Spoelstra, Watson N., an interview, December 15, 1971.

Stanley, Harry M., Jr., retail advertising manager, the *News*, an interview, March 13, 1972.

Wheeler, Edwin K., an interview, March 2, 1972.

Witherspoon, John H., nephew of John C. Lodge, former Police Commissioner of Detroit and Corporation Counsel, an interview, September 1, 1971.

NEWSPAPERS

Detroit American, published by the Pol-American Publishing Company, April 1967–October 1968.

Detroit News, 1873 through 1972, on microfilm, Catlin Memorial Library, the *Detroit News*.

Detroit Times, 1900 to 1960, on microfilm, Catlin Library.

Free Press, June–August 1912 and various selected dates to 1972, on microfilm, Detroit Public Library.

New York Times, 1919 through 1970, on microfilm, Detroit Public Library.

News-Tribune, August 28, 1898, through January 30, 1915, on microfilm, Catlin Library.

MANUALS

Municipal Manual, City of Detroit, 1909–1915, 1919–1920. Detroit. Compiled by city clerk.

Time Capsule, 1923, 1925, 1927, 1929. New York: Time-Life Books.

RECORDS

American Audit Bureau. *Statistics for Period Ending November 1970.*
Detroit Election Commission Records for various years from 1900 to 1972.
Detroit News. Research department lineage reports.
Detroit Police Record Bureau, various records dating from 1919 to 1971.
Media Records. Media Records, Inc., New York, N.Y.
Standard Rate and Data Service. *Newspaper Rates and Data.* Chicago, 1971.

UNPUBLISHED MANUSCRIPTS

Evening News Association, corporate papers, including extracts from writings of James E. Scripps, his diary, testaments and trusts; addresses and letters of William E. Scripps. Not available for general use.
Gilmore, W. Steele. Reminiscences, recorded by E. A. Batchelor, Jr., 1970, William W. Lutz, 1971–1972.
Hayden, Jay, "James Couzens."
Player, Cyril Arthur, "The Story of James E. Scripps." Catlin Library. Not for general circulation.
Player, Cyril A., and Majorie, *Hazen S. Pingree.* Catlin Library.
Wade, Harry V., "Reminiscences," 1971.

INSTITUTIONAL MAGAZINES

Cranbrook Magazine, Summer, vol. 2, no. 4, 1971.

BOOKLETS

A Chronicle of the Automotive Industry in America, 1893–1952. Detroit: Automobile Manufacturers Association, 1953.
Claremont College, An Unfolding Story. Pomona, Calif.: *Pomona College Bulletin,* September 1929.
The College at the Crossroads. Pomona, Calif.: *Pomona College Bulletin,* June 15, 1925.

Index

Adams, Jack, 164
Addes, George F., 73
Adler, Philip, 197
Advertiser and Tribune, 6, 29; and
    J. Scripps, 3, 14; and average
    man, 5; circulation of, 13; and
    H. S. Pingree, 18; and W. J.
    Bryan, 24
"Advice to the Lovelorn," 111
Alderman, Frank R., 54
Alexander, Samuel, 188
Alger, General Russell A., 19
Algiers Motel, 138–139, 140
Algiers Motel Incident, The, 138
Allen, Albert, 83
Alphonse (King of Spain), 58
"American Firsters," 168
American Federation of Labor, 15
American Motors Corporation, 56
Anderman, Al, 69–70
Arnold, R. K., 70
"Ask the News," 190
Assembly line, development of, 56
Associated Press, 12
Atlanta Constitution, 161
Automobile: effects of, 48–50; elec-
    tric, 52, 54; development of,
    50–55; *see also* Chevrolet; Model
    A; Model T; Olds; etc.

Baer, Max, 166
Bagley, Governor John J., 8

Baker, Frank "Home Run," 159–160
Baker, Patrick C., 51
Ball, Ernest, 85
Baltimore News-American, 152
Bannister, Harry, 91
Barker, Ma, 93
Barnes, Russell, 179
Barnett, Eddie, 46
Barrymore, Ethel, 90
Batchelor, E. A., Jr., 199–200
Baugh, Sammy, 170
Bay City Times Company, 29
Belanger, Duane, 136
Belle Isle: purchase of, 10; sunrise
    services on, 119–123; Peace Caril-
    lon Tower on, 120–122; and 1943
    race riots, 127, 128; and 1967
    race riots, 139; aquarium on, 189
Belle Isle Bridge, 46
Bennett, Harry, 59, 60–61, 62, 63,
    64, 69–70
Bennett, James Gordon, 10
Bennett Field, 157
Beresford, John B., 196
Bernard, Keith, 81
Bingay, Malcolm, 37, 38, 189
Blacks, 126, 129, 130, 140–141,
    144–146; *see also* Detroit
Blades, Francis A., 19
"Blanket sheets," 4
Blind pigs, 96, 97, 98, 131

Blockbusting, 129
Bodnar, Fred, 150
Boldt, Herbert, 129–130, 132, 149
Bommarito, "Long Joe," 97, 103, 105, 108, 109
Booth, Clarence A., 181
Booth, Ellen Scripps, 188, 191–193
Booth, George Gough: joins *Detroit News*, 13; and H. S. Scott, 26; and J. Scripps's will, 29, 295; and exposé of aldermen's graft, 39; and riverfront development, 180–181; and Detroit Institute of Arts, 187–188; and Cranbrook estate, 188; and Catlin Library, 193
Booth, Henry, 180
Booth, Henry Lodge, 13
Booth, Henry S., 196
Booth, James Scripps, 55
Booth, Ralph, 29
Booth, Warren S., 75, 196
Booth Publishing Company, 29
Borglund, William, 196
Boris, Colossal, 87–88
Boston Globe, xiv
Boushaw, Billy, 33–34, 41, 46, 176, 187–188
Bowles, Mayor Charles, 97, 103–104
Boyes, Edwin G., 86
Bradner, C. C., 86
Brearley, William H., 18
Breitmeyer, Eleanor, 183
Brennan, Bert, 71
Brooks, Milton E., 72
Brookside School, 188
Brown, Gates, 172
Brown, Nancy, 111–124, 191
Brush automobile, 55
Bryan, William Jennings, 24
Buckley, Gerald, 103–104
Bugas, John, 62–63
Buick automobile, 55
Burdick, E. J., 48
Burgess, Fred H., 6

Burns, William J., 34–38, 40
Burroughs, Clyde H., 116, 117
Burroughs, John, 58
Busing, 40
Butzel, Long, Gust, Klein and Van Zile, 151

Cadillac automobile, 49, 55
Cadillac Automotive Company, 55
Cadillac Motor Car Company, 54
Cameron, William J., 60, 162–163
Cammarato, Frank, 99
Campbell, Anne, 128
Capone, Al, 93
Caputo, Frank, 108
Carlisle, Jack N., 94–97, 100–102, 109, 200
Carstairs, Barbara "Betty," 165
Carter, Danny, 173
Carter, Lawrence, 148
Cavanaugh, Mayor Jerome P.: and 1967 race riots, 134, 135, 136, 140; and *Detroit News*, 147; and Horace Dodge Foundation, 183, 184
Cedarbaum, Rabbi David, 120
Chapin, Roy D., 56
Chevrolet automobile, 55, 59, 60, 61
Chicago Cubs, 169
Chicago Sun-Times, 147
Chicago Tribune, 4, 100, 166
Christ Church Cranbrook, 188
Chrysler, Walter P., 50
Chrysler Corporation, 55, 59, 68–69
Cincinnati Press, 10
Circulation, and headlines, 101
Claremont College, 192
Clark, Earl "Dutch," 164
Clark, George "Potsy," 164
Clark, Peter B., 14, 186, 200–201
Clark, Ramsey, 136
Clark, Tom, 80, 81, 90–91
Clay, Cassius, 171–172
Cleveland Browns, 169–170

Cleveland Penny Press, 10, 191–192
Cleveland Press, 11
Clockwork Orange, A, 154, 155–156
Cobb, Tyrus Raymond, 157–162, 167
Cobo, Mayor Albert E., 182
Cobo Hall and Arena, 176, 182, 189
Cochrane, Mickey "Black Mike," 163
Collingwood massacre, 93–94
Colossal Boris, 87–88
Commercial Marine Terminal, Incorporated, 195
Conrad, Paul, 68
Conscription, 168
Constitution of the United States of America, 93, 94
"Contact 10," 191
Conyers, John, Jr., 133
Cooke, Jay, 9
"Corporationists," 14, 17
Corrado, Dominic "Fats," 109
Couzens, James, 45–47; 88–89
Cox, James M., 84
Cranbrook, 180–181, 188
Crane, Dr. Henry H., 121–122
Crellin, Jack, 79, 130
Crime, 93–94, 100, 143–145; *see also* organized crime
"Crime: A Search for Solutions," 148
Crockett, Judge George W., Jr., 148

Dallas Morning News, 152
Dearborn Independent, 57
Dee, Michael J., 6
DeForest, Dr. Lee, 81, 84–85
De Horatiis, Dr. Joseph, 128
Dempsey, Jack, 84, 166
Depression, 88–89, 104, 163–164
Derby Hill, 189
Detroit: in 1873, 3–5; aldermanic system in, 10, 32–41; lighting system in, 14–15; in 1890, 15; transit system of, 17, 21, 28, 47, 49, 53–54; machine politics in, 18, 21, 33; pavement of roads in, 20;

ethnic population of, 33, 125–126, 130, 157; city charter of, 41; and auto workers' strike, 66; and Mafia, 95–96, 109; crime in 95–100, 103–104, 108–109, 130, 141–142, 143–153; and Prohibition, 96–100, 102–104, 108; prostitution in, 98, 130; governmental corruption in, 98–99, 105–108; and narcotics, 100, 130, 142, 143–144; Paradise Valley, 125–128, 130; flight of whites to suburbs of, 125–126, 129, 130; race relations in, 125–142, 144–147, 166–167, 169, 175; race riots in, 125, 126–142, 143, 172, 191; black population of, 125–129, 130, 140–142, 165–166, 175; statistics on population, 126, 129, 132; Twelfth Street, 130, 141; busing in, 141; sports in, 157–175; and World War II, 68–69
POLICE DEPARTMENT OF: and transit rates, 45–46; corruption in, 46, 105–108; and attempts on Reuther brothers' lives, 74–75; and Prohibition, 95–96, 97, 98, 101; and blacks, 126, 130, 140–141, 142; and race riots, 127, 128–129, 131–134, 138–139, 140; complaints about, 141–142
Detroit American, 144–145
Detroit Automobile Company, 54
Detroit Chronicle, 92
Detroit Citizens League, 21, 41, 42, 107
Detroit Civic Center, 175, 181–186
Detroit Daily, 100
Detroit Daily Advertiser, 3
Detroit Daily Mirror, 100
Detroit Free Press: and *Detroit News*, 5–6, 20, 22; circulation of, 13; and H. S. Pingree, 18, 22; and Free Silver, 24; and public transit sys-

Detroit Free Press (continued)
tem, 47; and 1937 Rouge plant strike, 69; and 1955 Ford–United Auto Workers pact, 75; 1962 strike at, 91; and Prohibition, 100; and *Chicago Tribune,* 100; 1967–68 strike at, and crime, 144; and Golden Gloves, 166; "Action Line," 191

Detroit Gas Company, 23

Detroit Historical Museum, 184, 185

Detroit Institute of Arts, 115–119, 182, 187–188

Detroit Journal, 18, 20–21, 34, 46, 47, 180

Detroit Lions, 164, 169–170, 186

Detroit Mirror, 100

Detroit Municipal League, 42

Detroit News: and Pentagon papers, xiv–xvi; and political affiliation, xvi; independence of, xvi, 194, 195; original name of, 5; founding of, 5–6, 194, 195; offices and plants of, 5–6, 8, 13, 196–197; first issue of, 6; and advertising, 6, 10, 12–13, 25, 26, 42–44, 82, 88, 154–155; circulation of, 6, 7, 8, 10, 13, 21, 26, 100, 190–191, 194, 195; writing style of, 6–7; finances of 6, 7–8, 9, 10, 30, 194–196; price of, 6, 10, 12, 14; editorial policy of, 9, 11–12, 14–15; and Panic of 1873, 9–10; and syndication, 10–11; and local news, 11–12, 197; Sunday edition of, 14, 148; and H. S. Pingree, 18, 19–20, 22, 24, 25, 27; political endorsements by, 18, 19–20, 24–25, 27, 44–45, 137; and pavement of roads, 20; and eight-hour day, 21; and Detroit United Railway, 21; and reform, 21, 22–23; and public transit, 21, 42–48, 53–54; leadership of, 21; and *Detroit*

Free Press, 22; and gas rates, 23; and electrical rates, 23–24, and telephone rates, 24; and William Jennings Bryan, 24; organizes band, 24; and home rule, 25; and riverfront development, 25, 180–185; adds sports and women's pages, 26; introduces comics, 26; starts photographic department, 26; and aldermanic graft, 35–41; and city charter, 41; and T. Roosevelt, 45; and development of automobile, 51–53, 54; and Henry Ford, 51, 64–65; and Ford Motor Company, 59–60; and 1936–37 General Motors strike, 66–68; and "Listening in on Detroit," 67; and 1937 strike at Rouge Ford plant, 69–71; Pulitzer Prizes awarded to, 71, 72; and 1955 Ford-union pact, 76; and World War I, 81–83, 86, 87, 88; in Depression, 88–89; and television, 90–92; strikes at, 91, 92, 144, 191; Washington Bureau of, 94–95, 122, 177, 179, 184, 185, 190; and crime, 94–100, 106–108, 109, 142, 144, 145–153; and Mafia, 95–96, 109; and Prohibition, 95–100, 102–104; and slot machines, 101; purchases first airplane, 101–102; and corruption in Detroit government, 105–108; and 1939 numbers scandal, 106–108; and "Experience" column, 111–124; sells fish, 112; and conservation, 114–115; and race riots, 126, 128, 129–130, 133–134, 135–136, 137, 138–139, 191; and blacks, 141, 144–146; and "Secret Witness," 144, 147–153; and *Time* magazine, 146; and racism, 146–147; and decline in morals, 153–156; and underground newspapers, 154; "The Other Section" of, 154; and sports, 157–163, 165, 170–172, 173; and Muhammad Ali, 171–172; and revitalization of Detroit, 175–190; and St. Lawrence Seaway, 176–180, 182; and Detroit Civic Center, 181–186; and Horace Dodge Foundation, 183–185; and Detroit Historical Museum, 185; and Detroit Institute of Art, 187–188; and average reader, 189; and "Ask the News," 190; community service programs of, 190–191; special columns of, 190–191; special sections of, 190–191; subsidiaries of, 195; as "Home Newspaper," 196; 1971 contract of, 198

EDITORIALS OF: on page one, xiv–xv; and Pentagon papers, xiv–xvi; and H. S. Pingree, 27; and Republican party, 28; and public transit, 42; "Don't Die on Third," 60, 162–163; and W. Reuther, 78–79; on numbers racket, 106–107; on retailers' profits, 112; and Peace Carillon Tower, 120–121; and President L. B. Johnson, 137; and Judge Crockett, 148; and X-rated films, 154–155; and J. Louis, 166; and St. Lawrence Seaway, 177–178; and W. K. Kelsey, 198–199; and Civic Center, 181–182; and Rivera murals, 182; and Old City Hall, 183

Detroit Post, 13
Detroit Red Wings, 164
Detroit Tigers, 157–159, 162, 163, 164, 168, 169, 172–175
Detroit Times: and J. Scripps, 14, 19; and public transit system, 47; and Battle of Overpass, 69–70; and Prohibition, 98, 100; and "Experience" column, 113; and G. G.

Booth, 180–181; and J. Schermerhorn, 185
Detroit Tribune, 12
Detroit Daily Union, 6
Detroit United Railway, 14, 21, 42–48
Detroit Urban League, 145
Detroit Zoo, 189–190
Dillinger, John, 93
Dix, Dorothy, 111
Dodge, Horace, 50, 55
Dodge, Mrs. Horace E., 183–185
Dodge, John F., 46, 50, 55
Dodge Brothers, 55
Don, Kaye, 165
"Don't Die on Third," 162–163
Doremus, Frank E., 44
Dorris, James T. 195
Dow, Alex, 23–24
Dragonette, Jessica, 90
Durant, William C., 49, 55, 59
Durant automobile, 55
Duryea, Charles, 50
Duryea, J. Frank, 49, 50

Early Bird, 101
Edwards, Frank, 81, 82
Edwards, George, 95–96, 99–100, 108, 109
Eisenhower, President Dwight D., 191
Electricity, rates for, 23–24
Electric Vehicle Company, 57
Ellsberg, Dr. Daniel, xiv
Eppert, Ray R., 145
Evening News, 5
Evening New Association, 29, 192–193, 195–196
"Experience" column, 111–124, 191
Extras, 101

Fairfax, Beatrice, 111, 123
Ferguson, Judge Homer, 107
Ferry, Dexter M., 19

Fifth Amendment, 94
Films, X-rated, 154–156
Finlayson, John, 154
Finstad, William L., 147
Fitzgerald, Edward, 35, 37, 38
Fitzgibbon, John, 15, 53
Fitzsimmons, Frank, 79
Fitzsimmons, Robert, 166
Fleisher, Harry, 103
Fleming, Walter Reynolds, 149
Flint Trolley Coach Company, 66
Ford, Clara, 61, 62, 64
Ford, Edsel, 60, 61
Ford, Eleanor, 62–63
Ford, Henry: and public transit, 45, 46; and price of cars, 49; and minimum wage, 49, 56; first car of, 50, 51, 54; influence of, 57; and anti-Semitism, 57; generosity of, 57–58; and Model T, 58; and 1941 lockout, 61; will of, 62–63; death of, 64–65; and battle at Rouge plant, 70
Ford, Henry II, 61–63, 186–187
Ford, William C., 186
Ford Motor Company: founded, 54–55; success of 56–59; decline of, 59–62; revitalization of, 62–64; 1937 strike at, 69–71; 1941 strike at, 72–73; 1955 pact with union, 75; see also Model A; Model T
Ford Motor Company Fund, 182
Forest Club, 127
Frahm, Commissioner Fred W., 106
Frankensteen (United Auto Workers leader), 69, 70
Franklin, Rabbi Leo M., 57
"Foxy Grandpa and Toyland," 26

Gaertner, Fred, Jr., 68, 70, 98, 103
Gang warfare, 95, 99–100, 103, 147
Garner, June Brown, 148
General Motors Acceptance Corporation, 59

General Motors Corporation, 49–50, 55, 59, 66–68, 152; see also Chevrolet
George B. Catlin Memorial Library, 193
Giacalone, Anthony, 109
Giacalone, Vita "Billy Jack," 109
Gibson, Bob, 174
Gillespie, Commissioner John, 45, 46
Gilmer, Elizabeth. See Dix, Dorothy
Gilmore, W. Steele: and radio, 88; and crime reportage, 103; and Nancy Brown, 116, 117–118, 120, 122–123; and sunrise services, 120; and Peace Carillon Tower, 121; and Pearl Harbor, 122–123; and race riots, 126; and W. K. Kelsey, 178–179; career of, 199
Girardin, Ray, 100–102, 129, 132–134, 200
Glinnan, Thomas E., 34, 36, 37, 39–40, 41
Golden Gloves tournament, 166
Gompers, Samuel, 15
Good, Raymond, 131–132
Goodrich, Merton Ward, 102
Graham, Otto, 170
Grand Circus Park, 129
Gray, Pete, 168–169
Green, Andrew H., Jr., 35–37, 39, 40
Greene, Edgar "Doc," 158, 170–172
Greene, Robert L., 138–139
Greene, Sam, 158, 161

Hagen, Walter, 164
Hammond, Charles F., Jr., 84
Hampden, Walter, 85, 90
Handbooks, 97, 104, 106, 108
Harding, Warren G., 84, 85
Harmsworth Trophy, 165
Hart, Herschell, 88
Hathaway, Arthur, 70, 127

Hayden, Jay G.: and T. Glinnan, 34; and exposé of aldermanic graft, 34, 35; and T. Roosevelt, 44–45; and Depression, 88–89; and outbreak of World War II, 122; and 1967 race riots, 138; and X-rated films, 154–155; and B. Boushaw, 188

Hayden, Martin S.: and Pentagon papers, xiv–xvi; and United Auto Workers Union, 66–67; and organized crime, 95; and Muhammad Ali, 171–172; and Horace Dodge Foundation, 183–185; and W. S. Booth's resignation, 196; and *The News of Detroit*, 201

Haynes, Elwood, 50

Headlines, and circulation, 101

Hearst, R. A., 58

Hearst, William Randolph, 10, 49, 113

Henry and Edsel Ford Auditorium, 176

Henry Ford II, 64

Henry Ford Museum, 58

Herron, Ashel H., 6

Hersey, John, 138

Highland Park Ford plant, 56, 59

Hills, Lee, 75

Hitler, Adolf, 168

Ho Chi Minh, xiii

Hoffa, James R., 71, 77, 78, 79

Holden, James S., 34

Holliday, William F., 86–87

Home rule, 14–15, 25, 28

Hoover, Herbert, 85–86

Hopkins, Harry, 122

Horace Dodge Foundation, 183–185

Horton, Willie, 172

Hostetler, Jerry, 130

Houston Chronicle, 191

Houston Post, 152

Howard, Roy, 11

Howe, Gordie, 164

Hudson, Joseph L., 42–44

Hudson automobile, 55

Hudson Motor Car Company, 56

Humphrey, Hubert, 136

Hutchins, Jere C., 21, 45

Hutchinson, Palmer, 197

Idealism, 4

Immigrants, 157

Inches, James W., 48

Isle Royale, 114–115

Jackson, H. C. L., 67

Jacobs, Clarence, 74–75

James E. Scripps Corporation, 29, 181

Jeffries, Edward J., Jr., 126, 128

Jeffries, James J., 166

John and Horace Dodge Memorial Hall of Industry, 184

John P. Scripps Newspapers, 192

Johnson, Ban, 159

Johnson, Orlin, 165

Johnson, President Lyndon Baines, 136–137, 191

Jones, Dr. Edgar Dewitt, 120, 123

Journalism. See newspapers

Joy, Henry B., 54

Kahn, Albert, 54–55, 90

KDKA, 84–85

Keller, Helen, 87

Kelly, Governor Harry, 128

Kelsey, W. K., 178–179

Kelsey-Hayes Wheel Company, 66

Kennedy, Jack, 70

Kennedy, John Fitzgerald, 190, 196, 197

Kennedy, Robert Fitzgerald, 77, 95–96

Kerbawy, Nick, 170

Kidnapping, 104

Kilpatrick, James E., 69–70

King, Charles Brady, 50, 51

Kingswood School Cranbrook, 188
Kirk, Robert D., 149
Knudsen, William S., 50, 57, 60
Koehler, Henry W., 52
Koenecke, Len, 102
KOLD–TV, 195
Kornegay, Francis A., 145
Kracken, Jack, 166
Krehbiel, George, 117
Kreisler, Fritz, 58
Kubrick, Stanley, 155–156
Kuenzel, William A., 26, 54, 159–160

La Jolla, California, 192
La Mare, Chester, 103
Landis, Kenesaw Mountain, 89
Lauren, Asher, 71, 75
Layne, Bobby, 169–171, 172
LeDuc, Harry, 165
Leland, Henry M., 41, 49, 55
Leland automobile, 55
Lend-Lease Act, 168
Leslie, Mrs. J. E., 110–111; *see also* Brown, Nancy
Libel, 95
Licavoli, Dominic, 96
Licavoli, Peter, 96–97, 98, 100, 103, 105, 108, 109
Licavoli, Thomas Yonnie, 96, 99
Lincoln automobile, 49
Lindbergh, Charles A., 87, 104
Lindbergh, Charles A., Jr., 104
Lindbergh Law, 104
"Listening in on Detroit," 67
Lochbiler, Don, 199
Lodge, John C., 32–34, 38–39, 41–42, 47, 181
Lolich, Mickey, 172–174
Lombardo, Peter, 74
Louis, Joe (Barrow), 65–68, 169
Lovett, William P., 21
Lower East Side gang, 103
Lubeck, Robert E., 154

Lucido, Jack, 96
Lucido, Salvatore "Sam," 96, 105, 108, 109
Lycett, James M., 191

McBride, William, 105, 108
McCarthy, John, 105–106, 107
McClellan, Senator John L., 95
McCrea, Duncan C., 106–107
McDonald, Mrs. Janet, 105–106
McGill, Ralph, 161
McKinley, President William, 15, 24–25, 53
McKinney, Thurston, 165, 168
McLain, Dennis, 172–173, 174, 200
McMillan, Hugh, 19
McMillan, James, 19
McMillan, William C., 23
McNamara, James, 40
McRea, Milton, 192
Mabley, G. R., Company, 20
Mafia, 95–96, 109
"Mafia—The Inside Story," 95
Manning, Marie. *See* Fairfax, Beatrice
Marciano, Rocky, 167
Mariner's Church, 176, 186
Martin, Homer, 67
Marx, Oscar B., 44, 45, 46
Massei, Joe, 105, 109
Matney, Bill, 92
Maxwell automobile, 55
Maxwell-Chalmers automobile, 55
Meli, Angelo, 109
Merrill, D. Roy, 194
Metropolitan Spelling Bee, 189
Metzger, W. E., Company, 54
Michigan Avenue Slim, 149
Michigan Bell Company, 19, 24
Michigan Chronicle, 148
Michigan National Guard, 128–129, 134, 136, 137–138, 139
Miller, George E., 110, 117, 177, 178

Miller, Hattie, 98
Miller, Karl, 178
Milles, Carl, 90
Milliken, Governor William G., 171
Misky, Billy, 84
Miss America motorboats, 165
Miramar, California, 192
Model A Ford automobile, 60, 61
Model T Ford automobile, 48, 56, 57, 58, 59–60
Moody, Blair, 122
Morals, decline in, 153–156
Muggings, 104, 130, 143–144, 145–146
Muhammad Ali, 171–172
Muller, William, R., 98
Murfin, James O., 158–159

Narcotics, 100, 130, 142, 143–144
Nash automobile, 55
Nash-Kelvinator Corporation, 56
"New Detroit Committee, The," 140
Newhouser, Hal, 169
New Orleans Times-Picayune, 152
Newspaper Enterprise Association, 7, 196
Newspapers: and idealism, 4; size of, 4; and political affiliation, 4, 9; price of, 4, 10, 13–14, 49; evening and morning editions of, 5; cost of, and syndication, 10–11; chain and local, 10–12, 13; and reform, 21, 22–23; leadership of, 21, 110; and radio, 88; and coverage of crime, 93–94; responsibilities of, 94; competition among, 101–102; and readers' interests, 110; underground, 154; *see also* reporters
New York Daily News, 152
New York Herald, 10
New York Herald-Tribune, 161
New York Journal, 111

New York Times, xii–xiv, xv, 21, 59, 97, 155–156
New York World, 114
Nieber, Allen, 76
Nixon, Richard M., xiv, xv, 79
Noguchi, Isamu, 185
Northern Pacific Railway, 8
Numbers racket, 104–108

Oakland automobile, 55
Oakland Hills Country Club, 164
Oakland Sugar House gang, 103
O'Hara, Chester P., 107
Old Club, 80
Olds, Ransom E., 49, 54, 56
Olds Runabout, 49, 54, 55, 56
Organized crime: and Depression, 104; in Detroit, 95, 96–100, 103–104, 108–109; and Prohibition, 93, 104; and public apathy, 108
"Orphan Annie," 100
Oswald, Lee Harvey, 197
"Other Section, The," 154
Owen, Rolf, 127

Packard, James W., 54
Packard Motor Car Company, 126–127
Paige automobile, 55
Palmer, Arnold, 164
Panic of 1873, 9–10, 22
Paradise Valley, 125–128, 130
Parker, Buddy, 170
Patton, Harvey, 76, 94–96
Peace Carillon Tower, 120–123
Pearl Harbor, 122, 168
Peck, Barton, 52
Peerless automobile, 55
Pendergast, Tom, 33
Pennsylvanians, The, 86–87, 90
Pentagon papers, xiii–xvi
Perrone, Santo, 74
Peters, Albert E., 14

Philadelphia News, 152
Philippines, 53
Phillips, Jack, 134
Pickert, Heinrich, 106
Pierce-Arrow automobile, 55
Piersante, Vincent, 95–96, 108
Pingree, Mayor Hazen Senter: character of, 17–18; and J. Scripps, 17, 18–19, 22, 24, 25–26, 27; achievements of, 18; and newspapers, 18, 20, 22, 26; and *Detroit News,* 18, 19–20, 22, 24, 27; mayoral nomination and campaign of, 19; and telephone company, 19; and school board, 20; and pavement of roads, 20; and poisoning of horses, 20–21; and transit system, 21, 48; and potato patches, 22; and gas rates, 23; and telephone company, 24; and Free Silver, 24–25; and house of ill repute, 25; and bankers, 25; and trusts, 26; as governor, 26, 28; trip abroad, 27; death of, 27; monument to, 27; and reform, 28
Pipp, Edwin G., 35–37, 38, 57, 110, 197
Pittsburgh Steelers, 170
Plant, Elton, 82
Playboy magazine, 154
Player, Cyril Arthur, 200
Pol-American Publishing Company, 144
Poland, invasion of, 168
Polish Daily News, 144–145
Pomona College, 192
Pontiac automobile, 55
Ponting, Herbert, 194
Poorman, Paul, xv, 138, 142, 171, 198
Popa, Robert, 186
Pope, Colonel Albert A., 50
Portman, John C., 186
Pridgeon, John, 20

Priziola, John, 109
Prohibition, 19, 93, 96–100, 104, 111, 143
Prostitution, 98
"Public Letter Box," 178
Public Lighting Commission, 23–24
Pulitzer, Joseph, Jr., 10, 49, 114
Pulitzer Prize, 71, 72
Purple gang, 103
Puyear, Mrs. Nola, 149

Qualified privilege, 95
"Questions of General Public Interest," 190

radio, 30–31, 80–81, 84–86, 88
Rambler automobile, 55
Ransom, Rolland R., 173
Reader's Digest, 152
Reading, Mayor Richard W., 105–107
Reading, Richard W., Jr., 106
Reform, and newspapers, 21, 22–23
"Relief by Work," 22
Renda, Carl, 74–75
Reo automobile, 55
Reporters: relations with criminals, 94, 100–101; competition among, 101–102
Republican party, 18, 19, 28
Reuther, Roy, 66–67
Reuther, Victor, 66–67, 74–75
Reuther, Walter: and Kelsey-Hayes strike, 66; and Flint Trolley Coach Company strike, 66–67; and 1936-37 General Motors strike, 68; and 1937 Rouge strike, 69–70; and World War II, 73; and 1945 General Motors strike, 73; gains control of United Auto Workers, 73–74; attempt to assassinate, 74–75; goals and methods of, 77–78; compared to Hoffa, 77, 78; death of, 78–79

Richmond Palladium, 86
Ripley, Anthony, 197
"ripoffs," 143–144, 145–146
Ritchie, Don, 74–75
Rivera, Diego, 182
Robinson, Archie W., 69–71
Rochester Times-Union, 86
Rogers, Will, 87
Romney, Governor George, 128, 134, 135, 136, 137, 139
Roosevelt, Franklin Delano, 89, 122
Roosevelt, Theodore, 26, 27, 44–45
Rosenberg, Abe, 99–100
Rosenthal, David, 34, 38
Ross, Robert B., 6
Rote, Tobin, 170
Rouge Ford plant, 59, 69–71
Rowan, Carl T., 148
Rowe, Lynwood "Schoolboy," 173
Ruby, Jack, 197
Rumpa, Sylvia, 198
Runabout automobile, 49, 54, 55, 56
Rushville, Illinois, 193
Ruth, Herman "Babe," 161, 167
Ryan, Mrs. Dorothy, 172
Ryan, Elmer (Buff), 107
Ryan, Richard, 138

Saarinen, Eliel, 180, 188
Sacramento Bee, 153
Sahs, Harry, 98, 102–103, 200
St. Lawrence Seaway, 176, 180
St. Louis Browns, 168
St. Louis Cardinals, 174
St. Louis Chronicle, 10
St. Louis Post-Dispatch, xiv, 114
St. Valentine Day massacre, 94
Salsinger, H. G., 157–159, 161, 166, 167
Salt Lake City Tribune, 152
San Francisco Examiner, 86
Saturday Evening Post, 95
Schaefer, Nick, 98
Schermerhorn, James, 185

Schermerhorn, Jane, 185
Schmeling, Max, 167
Schmidt, Joe, 172
Schreiter, Edward R., 34, 36, 37, 38–39
Scott, Anna V., 29, 30
Scott, Charles, 192
Scott, Hereward S., 26, 42–44, 194
Scott-Paine, Hubert, 165
Scripps, Edward Wyllis: joins *Detroit News,* 7; jobs of, 8; and expansion of Scripps chain, 10–11; and syndication, 10–11; and James Scripps, 11–12, 193; and W. J. Bryan, 24; and *Cleveland Penny Press,* 191–192; and Catlin Library, 192; and Scripps League, 192; and United Press International, 192
Scripps, Ellen B., 7, 11, 196
Scripps, Ellen S., 30
Scripps, Ellen W., 13
Scripps, George H., 7–8, 10, 11
Scripps, Grace M., 30
Scripps, Harriet ("Hattie"): children of, 3; and founding of *Detroit News,* 3, 4, 6, 7, 9, 30; appearance of, 15–16
Scripps, James E.: and Republican party, xvi, 18, 28; stubbornness of, 3; children of, 3; newspaper experience before *Detroit News,* 3, 4; and founding of *Detroit News,* 3–6, 194–195; concept of a newspaper, 4–5, 9, 21; conservatism of, 6; and religion, 6, 187; daily routine of, 8–9; and *Detroit News* finances, 8, 9; health of, 9, 12, 28; and syndication, 10, 11; and expansion of Scripps enterprises, 10–12; and E. W. Scripps, 11–12, 193; and wire services, 12; and civic affairs, 14; art collection of, 15, 187; ap-

Scripps, James E. (continued)
pearance of, 16; and H. S. Pingree,
17, 18–19, 22, 24, 25–26, 27; and
Free Silver, 24–25; and bankers,
25; and advertising, 26; as state
senator, 27–28; municipal ownership of public services, 28; and
reform, 28; death of, 28–30; will
of, 29–30, 195; and T. E. Clark,
30–31; and radio, 30–31; and
transit system, 48; and price of
newspapers, 49; and P. Baker,
51; and H. Ford, 65; and average
man, 65, 189; and Trinity Protestant Episcopal Church, 187
Scripps, James Mogg, 7, 193
Scripps, John Locke, 4
Scripps, Nina, 80–81
Scripps, Robert W., 196
Scripps, W. A., Company, 181
Scripps, Will, 75; and radio, 80–82,
83, 90; and Depression, 88–89;
and *Detroit News*'s first airplane,
101; and Peace Carillon Tower,
121
Scripps, William E., 29, 30–31, 195
Scripps, William J., 80–82, 83, 90
Scripps-Booth automobile, 55
Scripps-Howard Newspapers, 10–11,
192
Scripps Institute of Oceanography,
192
Scripps League, 192
Scripps Memorial Hospital, 192
Scroy, Chris, 108
Scroy, Sam, 108
Seattle Post-Intelligencer, 152
Secret Witness, 144, 147–153, 100
Seiter, William, 73
Seldon patent, 57
Senate Crime Committee, 95, 108–
109
Senate Rackets Committee, 77
"Senator Soaper," 95

Sensationalism, and crime reporting,
93–94, 100
Shanahan, Jack, 19
Shurmur, Henry, 76
Simmons, Boyd, 67–68, 71, 76, 150–
151, 152–153, 199–200
Sit-down strikes, 66, 71
Sitenis, Renée, 115
Skinner, Edna Mary, 173
Sloan, Alfred P., Jr., 49–50, 59
Slot machines, 101
Smith, Mayor John W., 180–181
Soapbox Derby, 189
Sob sisters, 111
Sojourner Truth housing project, 126
Sorensen, Charles E., 47, 61
Spanish-American War, 53
Speed, Judge John J., 8
Spitzley, Richard M., 196
Spoelstra, Watson, 160, 161, 172–
174, 200
Standard Cotton Products Company,
68
Stark, Mrs. Anne, 186
Stark, George W., 128, 183, 185–
186
Stern, Max, 103, 108
Stoll, Albert, 114–115
Stout, William B., 55
"Straphanger, Mr.," 42
Streetcars, 48, 53; *see also* transit
systems
Street in Brooklyn, 118–119
Strickland, Joseph, 138–139
Stroeker, Monroe, 98–99
Studebaker automobile, 55
Sullivan, John L. 166
Supreme Court, xiv, xvi
Swan, John, 6
Sweinhart, James, 57–58, 59
Syndication, 10–11

Taft, William H., 45, 177
Tallman, Joe, 99–100, 103

Television, 90–92
Ter Horst, Jerry, 94–96, 185, 197
"Texas defense," 103
Thomas, Burt, 42
Thomas, R. J., 73
Thompson, "Big Bill," 33
Throckmorton, General John, 137
Time magazine, 146
Tin Lizzie. *See* Model A Ford
Tinney, Frank, 85
Tocco, William "Black Bill," 109
Tolan, Eddie, 165
"Tonight's Dinner," 86
"Town Crier, The," 86
Townsend, Charles E., 177–178
"Town Talk," 183
Transit systems, 14–15, 17, 21, 42, 47, 48, 49, 53–54
Tremblay, William, 183
Trenton Monitor, 156
Trinity Protestant Episcopal Church, 187
Trout, Dizzy, 169
Truman, Harry S, xiii, 191
Trumbo, Harold, 82
Tweed, William Marcy, 33
Tyson, Edwin L. (Ty), 87, 89

United Auto Workers Union, 61, 66–68, 72–74, 75, 78; *see also* Reuther, Walter
United Community League for Civic Action, 131
United Motors, 162
United Press International, 12, 192
Universal Communications Corporation, 195

"Valachi papers," 95
Valenti, Jack, 155
Valentiner, Dr. William R., 116
Vance, Cyrus, 136–137
Veterans Memorial Building, 176
Vietnam, xiii-xiv, xv, 191

Volkswagen automobile, 58
Volstead Act, 93

Wade, Harry V., 95, 179, 200
WALA-TV, 195
Waldmeir, Pete, 174
Wallace, Richard B., 196
Walter, John, 164
Ward systems. *See* aldermanic system
Waring, Fred, 86–87, 90
Washington Post, xiv
Washington Star, 152
Waverly electric automobile, 54
Wayne State University, 125
WBL, 83
Weaver, John B., 151
Webber, Richard H., 44
Wells, Robert L., 182
Westinghouse Electric and Manufacturing Company, 84–85
West Side gang, 103
Wheeler, Edwin K., 171, 195
Whitcomb, Edgar Bancroft, 29, 195
Whitcomb, James S., Jr., 196
White, Lee A., 180
White, Rex G., 86, 190
White, Stoddard, 180
Wierzbicki, Arthur J., 144–145
Wilcox, Sheriff Thomas, 106
Wilkie, James, 46
Wilkins, Roy, 148
Wilkins, Sir Hubert, 197
Wilkinson, Warren S., 196
William J. Burns Detective Agency, 34–38, 40
Willow Run Ford plant, 62
Willys-Overland automobile, 55
Wilson, Earl, 174
Winstead, Ralph, 74–75
Winton, Alexander, 50
Witherspoon, Commissioner John H., 129
Wolff, Joseph, 130, 133, 135
Wood, Gar, 87, 165–166

Woodward Avenue, 5, 12, 20, 128, 197
World Series, 163–164, 168, 169, 172, 174–175
World War I, 41, 47, 110–111, 112
World War II, 122, 125, 128, 168–169
Worthington, John H., 152–153
WWJ, 76, 195; early years of, 81–86; studios of, 81, 83, 90; programming of, 86–87; in Depression, 89; sixteenth birthday of, 90; and Pearl Harbor, 122–123
WWJ-FM, 90, 195
WWJ-TV, 90, 195

Yost, Fielding H., 87–88

Zerilli, Joe, 96–97, 109
Zuidema, Henry, 127